The American Indians

DEAN SNOW

THE AMERICAN INDIANS

THEIR ARCHAEOLOGY
AND PREHISTORY

PHOTOGRAPHS BY
WERNER FORMAN

THAMES AND HUDSON
LONDON

Title-page: *A Haida or Tsimshian craftsman of the Northwest Coast made this 20.5-cm.-high stone carving in late prehistoric or early historical times. The troughs were probably meant to hold special pigments. (The Robert H. Lowie Museum of Anthropology, University of California, Berkeley.)*

© 1976 Thames and Hudson Ltd, London

Printed in Italy

Contents

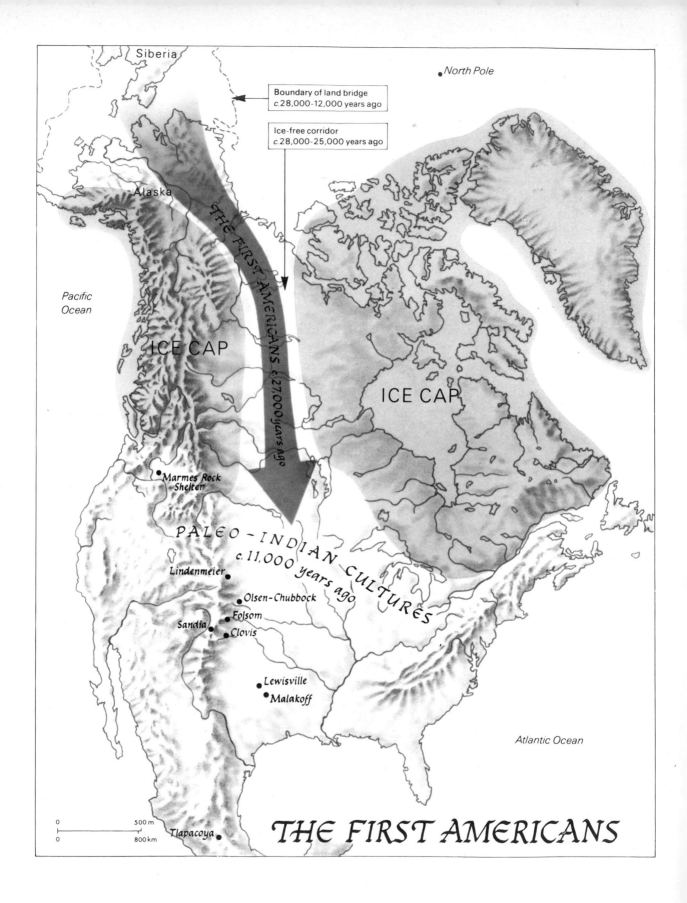

Siberia

•North Pole

Boundary of land bridge
c.28,000–12,000 years ago

Ice-free corridor
c.28,000–25,000 years ago

Alaska

THE FIRST AMERICANS c.27,000 years ago

Pacific
Ocean

ICE CAP

ICE CAP

•Marmes Rock
Shelter

PALEO-INDIAN CULTURES
c.11,000 years ago

•Lindenmeier

•Olsen-Chubbock

•Folsom

Sandia• •Clovis

•Lewisville
•Malakoff

Atlantic Ocean

0 — 500 m
0 — 800 km

•Tlapacoya

THE FIRST AMERICANS

Introduction

In January 1524, the Italian explorer Giovanni da Verrazzano gazed across a narrow strip of land that is now called Cape Hatteras, North Carolina. Seeing Pamlico Sound, he thought that he had discovered the Pacific Ocean and the isthmus that separated it from the Atlantic. Beyond the sound, unknown to Verrazzano, lay the earth's third-largest continent, with an aboriginal population of over a million. Between the Atlantic and the Pacific lived peoples with vastly different cultures, speaking at least 500 distinctly different languages. Yet the languages fell into a handful of language families, and in later centuries scholars would be able to trace the diverse cultures back to common roots. Verrazzano, however, saw little of the diversity before returning to Europe almost empty-handed.

A few years later, in 1541, Francisco Vasquez de Coronado, governor of the northwestern province of Mexico, pushed his overland expedition as far as Kansas. But he did not find his cities of gold, or even a small portion of the wealth that he hoped would make him rich. These are not unusual examples. Explorers of several European nationalities had their fantasies dashed by the sober realities of life in North America. Rumors of gold and silver led dozens to deposits of pyrite or mica, but never to the kinds of treasures found during the Spanish conquests of earlier decades. The incredible good luck of Cortés in Mexico and Pizarro in Peru was not to be repeated.

Modern readers are regularly treated to new volumes on the art and archaeology of Mexico, Central America, or Peru, and the riches of these regions are often displayed. At the same time, the historical arts of the North American Indians have also received considerable attention. All too often, however, there is a gap on the library shelf as silent verification of Coronado's verdict that there was nothing of value in precolonial North America, or Verrazzano's initial impression that there was nothing there at all. Yet what these and other early explorers saw or did not see was often a product of their own narrow perspectives. They were adventurers looking for the means to make themselves rich, famous, or powerful, according to a rather specific set of European values. The North American Indians did not prove to be a source of precious metals and gems, and the arts they did possess were therefore of little interest. By the time the colonists had decided to settle for the land itself, and the mundane bounty it could be made to yield, the Indian nations that had owned it were regarded only as obstructions to progress, fit to be expelled or exterminated.

What was missed by the explorers, the colonists, and their historians has been recovered by archaeology. Through it, we have rediscovered the achievements of the Indians of North America, achievements which range across the whole spectrum of human culture. Their monuments were built of earth, wood, and grass more often

1 Man probably first crossed from Asia into the heartland of North America some 27,000 years ago, when Ice Age glaciers locked up the waters of the Bering Sea – thus creating a land bridge between Siberia and Alaska – but were not so extensive that they blocked passage through Canada. Indian bands spread south, occupying sites like Tlapacoya, Mexico, by 23,000 years ago, and developing a successful big-game-hunting lifeway which reached its climax some 11,000 years ago.

15

20

II–VIII
2–8

I *Like a gigantic highway, Alaska's Yukon River shows the way inland from the Bering Sea. The first Americans traversed landscapes such as this 27,000 years ago in pursuit of big game.*

Overleaf:
Artifacts of the Hohokam, Sinagua, and Anasazi cultures which flourished in the Desert West from 300 BC to AD1500 testify to prehistoric Indian ingenuity in a variety of different media.

II, III *A Sinagua craftsman of northern Arizona used abalone shell imported from the Pacific coast and combined it with turquoise beads to produce the tiny beasts trapped in these pendants, each dating from about AD1200.*

IV *A Sinagua nose plug dating from about AD 1200 was made to fit through a hole in the nasal septum. The plug is of argillite, a fine-grained black stone, and is fitted with turquoise ends.*

V *A Sinagua pendant of argillite depicts an eagle, whose remote beauty and power charged the imaginations of virtually all prehistoric Americans.*

VI *Stone and shell beads alternate on this exceptionally long Sinagua necklace. Each bead was drilled for stringing without the help of metal bits.*

VII *A design painted in pitch was the 'negative' for the decoration on this shell pendant of AD1100. The acid of fermented saguaro fruit etched the shell left exposed, a triumph of Hohokam ingenuity.*

than stone. Their arts were practiced in fiber, clay, wood, or flint. Their most precious materials were copper, mica, shell, the volcanic glass, obsidian, and a lead mineral, galena, none of which have much intrinsic value to European minds. Yet these, and others even more commonplace, were the media of prehistoric North American artisans. It is the quality of their achievements in these media, not the intrinsic values of the materials themselves, to which this volume is dedicated.

Dozens of textbooks and hundreds of scholarly reports have been written on North American archaeology, but this is not one of them. Much of the special terminology that is found in such works has been avoided. Perhaps most importantly, there are no universal periods or stages superimposed upon this study. Periods are useful concepts where the details and dates of prehistory are poorly known, but become increasingly difficult to apply as archaeologists fill in the gaps in their knowledge. Stages, for their part, imply an evolutionary progression that can obscure important details. Consequently, the terms 'band', 'tribe', 'chiefdom', and 'state' are used more as descriptive categories than as developmental stages.

Bands are groups of a few dozen individuals each. They are usually exogamous, that is, unmarried members look for mates in other bands. In most other things, band members are inward-looking, living out their lives without formal ties to other bands. These small-scale societies are usually found where population densities are low and technology not well developed. The primary examples in North America were found by early explorers in the Great Basin of the Desert West, and the Arctic.

Tribes can be thought of as societies containing two or more band-like units. Tribes are often endogamous, that is, unmarried members look for mates within their own tribes. Usually, however, there are clan or other divisions within tribes, and individuals must seek mates outside their own divisions. Tribes often had populations numbering in the hundreds, and more often than not in fifteenth-century North America they were village-farmers.

By the usual definition, a chiefdom consists of two or more villages joined together under a single authority. We will see a prime example in the Natchez of Mississippi. In practice, the difference between a chiefdom and a loose confederation of tribes was often slight, depending upon the formality of the political structure or merely the charisma of a dynamic leader.

States are the largest and most complex of societies. Conditions appear to have precluded their development in North America until European state systems were transplanted into the New World. Only in Mexico and the Andes did native American states develop, with their diagnostic bureaucracies, organized religions, and urban populations.

For the most part, however, this volume is organized around the concept of cultural traditions, which come and go, change and develop, all according to their own schedules and the accidents of history. When it is necessary to discuss them, levels of cultural development are usually referred to as 'lifeways'. One cultural tradition may be responsible for the introduction of a new lifeway to a given region, for example, while another tradition perpetuates the old lifeway that no longer exists elsewhere. The use of additional archaeological terms would only confuse a general summary of North American prehistory.

II

III

IV

V

VI

VII

IX

There is order in all of this, however. The progress of American Indian cultures can be perceived in the gradual domestication of wild plants, the development of architectural forms both religious and secular, the advance of technology despite the absence of many important resources, and the growth of cities. The story of prehistoric North America is one of steady progress over thousands of years, studded by singular achievements. There are no lost tribes or boatloads of sailors from the Old World in this story, no superior visitors, either natural or supernatural. There are only the American Indians, and the events that transpired as a natural consequence of their humanity, their imagination, and the culture they carried with them when they arrived.

This combines the conclusions of many avenues of anthropological reasoning with the results of detailed scientific research, but leaves out both the huge body of specific data and the complex arguments they have spawned. We have only begun to understand the complexities of prehistory in North America, and it is not our intention here to suggest that any more than a few of the answers are known, or even that the answers we suggest are in their final forms. There is even speculation here, but it is the same speculation that gives life to conversations between respected scientists, not the ramblings of a sensationalist. Some of the ideas presented will be struck down by new knowledge, and others will be modified in time, this being only the best we can do with present information. But the central thesis, that the North American Indian contributed significantly to the cultural history of the world, will remain intact.

Birds had a strong symbolic significance for North American Indians, and two of the most commonly represented, ravens and birds of prey, are shown here in four different media.

5 Cut out and beaten from native sheet copper, and with a fresh-water pearl for an eye, this raven or crow, 38 cm. long, was made in Ohio by a craftsman of the Hopewell culture (300 BC – AD 500).

6 The claws of a bird of prey were the inspiration for this superb Ohio Hopewell ornament, 28 cm. long, cut from sheet mica.

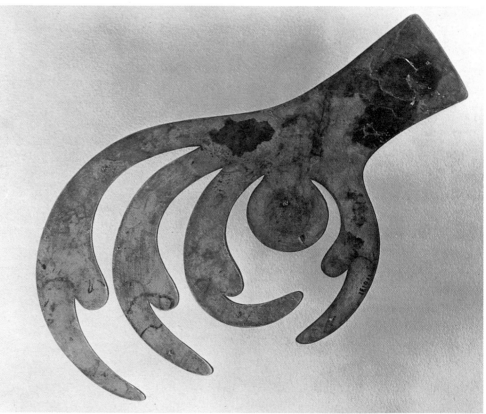

14

7 *A Haida craftsman from Queen Charlotte Island made this basalt tobacco mortar, 32 cm. long, depicting Raven, the culture hero, creator and trickster of Northwest Coast mythology. The carved wing shows an eagle head upside down.*

8 *A stylized panther confronts a fierce bird of prey on this 14-cm. shell pendant or gorget from Texas, engraved by a craftsman of the Mississippian culture (AD 700 – 1500), successor to Hopewell in the Eastern Woodlands.*

have killed large game animals outright except by a very lucky stroke. It would appear, therefore, that the strategy was to wound an animal, mortally if possible, and then pursue it until it dropped. The dying animal would then have been finished off at close range. Under these conditions, a spear that fell out was tactically superior to one that did not. It could be retrieved to be used again later on the same animal, and the wound it left behind would bleed freely.

People engaged in this kind of hunting economy could not have had permanent camps. They probably moved about in small extended family bands, that is, in groups larger than the basic family of parents and children, linked by close blood relationship. Teams of men might pursue a wounded animal for days, ranging far afield. Often the rest of the band would move up to the kill site, and all would camp somewhere nearby until the need for fresh food made them move on. Occasionally, two or more bands would meet under conditions that allowed them to camp together; less often, they would return to the same joint campsite. The Paleo-Indians were free-roaming nomads without a regular seasonal round of camps. Their lives were probably much like those of the Kalahari Bushmen of southern Africa. It is a kind of life that leaves little room for the accumulation of material possessions. Perhaps this is why something as utilitarian as point manufacture was raised to the level of an art form.

The bands traveled where the hunt took them. It was a centrifugal process that dispersed the small population very rapidly over the North American continent. Indeed, even though Clovis points are widespread east of the Rockies, they may have been scattered through that vast area over a matter of only a few centuries around 10,000 BC. Paleo-Indians camping in eastern Massachusetts left behind chert quarried in the Hudson Valley of New York. Pennsylvania Paleo-Indians used chert from central New York. At least some Paleo-Indians in New York brought chert with them from Ohio. A site in the Midwest shows evidence of a gathering of bands from two different regions, each with their own separate and regionally distinct chert. In these early Indians we must have one of the thinnest and most mobile human populations ever, scattered through one of the richest environments a hunting culture could hope to find.

Socially, the Paleo-Indians may well have resembled the historical Eskimos. A young person would not have been able to marry within his small extended family band, for that would have violated rules against marriage to a close relative. Periodic encounters with other bands would have provided a means by which such a young person could find a husband or a wife. A marriage would reinforce a distant relationship, or establish a new tie between unrelated bands. The tendency would probably have been for a young married couple to live close to the husband's rather than the wife's parents, so that the hunter would remain near men he knew and trusted, and near the hunting grounds he knew best. Under the free-roaming principle of Paleo-Indian nomadism, this tendency would not necessarily have been strong, but it became stronger as the centuries passed and the people settled into a more patterned lifeway.

A man with many brothers would probably have established his own extended family, perhaps in partnership with one or more of them. A man with few or no brothers might well have stayed close to his father after marriage, raising a family of his own and providing his parents with shelter in their old age. In any case, the rules were not rigid, and normally the ties of kinship kept closely related bands from drifting farther apart than was made necessary by the scarcity of wild food.

The bands were self-sufficient in most things. There was little room for specialization. Perhaps one person would be known for his stone-working, another for her hide-working, while still another would be widely respected as a magical curer or 'shaman'. But none of these talents could lead to a life of specialized activity. Each person was expected to be minimally accomplished in the range of daily activities dictated by sex and age. The nomads trudged through lives from which pleasure was extracted in small amounts, whether it be a chance encounter with old friends in another band or the manufacture of an especially fine spear point. For the most part, it was a strange mixture of extraordinary experiences and daily routine.

As time went on, and perhaps as the herds of Pleistocene animals began to diminish, new hunting techniques were developed. The earlier Paleo-Indians may well have hunted alone or in very small bands, stalking, maiming, and driving to earth one huge beast after another. Later bands may have been bigger, because we see a trend toward techniques involving the entrapment of whole herds. The makers of Folsom points, as we have seen, appear to have preferred the large bison that are now extinct. At several sites there is evidence that these later Paleo-Indians drove small herds into compounds or box canyons, killing several at a time, often more than they needed. If the main bison herds were as large as those seen in AD 1800, such a technique could have supported a larger Paleo-Indian band, moving in a more regular nomadic pattern than previously. In fact, population pressures and the disappearance of the larger mammals might have forced the shift. But the disappearance of one game species after another appears not to have reversed the trend towards overkill.

Fluted points were no longer made after about 7000 BC, but excellence of manufacture continued just the same. Projectile points gradually became a lanceolate 13 shape, the finest of them being very long and slender despite the absence of fluting; many points bear delicate patterns of long, thin, parallel pressure-flake scars. The change was a forerunner of a whole series of technological developments that were caused by the disappearance of the largest of the big game.

Unfluted points have been found embedded in some of the bison skeletons at the Olsen-Chubbock site in Colorado. Here, over a hundred terrified bison were stampeded into an arroyo or ravine. The first animals to enter were trampled to death by those behind, and Indians standing above on the rim of the arroyo had only to kill those on top of the heap. A minority of the bison were butchered. Prized parts were removed from some others. Most of the meat was left to rot.

Elsewhere in the West there are buffalo jumps where bison herds were stampeded over cliffs in huge numbers. The waste was often great, for although they had the capacity to preserve meat, these nomads had no means to take it along with them. It is unfair to blame them, because the idea that they could help to exterminate whole species would have been as incomprehensible to them as it is to most modern readers. Nevertheless, the large bison species must have been particularly vulnerable, for they all died, leaving the Plains to the smaller modern American bison.

The beasts of the Pleistocene were disappearing rapidly by 7000 BC. While some were hunted to ground, others died naturally in herds no longer large enough to be viable. With so many others went the horse, and with it the American Indian's later chances for plow agriculture and wheeled transportation. There remained no other large animals that were suitable for eventual domestication as draft animals. Every-where, Paleo-Indians were forced to adjust to the new conditions, and in their camp sites we find food-grinding implements for the first time. Their seasonal round became more regular, and their diet came to be a more balanced mixture of meat and gathered plant foods. It was the beginning of a new lifeway involving an intensive exploitation of a wide variety of food resources, an efficient adjustment that has been labelled the 'Archaic' lifeway. By 5000 BC the ecological pattern in North America had changed completely. The exotic animals of the Ice Age were gone, and neither they nor the human cultures they supported would ever be seen again.

13 *Late Paleo-Indian point types lack flutes, but many show the same superb craftsmanship as Folsom points. These chert lanceolate blades from the Eastern Woodlands, 6 – 10 cm. long, date from about 7000 BC.*

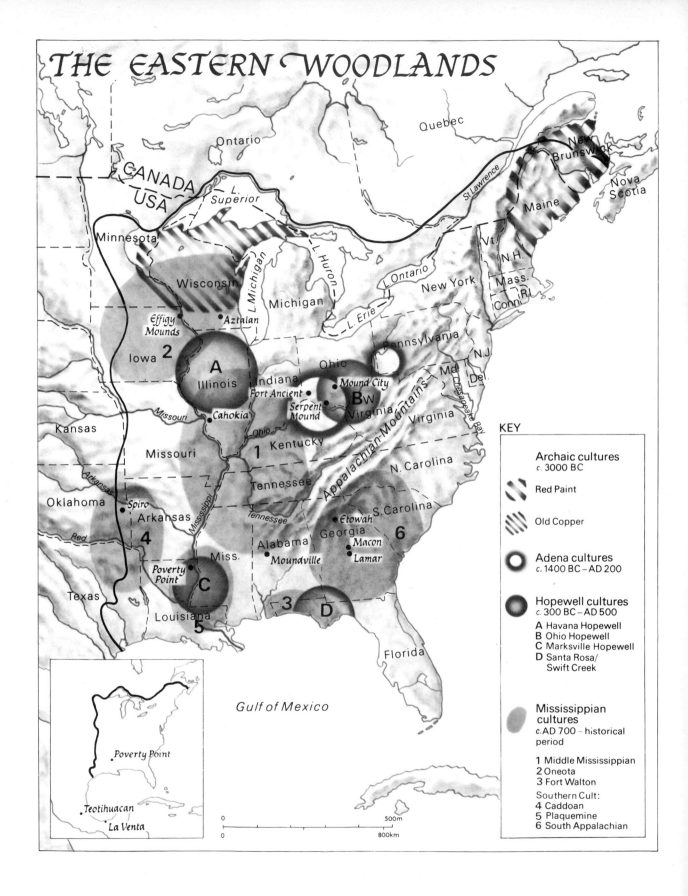

THE EASTERN WOODLANDS

Quebec

New Brunswick

Nova Scotia

CANADA
USA

Ontario

L. Superior

Maine

Minnesota

Vt.

N.H.

L. Michigan

L. Huron

Wisconsin

Michigan

Mass.
R.I.

L. Ontario

New York

Conn.

Effigy Mounds

•Aztalan

L. Erie

Pennsylvania

N.J.

Iowa **2**

A

Ohio

Md.

Del.

Illinois

Indiana

•Mound City

Chesapeake Bay

Fort Ancient

B W.

Serpent
Mound

Virginia

Virginia

•Cahokia

Ohio

Kentucky

Appalachian Mountains

Kansas

Missouri

1

N. Carolina

Tennessee

Arkansas

Oklahoma

•Spiro

Arkansas

Tennessee

•Etowah

S. Carolina

Georgia

6

4

Mississippi

•Macon

Red

Miss.

Alabama

•Lamar

Texas

Poverty
Point

•Moundville

C

3

D

5

Louisiana

Florida

KEY

Archaic cultures
c. 3000 BC

Red Paint

Old Copper

Adena cultures
c. 1400 BC – AD 200

Hopewell cultures
c. 300 BC – AD 500

A Havana Hopewell
B Ohio Hopewell
C Marksville Hopewell
D Santa Rosa/
   Swift Creek

**Mississippian
cultures**
*c.*AD 700 – historical
period

1 Middle Mississippian
2 Oneota
3 Fort Walton

Southern Cult:
4 Caddoan
5 Plaquemine
6 South Appalachian

Gulf of Mexico

•Poverty Point

•Teotihuacan

•La Venta

0   500m

0   800km

The Eastern Woodlands

The Eastern Woodlands is an immense region that has been the setting for a diverse array of environments and Indian cultures. Despite the diversity, there are no convenient internal barriers that would allow us to divide the region into smaller and more easily understood areas. We are forced to look at the prehistory of the Woodlands as a single unfolding drama. There is a temptation, which has claimed too many victims, to seek a simple explanation for the complexities of the region. Eighteenth-century readers quickly accepted the idea that the prehistoric earthworks of the East were built by 'Mound Builders'. By itself, this is a harmless concept, for it simply says that the builders of mounds were mound builders. Yet, all too soon a companion notion arose to the effect that the Mound Builders were a superior race that was wiped out and replaced by the Indians who were later encountered by European settlers. In the eighteenth century, Indian cultures were being vigorously exterminated or expelled westward ahead of the tide of European civilization. To attribute the prehistoric monuments of the East to these cultures would have been to grant them civilization and a status approaching equality. It was an unthinkable concession, and its rejection fueled the myth of the Mound Builders.

Even in the eighteenth century convincingly sober explanations were available for the prehistoric remains that were known. In 1784, Thomas Jefferson turned his surpassing talents to the archaeology of Virginia. He had noticed burial mounds near his home, and his curiosity was aroused by the variety of local stories that circulated about them. He decided to excavate one, and he recorded his findings in detail and with accuracy. The local belief that the Indians buried their dead standing up proved to be false. What he found were 'bundle' burials, that is, secondary interments of disarticulated bones. He did not excavate the entire mound, but on the basis of his sample, he concluded that the structure could contain as many as a thousand such burials. He also noted that none of the remains showed signs of violent death, and that they appeared to have accumulated a few at a time. That observation should have put an end to the still popular belief that mounds were built as monuments to the assembled victims of bloody battles.

The myth of the Mound Builders spawned many offspring. The Eastern Woodlands has yielded the forged or imaginary remains of Vikings, Phoenicians, Egyptians, medieval Irish monks, Welshmen, and dozens of others over the last century. The evidence for Norsemen in North America does not appear outside Greenland and Newfoundland, as we shall see in our final chapter, and for the others there is no convincing evidence at all. When the myths are stripped away, we find that what happened over the course of 12,000 years in the Eastern Woodlands

14 *Map of the Eastern Woodlands, showing ancient sites and cultures, and, in the inset, the relationship of the Woodlands to La Venta and Teotihuacan, centers of Olmec and early Mexican civilization respectively.*

was an indigenous phenomenon. Sometimes influenced by Mexican developments, sometimes acting upon their own inspiration, the Indians played out a story that is indisputably American.

The eastern and southern boundaries of the region are neatly defined by the Atlantic and the Gulf of Mexico. Elsewhere, the boundaries are not so clear. In the north, the region extends to the southern limits of the Canadian coniferous forests, a vague and uneven line that runs east to west, north of the St Lawrence River and the Great Lakes. The western boundary is a ragged line parallel to, but generally west of, the Mississippi. Here, the forests of the East give way to the grasslands of the Prairies. The Woodlands persist west of the boundary only as long tentacles following the fertile valleys of rivers that rise in the Great Plains and flow eastward to the Mississippi.

In the simplest terms, the modern Eastern Woodlands are composed of both broadleaf and coniferous trees, but there are marked differences from place to place. Hickory, oak, chestnut and other broadleaf trees flourished in the Appalachian uplands. Conifers predominated in the Atlantic and Gulf coastal lowlands. Hemlock and pine predominate over broadleaf trees in the north. It is a mosaic of subtle changes from one area to the next that is complicated by variations over time as well. Since the retreat of the last glaciers began 14,000 years ago, the forests and grasslands of the East have undergone constant change. Throughout this long period all the plants in the region produced vast quantities of tiny pollen grains, and these have been preserved in bogs and other deposits that can be accurately dated. Pollen grains from different plants can be identified and counted, and the forest cover for a given place and time can be reconstructed on paper. Thus, through the painstaking analysis of microscopic samples of pollen we are beginning to understand the changing environments that confronted prehistoric Indians.

There were no major barriers to prevent or retard the spread of prehistoric innovations within the region. Even the northward spread of agriculture after 1000 BC was slowed only by cultural conservatism, and the constant need for the selection of more rapidly maturing plant species. Farming eventually stopped at the northern fringes of the region, and has been advanced only a little farther by modern technology. As each local Indian culture adopted agriculture, it did so according to its own special traditions and environment. But the general trend was always the same, the universal human current of increasing complexity and integration, the cultural equivalent of biological evolution that we sometimes call 'progress'.

To find the roots of the historical Indians of the Eastern Woodlands, we will reach far back into their linguistic past and try to match what we find with archaeological remains. Languages can be classified much like species of animals, and common ancestors reconstructed from clues embedded in their modern descendant forms. This is fortunate, for unlike biological species languages leave no separate fossil record. Two of the region's three main aboriginal language families, the Iroquoian and the Algonquian-Muskogean, have probably been present in the East for 10,000 years or more. As bands slowly settled into regular seasonal movements within specific territories, linguistic subdivisions began to appear within these families. By the end of prehistory, they had fragmented into dozens of mutually unintelligible languages. Yet even this diversity of languages was not sufficient to prevent the relatively rapid spread of innovations, or erase common heritages. The focus of prehistoric development shifted from time to time; a given culture might lead the way during one century, only to fall behind in the next. Yet even though some localities seem to have been permanently marginal, all the prehistoric peoples of the Eastern Woodlands participated in some way in the developments discussed here.

15 *Map of the principal North American language groups.*

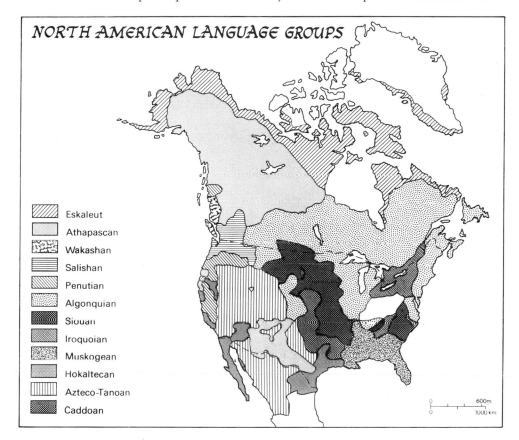

The Archaic lifeway

The environmental changes that followed the retreat of the continental glaciers were not sudden or catastrophic. Children were born and grew to old age without ever perceiving the slow and widespread evolution of their habitat. Even so, the cumulative effects were profound. By 7000 BC, most of the dominant animal species of the Ice Age were extinct in the East, or had dwindled to tiny refugee herds. The people who had depended upon these meat sources for so long gradually had to shift their attention to other kinds of food. More and more plant and animal species were utilized within each local area, and the free-roaming nomadism of the Paleo-Indians gave way to a pattern of regular seasonal movements. The Indians of this new, Archaic lifeway came to count on the availability of particular resources at particular times and places, and planned their movements accordingly. Under these conditions, chance encounters with other bands were less likely, but organized

33

contacts increased. Regular meetings of bands could be planned into the predictable seasonal round, fostering the growth of social and economic ties that went beyond band limits. Even in the absence of agriculture and sedentary life, the cultures of the Archaic period began to form the dynamic network that would later lead to the development of extensive trade in luxury goods, and the dissemination of elaborate religious cults.

The oldest evidence for the Archaic lifeway, dating to about 8000 B C, comes from camp sites in the southern part of the Eastern Woodlands. Evidence from northern sections for this period is generally scanty or absent, despite intensive archaeological research. Large portions of the region must simply have been unoccupied for many centuries following 8000 B C. The explanation may well lie in the progression of environmental changes that followed the retreat of the last glacier. As the glacial ice melted back, the tundra along its margins and the forests that had been compressed into refuge areas began to shift northward. Unfortunately for the Indians and the animals they hunted, it was not simply a matter of moving with their environments, for the tundra and the forests were changing in character as well as location. The tundra of the Ice Age had been an ideal environment for many species; but with the retreat northward, it entered a part of the continent recently scoured by ice, where the sun comes and goes on a seasonal rather than a daily basis. Its ability to support large animal populations and the Indians who depended upon them was drastically reduced. As the result of a similar process, around 8000 B C the northern part of the Eastern Woodlands came to be dominated by spruce, fir, and pine forests, which offer little food for herbivores or carnivores, and therefore little for humans either. Thus, the development of the Archaic lifeway was primarily a southern one, and many northern areas were simply abandoned.

By 5000 B C, however, the silent conifer forests of the north were beginning to change as broadleaf trees became established. By 3000 B C, much of the northern section was covered with a mixed forest that attracted game animals and man. Probably most, if not all, of the Indians who moved into the northern Eastern Woodlands were ancestors of the Algonquian-speaking tribes that occupied the same territory in the colonial period. By now they had diverged substantially from their Muskogean relatives in the south, separated from them by the large block of Iroquoian-speakers in the Appalachian uplands.

Archaeological evidence indicates that it was here, in the north, that the ideological foundation for much of what followed later was laid. Mortuary practices were increasingly complex all across the Eastern Woodlands, but by 3000 B C they were particularly elaborate in the north. Although careful burials with grave offerings can be found almost anywhere, really elaborate examples are generally discovered only in sedentary and usually agricultural contexts. Perhaps these northern hunter-gatherers found stimulation in the natural richness of their environment, only recently reoccupied and still not supporting a large human population. Whatever the specific ecological and ideological forces were, we can assume that the northern mortuary complexes developed without significant external influence.

The axis of the northern Archaic developments stretches east–west through the Great Lakes, New England, and the Maritime Provinces of Canada. One of the most outstanding examples of elaborate mortuary ceremonialism in the region was once

15

attributed to a mysterious race of 'Red Paint People', so-called because the farmers who found the first burial pits were impressed by their linings of bright red hema-tite. Indian cemeteries of this kind, with stone tools as offerings, have since been found scattered throughout New England and the Maritimes. Red pigment, with its strong suggestion of blood and life, has been used in a similar way for thousands of years, and in many parts of the world. Here, as elsewhere, the key seems to have been the availability of the pigment in natural deposits.

The northern soils do not afford good preservation, and skeletal remains have rarely survived the millennia. Most graves contain celts (axes), adzes and gouges, often highly polished and sometimes still sharp enough to inflict a deep cut on a careless archaeologist. All three forms are heavy woodworking tools, probably designed for the construction of dugout canoes, which these fishermen and hunters of sea mammals and caribou used in their everyday activities. Other equipment included fire-making kits of iron pyrite and flint, and whetstones to sharpen the edges of the woodworking tools. The finest whetstones are long slender tablets, pointed at both ends, and holed at one end for suspension. Certain graves also contain spear points ground from sheets of slate. Some are long bayonets, exquisite artifacts so slender that it is difficult to imagine how they could have survived use in the real world, or even the strains of their own manufacture. Some were skillfully faceted until they had the cross-sections of flattened hexagons, and the facets were incised with delicate geometric designs.

The cemeteries allow us to probe the ideology of these people. Here was an egalitarian society, with few favors shown according to birth, age, or sex. The dead were buried with the tools they valued most or could use most skillfully. Perhaps they needed such tools to build the spiritual boats that would take them to the next world. Like people everywhere, they perceived that journey and its end in terms of the world they already knew.

The exotic and beautiful artifacts found in graves are rarely discovered even as fragments in habitation areas. What we find in the refuse of day-to-day living are more practical and mundane implements. Perhaps the finest craftsmanship and the rarest materials were reserved for grave goods, or the prized possessions and status symbols of individuals during their lifetime, accompanying them even after death. In any case, the finest works of these ancient artisans were removed from the world of the living at a rate that nearly equalled their manufacture, a pattern of conspicuous consumption that was to continue in the East for 3500 years.

It is possible that the finest grave goods were made by specialized craftsmen, but this seems improbable. The economy of people subsisting upon hunting and gather-ing is unlikely to have supported craft specialists. The grave goods themselves also argue against such an interpretation. Each grave lot uncovered appears to be a special collection of unique pieces. One grave may contain a dozen slate bayonets, no two of them identical, with no artifacts of any other type. Another grave may contain only three or four finely made adze blades. It seems likely that each person produced his or her own grave goods in the course of day-to-day living, keeping them as treasured possessions even after death.

Some of the Red Paint artifacts are known not so much for the excellence of their manufacture as for the material from which they were made. Many projectile points are fashioned out of an attractive translucent quartzite, known to occur naturally only on the Labrador Peninsula. Notwithstanding the artistic qualities of these points, their real significance is that they provide clear evidence for the early establishment of long-distance trading in luxury goods. As we shall see, this later grew to almost continental proportions, facilitating the development of widespread prehistoric art forms and the distribution of finished pieces.

The most extraordinary Red Paint cemetery found so far is the site at Port au 137 Choix in northern Newfoundland. The site is at the northern extremity of the area penetrated by peoples practicing the Red Paint cult. It is in an area where the closed conifer forest still predominates, 4000 years since the site was used, and thousands more since the disappearance of the last glacier. Then as now, human habitation would not have been possible without the resources of the sea.

The Port au Choix cemetery is situated on an old abandoned beach several meters above the present shore of the Gulf of St Lawrence. The beach is salted with tiny fragments of shell that have served to neutralize the normal acidity of the soil, and permit the preservation of bone and antler. Here, the skeletons of people buried 4000 years ago survive in near-perfect preservation. Some 100 individuals were unearthed, a population almost equally divided between males and females. About half were adults, the other half children. These people appear to have been healthy and robust, probably quite similar in appearance to the historical Indians of New England. Tooth wear was heavy, no doubt because hides had to be softened by chewing, and some adults had lost teeth. But tooth decay, which afflicts people with diets high in starch and sugar, was almost nonexistent. Their bone and antler artifacts have also survived, along with the more durable tools already well known from sites elsewhere. Among other things, they show us that bayonets and other fine slate artifacts had bone prototypes. The site has yielded many implements that are duplicated in both materials. Finally, Port au Choix has produced beautifully made combs, pins, effigies and other items of bone and antler that have apparently perished elsewhere. We can infer that such trinkets were widespread, but we are unlikely to find many more sites with preservation as good as at Port au Choix.

The Red Paint Indians were not the lost race that some eighteenth-century farmers thought them to be. They were among the ancestors of the historical Algonquians of the Northeast, and for fifteen centuries they supported an elaborate mortuary cult along the streams of the northern forests. This rich ceremonialism was already in decline by 1500 BC, for reasons that we are only now beginning to understand. By 500 BC, the clear ponds of the inland forests were evolving into bogs as a natural consequence of post-glacial erosion. The northeastern Woodlands seem to have lost their capacity to support human occupation. As the population thinned, and the traditional seasonal patterns became untenable, the old cult faded too. The area reverted to a cultural backwater for the remainder of prehistory.

Far to the west, at the opposite end of the northern Archaic axis, are found the remains of what has long been called the 'Old Copper' culture, dating from around 14 3000 BC. The culture takes its name from the copper objects that the Indians of the time produced. Glacial deposits near the southern shore of Lake Superior and on Isle Royale contain lumps of native copper. The prehistoric Algonquians learned how to mine and beat these 'stones' into useful shapes. They never developed true metallurgy, or progressed to the stage of smelting or casting. But they knew how to keep the metal from becoming brittle by annealing it, that is, by repeatedly heating the copper and plunging it into cold water, and this enabled them to fashion a much greater variety of shapes than cold hammering itself allowed. Many copper tools were modeled on earlier prototypes made of bone, stone, or other materials.

Old Copper implements include long broad spear points with long pointed tangs, short stems, or flanges for hafting. Knives are straight and pointed, or curved like the semilunar 'woman's knife' of later Eskimo culture. The knife prototypes were clearly slate, whereas barbed copper harpoon points came from bone originals. Copper adzes duplicate stone examples found elsewhere. Other forms include double-ended awls and punches, always well made.

As a subtradition, Old Copper paralleled the Archaic Red Paint culture of the Northeast. Curiously, there is little to equal either of them in the lower Great Lakes area. Old Copper is restricted to the vicinity of the upper Great Lakes. It may be that something similar will yet be found in the intervening region, around Lakes Ontario and Erie. Alternatively, perhaps this area was ecologically unsuitable for earlier Archaic developments. This was certainly not the case in later periods, for the focus of the Archaic tradition shifted southward into Ohio as the exotic Red Paint and Old Copper cultures waned.

Adzes, celts, and gouges were not the only artifacts of ground and polished stone produced by Archaic cultures. The craftsmen of the time also produced beautifully made 'boatstones', effigy 'birdstones', and holed 'bannerstones'. Their function went unrecognized for decades, but it now seems clear that all were used as weights on spear-throwers. Boatstones and birdstones were simply lashed to the wooden shafts, 16 the latter carved to look like birds primarily for magical purposes. Bannerstones, 17 so-called 'winged' objects, were attached to the shaft through a long cylindrical hole.

As we have already observed, the spear-thrower was used mainly before the introduction of the bow and arrow as a means of increasing the length of a man's throwing arm, and therefore the velocity of his throw. Simple physics shows that the addition of a weight to a rigid spear-thrower shaft does not improve its effectiveness. The small size of the shaft hole in most bannerstones provides a clue, however. If rigid, a shaft of the size indicated by this hole would snap on the first throw. The conclusion must be that the Archaic peoples were using flexible shafts. Indeed, there is some archaeological evidence indicating that extremely tough but flexible ironwood shafts were used with stone weights. It seems that the advantages of flexible shafts now universally recognized by golfers and fishermen were discovered and developed by Indians in North America over 7000 years ago, long before the invention of fiberglass. It would appear to be no simple coincidence that ironwood trees and spear-thrower weights have very similar distributions in North America.

16 *This 14-cm.-long birdstone of banded slate, about 3500 years old, would have been strapped as a weight to the flexible shaft of a spear-thrower, thus giving added spring and power to the hunter's throw.*

Poverty Point and Olmec influences

The cultural center of the Eastern Woodlands in the centuries after 1500 BC was the 'Adena' complex of Ohio, named after the mound group and modern town of the same name. The ideological basis for the new development was probably derived from the earlier mortuary cult to the northeast, but something more was added. The earthen mounds, huge when it is remembered that they were built by hand, were new to the Eastern Woodlands. The 'Glacial Kame' culture, which centered in southern Michigan, Ohio, and Indiana, and which flourished at about the same time as Adena, was for many years generally accepted as the innovator of burial mounds. Early burials of this culture are often found in kames (small abrupt hills) left behind by the last glaciers. Later burials are in artificial mounds. It was reasoned that the prototype burial mound was a natural kame. However, radiocarbon dating has shown that artificial Adena mounds are as old as Glacial Kame burials, suggesting that the latter were the work of country cousins trying to duplicate more elaborate Adena practices. The Glacial Kame badge was the sandal-sole gorget, an asymmetrical tablet presumably worn around the neck. These occur in many burials of this culture, and a few of them have carved designs.

The use of glacial kames and other natural hills is known for the earlier Red Paint burials as well as for other relatively early cultures across the northern zone. Certainly this was part of the Adena heritage. But there is also evidence of a strong stimulus from Mexico, which comes in the form of a single extraordinary site that is not duplicated anywhere else in North America, the site of Poverty Point, Louisiana.

Poverty Point is incredibly huge. The main complex, or 'village', built around 1500 BC and therefore early enough to predate most of Adena, is a series of six concentric octagons nested within each other. Each is composed of eight ridges of earth about 2 meters high. The outer octagon is about 1300 meters in diameter. The inner octagons are progressively smaller, each about 100 meters less in diameter than the last. Mound A, to the west of the 'village', is over 20 meters high and over 200

14

18

14

17 Once thought to have been symbols of authority – hence their name, 'bannerstones' – these objects, averaging 10 cm. in width, are now explained as spear thrower weights. Like birdstones, of similar age and function, their forms are often winged.

18 A strange animal, with eyes and ears askew and umbilical cord still attached, decorates this rare engraved sandal-sole gorget, 18 cm. long. Gorgets of this type, usually undecorated, were characteristic of the northern Woodlands Glacial Kame people, who often buried their dead in natural kames or hills in the centuries following 1500 BC.

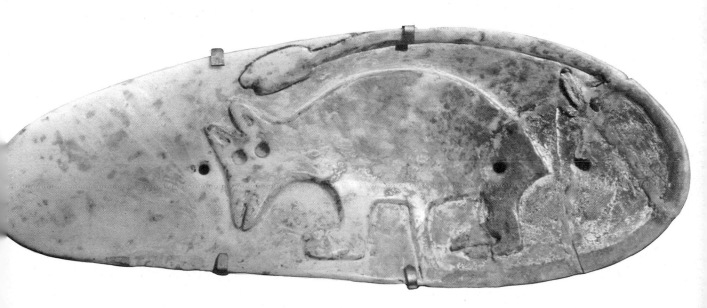

meters long. A long ramp descends toward the 'village' to the east. Another somewhat smaller mound stands to the north. A person standing on Mound A can view the vernal and autumnal equinoxes directly across the center of the 'village'. This is the point at which the sun rises twice a year, on the first day of spring and the first day of autumn respectively.

Artifacts found at Poverty Point include most notably thousands of fired-clay balls, apparently used to boil food. Instead of preparing meals directly over open fires, the Indians would drop hot clay balls into their cooking vessels to heat up their food. Hot stones were more often used in other regions – hence the usual name given to the practice, 'stone-boiling'. Also found are small bird effigies and clay figurines. The latter are small human figures that bear a close resemblance to those found along the Gulf Coast of Mexico, produced by the Olmecs, the creators of the 14 first American civilization. Poverty Point itself is reminiscent of La Venta and El Corral, both well-known Olmec sites that were occupied at about this time. It is difficult to avoid concluding that Poverty Point was a product of Olmec influence, and the gateway through which the idea of monumental architecture passed into the Eastern Woodlands.

To understand Olmec influences in the Eastern Woodlands, we must examine the origins of this early civilization. The retreat of the Canadian ice sheets and the environmental changes that ensued across the continent forced the Indians of Mexico to an early abandonment of the Paleo-Indian lifeway. The new pattern that emerged was one of intensive exploitation by hunting and gathering, an Archaic lifeway much like that of the Eastern Woodlands. The important difference was that the Mexican highlands were relatively rich in plants that had some potential as domesticates. Among them was a kind of grass that was knee high at maturity, and produced only a small stem of seeds just under a tassel at the top of the plant. Together, the seeds formed a cluster about the size of the last joint in an adult's little finger. This, however, was wild maize, ancestral to the modern plants that sometimes produce cobs of corn the size of a man's forearm. The Indians of highland Mexico selected this plant and others, such as beans and squash, because they could be planted with a pointed stick and tended with a hoe. Without the plow, plants that had to be sown broadcast were beyond consideration. Once under development, the crops were distributed outside their natural environments in the Mexican highlands, and into the hot humid Gulf lowlands. Here, simple slash-and-burn agricultural techniques, involving the planting of crops in the ashes of burned-down trees and shrubs, allowed heavy production along with a settled and relatively dense human population. It was on this basis that Olmec civilization began to flourish in the centuries preceding 1500 BC.

The Olmecs built clay-sided temple mounds, and mosaic pavements of serpentine blocks. Colossal heads were hewn from solid basalt, while smaller pieces were carved from Mexican jade. Pervading much of their art was the feline god motif 19 which has come to be regarded as their hallmark. Sometimes drastically stylized, sometimes disarmingly natural, the art of the Olmecs was the starting point for much of the later art of prehistoric Middle America or 'Mesoamerica'. In much the same way, later Mayan calendrics and Mesoamerican architecture can be traced back to the Olmecs. The sources of their inspiration are still obscure, but the faint trails

19 *This 31-cm.-high jade celt represents the 'were-jaguar', mythical product of the union between woman and jaguar and hallmark of Olmec civilization (1500 BC–AD 100) which flourished along the Mexican Gulf Coast. Olmec arts profoundly influenced those of later Mesoamerica and the Eastern Woodlands.*

seem to lead to the Mexican highlands, Central and South America. Certainly there is no reason to presume influences from overseas. Olmec architecture, which is only superficially similar to architecture of the same age in the Old World, has many descendants, one of them Poverty Point.

Thus, the prehistory of the Eastern Woodlands after 1500 BC can be linked to Olmec civilization in Mexico. The immense architecture of Poverty Point, wedded to the ideology that already existed in the northern part of the region, gave rise to the burial-mound cults that dominate the prehistory of the Woodlands for the next 2000 years.

Adena-Hopewell culture

A conservative Archaic lifeway persisted in some areas, but by 1000 BC it had been abandoned over much of the Eastern Woodlands. In very broad terms, the new lifeway was characterized by the manufacture of pottery, burial mounds, and the beginnings of agriculture. The economy was based upon the cultivation of sunflower, goosefoot, pigweed, marsh elder, gourd, squash, and maize, the last two belonging to the maize-beans-squash trio of staple crops that, as we have seen, had been developed in Mexico over the previous millennia. Thus the Woodland Indians adopted the most suitable Mexican plants, and extended the idea of domestication to some local plants as well. What emerged was a variety of localized agricultural systems, which provided these Indians with both the stimulation and the economic capacity to embark upon a vigorous cultural florescence. Huge earthworks were built, a basketload at a time, and raw materials from great distances were transformed into artistic masterpieces. It was one of those rare periods that follow the sudden opening of new potentials, but precede the subsequent rise in population and competition for resources. For so long as that economic climate prevailed, the Indians of the Eastern Woodlands were in a golden age.

At the heart of it all was Adena culture, centered in southern Ohio and the adjacent 14 portions of Indiana, Kentucky, Pennsylvania, and West Virginia. Over 200 Adena sites are scattered throughout the heartland. Each shows features that link it to Adena culture as a whole. Yet each also provides an idiosyncratic twist on the central theme, a theme uniformly preoccupied with death.

In southern Ohio, earthworks are both early and extensive. Like hedgerows, sharp ridges of earth define large circles, squares, and pentagons, or sometimes follow the irregular edges of flat-topped hills. The enclosed fields average about 100 meters in diameter, and seem to have been for ceremonial rather than defensive purposes, hence their common name, 'sacred circles'. The earth from which the walls were constructed was most often taken from just inside the perimeter, giving the false impression of an interior moat. There are usually openings into the enclosures, and there are examples of two or more enclosures linked together as a single huge structure.

Adena burials might be in simple clay-lined basins, or in large log tombs built to contain one, two, or three individuals and buried under a mound. Many corpses, especially in the simpler graves, were cremated. The occupants of more elaborate tombs were apparently often smeared with red ocher or graphite, and in these cases grave goods are more frequently present. The burial mounds occur both inside and outside the large sacred circles. Some are small, built in one stage as a tomb and monument to a single important person. Others are larger, often over twenty meters high. The mounds sometimes lie over subsurface posthole patterns that indicate that they were constructed on top of pre-existing round houses. These houses may have been ossuaries, shrines, or simply dwellings. In any case, they were usually burned down as part of the burial ceremony.

Some log tombs appear to have been provided with entrances and left open so that additional burials could be added from time to time. Once sealed, these tombs eventually collapsed under the weight of the earth above, leaving the archaeologist to reconstruct the originals through careful excavation. Except in cases of cremation, Adena burials are usually in an extended, face-up position. Occasionally an additional severed skull was included, but it is not clear whether this belonged to a respected ancestor or an unfortunate enemy. There were further elaborations of these rites, but the important central factor is the attention given to the disposal of the dead in Adena culture. Creative energy was directed toward this apparent cult of the dead almost to the exclusion of everything else.

Although the Adena peoples made pottery, it was not the subject of much artistic elaboration, and played no role in burial ceremonialism. In fact, Adena grave goods of any sort are not common. A few impressive pieces exist, however. 'Reel-shaped' gorgets, usually with two perforations near the center, were made from stone tablets, often banded slate or some other attractive, fine-grained stone that takes a high polish. The tablets varied in shape from rectangles with slightly concave sides to extreme H-shaped forms. Other tablets were engraved with elaborate curvilinear designs on one or both sides, usually abstract zoomorphic motifs, most commonly a bird of prey. The uses of all these artifacts are not clearly understood. At least some of the gorgets were probably used as spear-thrower weights. The engraved tablets might have served as dye stamps for textiles, but a more likely explanation is that they were used for the application of tattoo designs. Bone awls, which would have been needed for tattooing, are often discovered with the engraved tablets, and the tablets themselves often bear grooves used to sharpen the awls.

Another important Adena artifact class is the tubular pipe. A few examples are elaborately carved, such as the famous one showing the effigy of a standing man, a goitrous dwarf. The first appearance of pipes probably marks the first appearance of tobacco in the Woodlands. All tobacco species originated in South America. The tobacco smoked by the Indians of the East appears to have arrived in North America by way of the West Indies or perhaps Mexico. The plant and smoking equipment were probably transmitted together. It is unlikely that North American Indians smoked other substances before the arrival of pipes and tobacco from the south, but they soon learned to use local plants in addition to tobacco, and sometimes in combination with it. The hardy tobacco species popular in the East eventually spread beyond the growing limits of most other important prehistoric crops, growing in areas where other domesticated plants could not grow. The English quickly adopted tobacco after 1600, but introduced a West Indian species into Virginia. It is this species, not the original hardy species, that came to be so popular with Europeans.

Other Adena artifacts include many made of native copper imported from northern Michigan. The metal was most often hammered into bracelets, beads, rings and gorgets, although there are a few copper axes. Enough tiny textile fragments have been preserved to tell us that the Adena people were accomplished in this craft too.

The Adena cult was not simply an extension of the pattern set by the Red Paint and other earlier developments. As we have seen, the emphasis in earlier centuries was upon more or less equal treatment for all the deceased, and burial with whatever prized goods each may have possessed. Adena burials, however, fall into broad classes, suggesting that now people had different standings in society, and received different burial rites accordingly. We can conclude that persons cremated in simple graves did not enjoy the same high status as those buried with offerings in log tombs. The general implication is that Adena society was not composed of small bands of equals as earlier societies had been. The comparative consideration of historically known cultures around the world suggests that Adena society was organized in lineages, groups of families linked by descent from a common ancestor. There may even have been clans, groups of linked families which could unite lineages living in different villages. Kin units of this sort often have formal leaders, and it may have been these powerful individuals who were given the most impressive burials. Alternatively, high status burial could have been accorded to persons who managed to become first among equals in a village, regardless of family connections.

Whatever specific principles may have been involved, it is apparent that Adena culture fostered the early stages of what anthropologists call 'stratified' society. But this does not necessarily imply the emergence of large and compact towns. The Adena people themselves appear to have been neither numerous nor territorially expansive. Their small communities were often composed of no more than four or five houses, each of which probably sheltered an extended family of closely related people. The houses themselves were circular, with a typical diameter of less than ten meters. This does not even approach the size of some historical Indian towns with their populations of hundreds or even thousands packed into communal houses. The Adena and other Eastern Woodland cultures of the time still had no plant domesticates that would provide an adequate substitute for animal protein. They avoided malnutrition by hunting and gathering wild foods to combine with their domesticates. It was a subsistence pattern that required small scattered settlements for the best use of limited wild resources.

The Adena burial cult was focused in Ohio, but its influences can be seen as far away as the Atlantic coast. Adena artifacts are found near Chesapeake Bay, and Adena burial mounds occur in New York State. These remains were once thought to have been the result of colonization by small groups moving out of Ohio. Now, however, it seems more likely that they resulted from trade contacts and the adoption of the cult by the native tribes of the coastal regions. It may be that the people of the Ohio Adena were seeking raw materials or other goods from these areas, and were able to obtain them in exchange for finished goods. The beautiful finished pieces could have stimulated interest in the cult among tribes not familiar with it, and that interest could have been further enhanced by the prospect of obtaining more finished pieces.

Adena culture waned by about AD 200, not because of internal decadence or external catastrophe, but simply because it was in the process of becoming something else. The people did not disappear, but the complex of artifacts and burial practices that we conveniently refer to as Adena went out of fashion. At its height, Adena culture spawned a new series of developments that were to spread burial mound ceremonialism and trade in luxury items through most of the Eastern Woodlands.

These new developments are called 'Hopewell', a name which like 'Adena' derives from an Ohio mound group. The earliest such development, the Havana Hopewell, appeared in what is now Illinois by 300 BC. It may have evolved out of 'Red Ocher' culture, an Illinois culture not to be confused with the Red Paint culture of the Northeast, with strong influences from the Adena of Ohio. The resulting synthesis then spread back to Ohio, leading to the development of Ohio Hopewell around 100 BC, apparently while some nearby tribes still perpetuated the old Adena culture. Elsewhere, Hopewell sites developed at later dates and all flourished until about AD 550.

14

The rapid spread of Hopewell from one local group to another suggests that we should view it as a religious cult, rather than a whole culture. In a complex chain reaction, cultures scattered over much of the region began to interact with the Hopewell heartland, making the cult their own, and trading what they had for strange and beautiful finished artifacts. It was the logical consequence of the trends initiated by Adena.

Much of the excavation of classic Hopewell remains was carried out in the last century when antiquarianism was at its peak. Mounds were excavated in large numbers but with little care, all to the exclusion of village sites. As a result, we still know little of the daily lives of these peoples, and much important data from the mounds was lost in the excavators' rush to acquire valuable antiquities. We are not entirely in the dark, however. We know that Hopewell mounds tended to be built in two stages. The first was usually a low construction containing a log tomb or a series of crematory basins. Later, this was usually covered by a mound of earth, sometimes twelve meters high and often more than thirty meters wide. Unlike most Adena burials, Hopewell burials were usually accompanied by lavish offerings of grave goods.

In Ohio, Hopewell mound-earthwork complexes are larger and more complicated than Adena examples. Circular, rectangular, or octagonal earthworks sometimes exceed 500 meters in diameter. Two or more may occur linked, as in some Adena cases. The internal 'moats' are trenches dug to provide material for the earthworks; their use as fortifications is quite improbable. Burial mounds are usually within the enclosures, as is the case at the Mound City site near Chillicothe, Ohio, which is preserved as a National Monument. Here, twenty-four mounds lie within a rectangular enclosure covering thirteen acres of land.

Another extraordinary site is Serpent Mound, southwest of Mound City. Here, an earthwork like an uncoiling serpent winds for half a kilometer along a hilltop. A hemispherical mound lies at one end, clasped in the jaws of the serpent. The other end of the monument tapers off to a tightly coiled tail. Apparently, the monument was a religious effigy that did not function primarily as a burial place.

20

20 *Serpent Mound winds for nearly half a kilometer between modern pathways on an Ohio hilltop. Built about 2000 years ago by the Adena–Hopewell peoples, earliest of the mound builders, this unique religious effigy was perhaps inspired by a comet or some other rare natural phenomenon.*

21 *A well-dressed man of the Hopewell culture (300 BC–AD 500) wore ear-spools and pendants of beaten native copper, and pearl beads of fresh-water shellfish. The ear-spools resemble blossoms of the dogwood tree, the bark of which may have been smoked with tobacco as a mild narcotic.*

Some Hopewell mounds are large structures containing hundreds of individual burials that must have taken decades to accumulate. Whether cremated or placed in log tombs, the dead were given grave goods in accordance with their status in the community. The most important persons appear to have been buried singly with large offerings under small mounds. One such burial had with it more than 135 kilograms of imported obsidian, over half of all that found to date in Ohio Hopewell sites.

Hopewell artisans produced much of the finest prehistoric art of North America. To say that they were competent is to understate the case. They were highly skilled in working a wide variety of raw materials, imported from great distances, into an astonishing array of forms. Large amounts of native copper were imported from the southern shore of Lake Superior and beaten into cut-outs, ear-spools, artificial noses (presumably for the dead), beads, gorgets, and even panpipes. Two-dimensional drawings were sometimes embossed on sheets of copper, and thicker sheets were used as breastplates. Other nuggets were shaped into celts, axes, adzes, and awls. There is even a copper imitation of a deer-antler headdress accompanied by a pair of copper ear-spools, each beaten into the shape of a flower. The ear-spools resemble the blossoms of the dogwood tree, the inner bark of which Indians discovered to be mildly narcotic when smoked with tobacco. It seems likely that these and the headdress were part of the magical paraphernalia of a 'shaman', or sorcerer.

21

Meteoric iron was also sometimes used, usually in conjunction with copper. It was beaten into foil, and used to jacket such things as copper ear-spools, axes, adzes, and even in one case a human arm bone.

Small nuggets of silver were imported, apparently from Ontario, and tiny amounts of gold have also been found. Cubes of galena, a lead mineral, came from the Mississippi valley. Mica was imported from the southern Appalachian area, and sheets of it were transformed into exotic cut-outs. Like the copper cut-outs, they often take the shapes of serpents, animal claws, human heads, hands, swastikas and other geometric designs. There are extraordinary examples of abstract profiles of the claws of birds of prey, and still others of long tapering human hands. The area that 6, 22 produced mica for Hopewell consumption also provided quartz crystal and chlorite.

Large conch shells and smaller shells were imported from Florida and the Gulf Coast. The same area provided the teeth of barracudas, sharks, and alligators, turtle shells, and the jaws of various marine fish. Grizzly bear canine teeth came from far to the west, probably the Rocky Mountains.

Hopewell artisans were also skilled knappers, and the obsidian they used was imported all the way from Yellowstone Park, Wyoming. Chert was obtained for 3 the same purpose from closer sources in Ohio, Indiana, and Illinois, and a mottled 4 chalcedony was brought in from either North Dakota or Montana. A translucent knife was chipped from quartz imported from Arkansas. All these materials were 2 used to make knives and projectile points. Some of the tools may have been utilitarian, but many others are so large, thin, or elegant that they seem to have been designed only for show.

The utilitarian pottery of the various Hopewell cultures resembles that of Adena. Unlike Adena, however, Hopewell artisans made a series of especially fine types that appear to have been intended only as grave vessels. Some of these bear panels or zones, each decorated separately with incised lines. Various plastic techniques were used to produce an almost endless variety of decorative motifs. Hopewell potters also made copies of stone pipes and copper ear-plugs in clay. Finally, there are a few extraordinary examples of naturalistic human figurines. These are unlike any clay 26, x figurines found in Mexico or the Desert West. From these, and from the careful excavation of burials, it has been possible to show the dress and personal ornamentation of Hopewell people. Even hairstyles with elaborate braids, topknots, and shaved x patches are discernible. Still, it would be a mistake to conclude that either the figurines or the more elaborate burials represent ordinary Hopewell men and women. We must conclude that the more extraordinary the find, the more extraordinary the person or persons represented. At least some of the figurines appear to represent shamans, people whose high status would have been intertwined with magical powers. One depicts a man with his hair pulled into a large knot over his x forehead. The knot may in fact represent the single horn that is a shaman's symbol in both Asia and the Americas. The wide distribution of the symbol suggests that it is a very ancient one, part of the ideological baggage of the first Americans.

Textile fragments sometimes survive next to copper ornaments, protected from decay by the copper salts. These small bits of cloth show the Hopewell to have been accomplished weavers, producing tightly woven fabrics, frequently decorated with batik-like designs.

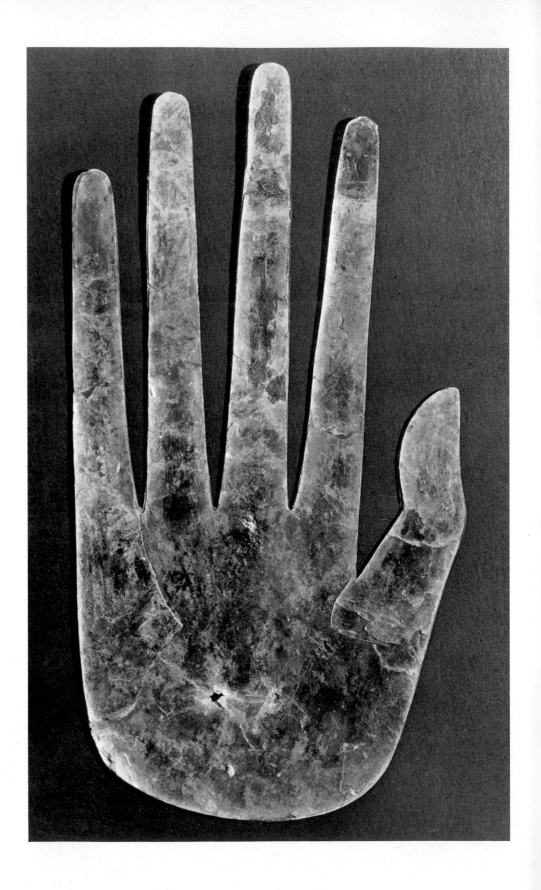

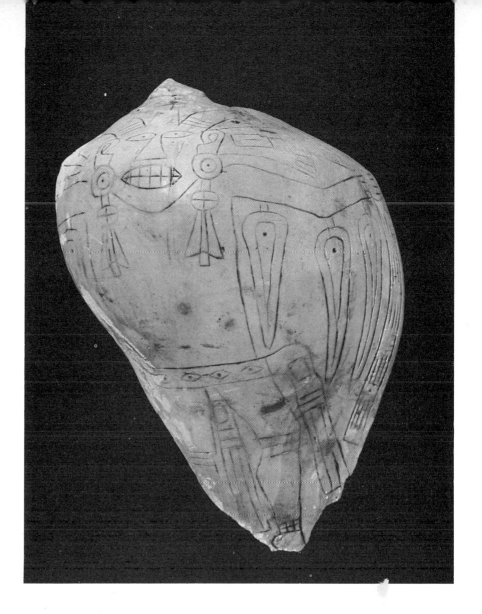

Thus, running through all the later local expressions of Mississippian culture is a common thread that is usually called the 'Southern Cult'. Archaeologically, the cult appears as an interrelated series of ritual objects and design motifs. These were clearly used in ceremonies connected with the large earth temple mounds, and appear most frequently in the largest sites. Favorite motifs are a human hand with an eye in the palm, a sunburst, an elaborate cross, an arrow splitting a disk (bi-lobed arrow), the forked, weeping, or winged eye, death motifs, and several more abstract designs. Such motifs appear frequently incised or painted on pottery, carved in shell, sculpted in wood and stone, knapped in flint, painted on cloth, and even embossed on thin sheets of native copper. Some of the symbolism can be easily interpreted in terms of historical Indian ideologies, and much of it seems to be derived from Mexico. Wind, sun, fire, and human sacrifice are all familiar themes. Still, there are also elements of the older indigenous Adena-Hopewell religious cults, and the Southern Cult cannot be viewed simply as a Mexican transplant.

30–36,
XI

Opposite: one image seen commonly in Southern Cult art is the figure of a leaping man, adorned with headdress, ear-plugs, weeping eyes, tail, and bands on wrists and ankles. The bird-like attributes of many of the depictions suggest that this is a flying shaman, perhaps even a god.

35 This 10-cm. shell gorget from Tennessee shows a flying shaman with a death's head in one hand and a ceremonial mace in the other.

36 The flying shaman on this 7-cm. shell gorget from Etowah, Georgia, has the wings and talons of a bird of prey. See Plate 34.

Right: Mississippian men wore elaborate ornaments and facial paint.

37 A shell gorget depicts a man with Southern Cult headdress and ear-plugs similar to those of the Tennessee figure (Plate 35).

38 The topknot hairstyle, dating back to Hopewell times (Plate X), is shown incised together with a weeping eye and other facial decoration on this 6 cm. shell head.

One figure is seen frequently in Southern Cult art, and we have it repeated in three different forms here. Basically, it is the figure of a human male, his face always in profile and his limbs flung out or flexed in any of a variety of postures. Feathers are shown as either hanging from or attached behind his arms, and he is usually provided with a tail as well. Frequently there is a bird-like headdress, and the area around the mouth is decorated in a manner very much like that seen on the effigy pots examined earlier. Bands often appear on wrists, ankles, calves, and upper arms. The variety of postures depicted has led to statements that the man is dancing, jumping, running, squatting, sitting, and so on. However, many examples show postures that are physically impossible for terrestrial man. The legs are so positioned that they could not support the body, and the appended tail extends far below the feet. Yet neither is this just the product of artistic license or naïvete. There is in fact a single explanation that fits all the cases, and this is that the figure is flying. Thus we have not a man disguised as a bird, but another case of a shaman having *become* a supernatural being. In the art of the Southern Cult, we see portrayed the god himself, not a series of cartoon records of ancient ceremonies.

The god, whatever his name may have been, is laden with the symbolic trappings of the Southern Cult. In an embossed-copper specimen, a bi-lobed arrow extends from the god's headdress. In his left hand he carries a disembodied human head, which in turn bears the weeping- or forked-eye motif. Another specimen is carved on the exterior of a conch shell. In this case, the feathers that attach to the arms are made to double as winged eyes. In the god's ears are sun circle ear-plugs, and hanging from them are examples of the simple cross motif. Eyes appear again on the belt. Bands on knees and ankles complete the attire.

We see two other examples on shell disks. The death's head is repeated on one, and both have several sun circles. One has bi-lobed arrows connected to wrist bands, and in place of hands there are the talons of a bird of prey. One hand remains in human form on the other example, but here both feet have become talons.

A third example of shell disk carving bears a spider within a sun disk. To many American Indians the spider's web symbolized universal symmetry and order, at the center of which resided the spider, which in the real world was often accorded great respect. In this case, the spider's thorax bears the Southern Cult cross symbol, which probably represents the sacred fire. It is clear that, as with the other specimens, we have in this piece much more than a pretty ornament. It is superficially simple, but nevertheless contains a complex religious symbolism that must have been important to its wearer.

The Southern Cult does not appear fully formed until after AD 1000. By this time the Mexican center of Teotihuacan had been a dusty ruin for over 200 years, and the highland city of Tula was the capital of the new Toltec Empire. It was a period of warfare and turmoil in Mexico, and one of continued Mexican influence in the Eastern Woodlands. One of the most common artifacts of the Southern Cult is the small copper long-nosed-god mask. Examples are known from many sites, and it may be that the small mask represents the patron god of the Mexican traders we have called 'pochteca'. The small masks do indeed resemble known representations of this god that have been found in Mexico. The bi-lobed arrow motif may have had a similar origin among the pochteca, but for now we can do little more than speculate.

x This naturalistic Hopewell clay figurine from Ohio depicts a man with his hair pulled into a knot over his forehead. The knot may represent the single horn, a shaman's symbol both in Asia and America. See Plate 38.

X

XI, 39 Details of hairstyle
and facial decoration are
emphasized on these two
powerful Mississippian
faces, possibly portraits,
embossed in copper. The
forked eye and ear-spool
(opposite) and the wide
band across the cheek
(right) are typical Southern
Cult conventions.

40 One of the commonest artifacts of the Southern Cult is the small long-nosed-god mask, which may represent the patron god of the Mexican traders or 'pochteca' who helped transmit Mexican influences to the Eastern Woodlands. These two tiny masks, 5 cm. high, are made from bone, but examples are also known in wood and copper.

The Mississippians often wore shell disks suspended on the breast, and engraved with complex religious images.

41 Crested woodpeckers guard the four directions that encircle the central sun on this 8.5-cm. disk from Tennessee. Woodpeckers were symbols of war to the Mississippians.

42 Spiders were sacred to many North American Indians. The cross symbol on the thorax of this example from Illinois symbolizes the Mississippian sacred fire.

The contacts between Mexico and the Eastern Woodlands may have involved the long-range exchange of portable luxury goods. This was probably not the same sort of network of individual exchange partnerships that has been suggested for the Hopewell. Rather, this trade would have been carried on by the economically specialized pochteca and their counterparts in the Eastern Woodlands. The emerging economic systems and political power structures were quite capable of supporting this more expensive kind of long-distance trade and the special privileges for an élite minority that it implies. At least some of the goods were probably acquired by priests and used in public ceremonies connected with the Southern Cult. But although general economic conditions benefited whole societies, only those at the top of the emerging social hierarchy would have enjoyed real luxury.

In AD 1000, the southern Mississippi valley was still inhabited by Muskogean-speaking peoples. The cultural tradition that was responsible for the construction of the Poverty Point site now participated in the Mississippian tradition. This local expression of the tradition is called the 'Plaquemine' Mississippian. The region may in fact have been the corridor through which Mexican influences reached the middle Mississippi area. One of the chiefdoms of the Plaquemine, the Natchez, survived long enough to be described by French writers in the eighteenth century. Their writings give us some insight into aspects of the Mississippian tradition that archaeology can never hope to discover.

There were two basic classes in Natchez society, nobles and commoners. The nobles referred to the commoners as 'stinkards' in private conversation, as a handy means of reinforcing their position. The nobility was itself divided into three grades, called suns, nobles, and honoreds respectively. The Great Sun was at the peak of the social pyramid. The whole system was maintained by, among other things, an elaborate etiquette and strict rules of inheritance, descent being reckoned through the female line. But added to this relatively common rule were some others that are unusual. All members of the nobility, whether male or female, were required to marry commoners. Children whose fathers were commoners inherited the ranks of their mothers. Children whose mothers were commoners were born to the next rank below that of their fathers. Thus, the son of a sun was a noble, the son of a noble was an honored, and the son of an honored was a commoner. A man, and sometimes his wife too, could climb the social ladder by making a sacrifice, taking a scalp or performing some brave deed in war. The French settler Le Page du Pratz tells us of one couple who moved from commoner to honored status by sacrificing their own child on the crematory fire of a deceased Great Sun. Another commoner, whose deceased wife had been a sun, rose to honored status when two old women related to him took his place next to her on the crematory fire. We must assume that there were additional rules or informal practices that helped to keep a balance between classes, but the examples we have seen are strong evidence of a stratified society.

The Great Sun, whose father was necessarily a commoner, inherited his office from his mother, the 'White Woman', who was in turn the eldest sister of the last Great Sun. The Great Sun's brother was called 'Little Sun', and held the office of Great War Chief. Normally, the Great Sun would pass his office to his sister's son when he died. One such death of a Great Sun was observed by early French settlers. The event, like others of this magnitude, was accompanied by human sacrifice, including ritual suicide by some. Du Pratz and other French observers were able to keep the deceased's younger brother, a man called 'Tattooed Serpent', from killing himself only with the greatest difficulty. The wives and retainers of the Great Sun were marked for sacrifice, and prepared themselves accordingly. For days they alternated between standing on special scaffolds in the plaza and climbing down to dance together. In the end, the dead Great Sun and his wife were borne on a litter to the temple, on a path paved with the bodies of strangled infants. Those who were to accompany them in death took potions of tobacco, lost consciousness, and were strangled by their closest relatives. All were buried or cremated, and the house of the Great Sun was burned. Eventually his bones were exhumed and placed in the main temple, as befitted a person of his importance.

A funeral ceremony was no less important in the case of a White Woman. It was the custom for her commoner husband to be sacrificed by strangulation by their eldest son, a person who was either already or would become a Great Sun.

Perhaps the Natchez were an extraordinary example, but the case serves to demonstrate the striking contrasts between the chiefdom societies of the Mississippian tradition and the tribal societies of the Adena-Hopewell. These were people who had adopted the rigid political and religious principles of Mexican civilization. Although they perpetuated the female descent principles that usually characterize tribal farmers, they were in other ways much like the Mexicans. Seed was brought to the temple before sowing, and the first fruits of the fall harvest were presented as ritual offerings. Thus, nearly all aspects of social, political, and economic life were tied to public ritual, a pattern not previously seen in the Eastern Woodlands. Public ceremonies marked the new year in early spring, and harvest in the fall. Through it all, the trappings of the Southern Cult provided both symbolic meaning and material substance to the ritual.

The example of the Natchez is echoed by historical accounts of several other chiefdoms of the Woodlands. None of the others were quite as bizarre, but all seem to have taken the giant step toward full-time agriculture, public religion, elaborate political organization, and social stratification.

To the west of the Plaquemine Mississippian, in parts of Louisiana, Arkansas, Oklahoma, and Texas, there developed another branch of the tradition called the 'Caddoan Mississippian'. The people responsible for this culture were speakers of 14 Caddoan languages, a part of the larger Siouan family. In early historical times, most 15 of them moved onto the Plains, where we know them by names like 'Wichita' and 'Pawnee'. But in AD 1000 they were settled farmers, actively participating in the Mississippian tradition. There is even some evidence to suggest that Mexican influences into the Eastern Woodlands entered by way of this western fringe area.

Perhaps the best known Caddoan Mississippian artwork comes from Spiro in 14 eastern Oklahoma. The Spiro Mound materials that have survived include artifacts of textile, shell, copper, clay, and stone. A single cache contained thirty copper- 43–45 sheathed masks. Pottery and many other artifact styles from Spiro are distinctly local, but artifacts that were part of the Southern Cult paraphernalia were made in styles recognizable all across the south.

The Caddoan and Plaquemine developments were heavily influenced by the geographically more central Middle Mississippian. They were linked together by 14

Some of the finest Southern Cult artwork comes from Spiro Mound, Oklahoma.

43 This 29-cm.-high mask with deer antlers, carved from one block of cedar and inlaid with shell, was probably worn by a shaman during the Deer Ceremony, a ritual dance to promote good hunting which lasted into historical times.

44, 45 Two stone effigy pipes, 25 cm. high, represent a warrior decapitating a victim (right) and a maize grinder with mortar (opposite). Smoking had religious overtones for prehistoric Indians; elaborate pipes such as these were used for ceremonial smoking only.

the ritual bonds of the Southern Cult with all its trappings. Middle Mississippian influences radiated into other areas as well, but often they were much less direct. In some cases, the influences appear to have been carried by intrusive colonies moving out from rapidly growing centers like Cahokia. An example of such an intrusive colony is Aztalan in southern Wisconsin. 14

The inhabitants of Aztalan appear not to have been welcome in Wisconsin, for they lived in a rectangular village surrounded on three sides by a high palisade, complete with long corridor entrances and watchtowers. The fourth side was protected by a river. The reconstructed village measures about 200 by 500 meters. There are two temple platforms, one near each of the two corners of the palisade. The platforms are terraced mounds, like their remote prototypes in Mexico.

Aztalan was established relatively early, perhaps not long after AD 1000. Its inhabitants carried northward much of what we have come to recognize as Middle Mississippian, but neither they nor any of the other northern colonies took on the Southern Cult. Aztalan persisted until the end of prehistory, and the people who built it survive, known now as the Winnebago.

The Aztalan people were probably Siouan-speakers, like other Middle Mississippians. Together with neighboring Siouans, they developed what has come to be called 'Oneota' culture, a sort of second-hand Mississippian. Theirs was a marginal participation in the larger tradition, a participation that they abandoned when they moved onto the Plains in early historical times. Here they developed into what was essentially a new culture, one that has ironically become stereotyped as the quintessence of the American Indian. Many of the mounted nomads of the historical Great Plains were Mississippian farmers only a few decades earlier. 15 14

Oneota was really a cultural blend, still as much rooted in Adena-Hopewell as in the new Mississippian tradition. Another such culture was that of Fort Ancient in Ohio. The Adena-Hopewell cult was long gone, but the Fort Ancient people continued to bury their dead in mounds, suggesting that they may have been directly descended from the earlier Ohio culture. They built no temple platforms despite their contacts with the Middle Mississippian. Earthworks that in earlier times were purely ceremonial were now erected as defensive walls ringing the summits of hills. The Fort Ancient people persisted into early historical times, and were perhaps the ancestors of the Shawnee. 14

Indians farther to the northeast, such as the Iroquois tribes, were even less affected by the Mississippian. Improved crops and a few other influences reached this area, but none of the opulent ceremonialism came so far. In the northeast, the Iroquoians and the eastern Algonquians remained firmly rooted in the old tribal lifeway, just as people farther north still followed the even older Archaic lifeway.

Mississippian influence in the southeast was greater, appearing both indirectly, and in the form of colonial incursions. One such colony is the Macon site in Georgia, a kind of southern version of Wisconsin's Aztalan. The site is clearly Middle Mississippian, yet far away from its source, and in the midst of an indigenous local culture area. The people of Georgia and South Carolina were primarily Muskogean-speakers, probably unrelated to the inhabitants of Macon. The site is surrounded by two earthwork enclosures, and contains the remains of mounds, public buildings, and houses. One of the large public buildings is a circular semisubterranean structure 14 15 about thirteen meters in diameter. It was evidently a council chamber. There are forty-seven seats on a low bench around the room, and another three on a raised 'throne'. The latter is an effigy of an eagle, and stands opposite the entrance to the room. Taken as a whole, it is an architectural form similar to some found in the Caddoan area. Much of the art and architecture of the Macon Plateau is preserved in Ocmulgee National Monument.

Apparently the Macon colony was not an unqualified success. Its Middle Mississippian culture is limited to the primary site and a few minor ones nearby. It did not expand and send out colonies of its own in the years leading up to the arrival of Europeans. Instead, the local Muskogeans continued to dominate the area, adopting a few of the foreigners' innovations and becoming what is known as the 'South Appalachian Mississippian'.

Of all the South Appalachian Mississippian sites, one of the largest and best known is Etowah, located in northwestern Georgia. Another is Lamar near the Macon colony. Both were palisaded. Etowah was a particularly large community with temple mounds and other public structures. The site has produced some very fine cut-outs and embossed sheets of native copper. There are also sculptures of kneeling human figures like those of Tennessee, in this case carved from solid marble.

Etowah and a few other nearby sites were built and occupied by the prehistoric Cherokee, people related to the Iroquois of New York. Many of the Muskogean-speakers of the area were later known as Creek Indians. These were the chiefdoms whose villages Hernando De Soto visited when he made his famous trip through the Southeast in 1540–42. He observed much the same sort of civilization later seen by the French when they visited the Natchez. The Creek had a strong and highly structured political and social system. There were public rituals conducted around the temple platforms, and ball games were played in town plazas. Large towns dominated their surrounding countrysides, and were linked together in a loose confederacy. European colonization eventually forced the confederacy to become more tightly knit, but by the eighteenth century the Indians were too weakened by war and disease to put up further resistance to incursions. In 1835–40, they were forced to move to Oklahoma, along with the Cherokee, Choctaw, and Chickasaw. A branch of the Creek called the Seminole resisted and held out in Florida while some Cherokee did the same in the mountains of North Carolina. After seven years of fighting, most of the Seminole moved to Oklahoma, but branches of both tribes still remain in their homelands. The episode, called the 'Trail of Tears', is a bitter one in the history of the Indians of the Eastern Woodlands.

Archaeologists once thought that Mississippian culture was already in decline when the first Europeans arrived in North America. However, this impression appears to be a false one. De Soto and his party encountered a vigorous civilization in 1540, one that had not yet reached its full potential. But the effect of his visit was swift and disastrous. Smallpox and other unfamiliar diseases swept ahead of the Europeans, decimating local populations and thus destroying the economic and social foundations of their cultures. By the time seventeenth-century European colonists made direct contact with most Indian communities, disease had already ended their glory, and made them the objects of unfair contempt. Some of the Mississippian people postponed subjugation by adopting the horses introduced by

14

15

the Spanish, and moving onto the Great Plains, but the escape proved to be only temporary.

The northerners who still perpetuated the lifeway of Adena-Hopewell or the older Archaic societies fared a little better. The new fur trade allowed them to become participants in European colonization, rather than just the victims of it. A few, like the Iroquois and the Penobscot, survived by learning to play the European game of power-politics. Often it was a matter of maintaining a precarious position between the French and the English, the primary competitors for colonial power in

46, 4

The Iroquois, a league of five northeast Woodlands tribes formed probably in the 16th century, was one of the few Indian groups to maintain its identity in the face of European colonization.

46 The scalloped-collar incised designs on this pottery vessel are typical of those made by Iroquoian women in New York State and Ontario.

47 The Iroquois believed that evil spirits or 'False Faces' in the forest caused sickness. Miniature basswood masks like this 5-cm.-high example were once used as powerful charms or amulets in ceremonies of the False Face medicine society to help appease the spirits.

the Eastern Woodlands. This unpleasant but serviceable strategy collapsed with the expulsion of the French from North America. The Indians were less successful in playing the English off against the American-born colonists, although in the end the strategy enabled several tribes to escape extermination. Many other tribes, from the Atlantic to the Mississippi, were simply dispersed or destroyed by the European invaders and the diseases they brought with them. The survivors who still persist maintain reservations, where the cultural achievements of more than 12,000 years are only distant memories.

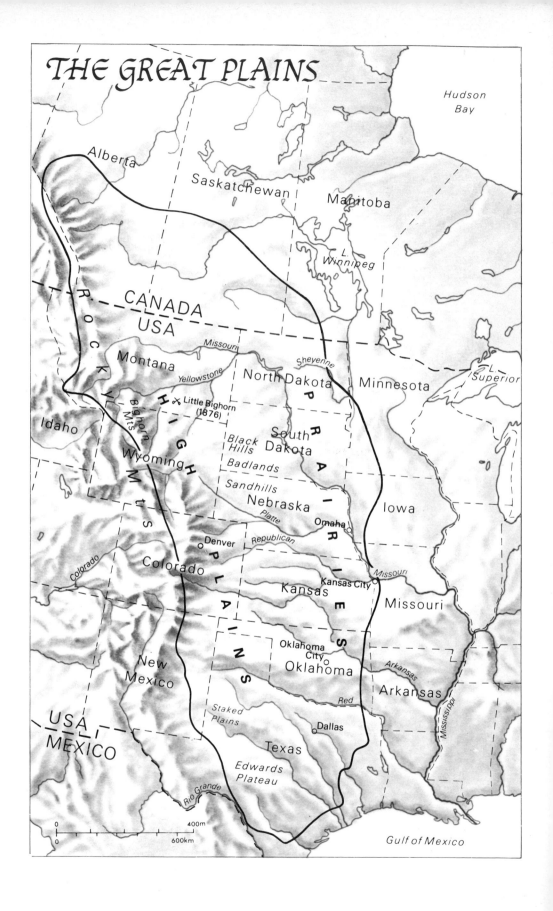

THE GREAT PLAINS

Hudson
Bay

Alberta

Saskatchewan

Manitoba

L.
Winnipeg

CANADA
USA

Missouri

Montana

Sheyenne

North Dakota

Minnesota

L.
Superior

Yellowstone

R
O
C
K

Y

Little Bighorn
(1876)

Idaho

Bighorn
Mts

H
I
G
H

South
Dakota

Black
Hills

Badlands

Wyoming

M
t
s

Sandhills

Nebraska

P
R
A
I
R
I
E
S

Iowa

Platte

Omaha

Colorado

Denver

Republican

Colorado

P
L
A
I
N
S

Kansas

Kansas City

Missouri

Missouri

New
Mexico

Oklahoma
City

Oklahoma

Arkansas

Arkansas

USA
MEXICO

Staked
Plains

Red

Dallas

Mississippi

Texas

Edwards
Plateau

Rio Grande

0
400m
0
600km

Gulf of Mexico

82

The Great Plains

West of the Woodlands and east of the Rockies lie the vast grasslands of mid-continental North America. The Great Plains are difficult to define geographically even on the west, because the Rockies do not always occur as a solid wall. Ranges like the Black Hills and the Bighorn Mountains stand apart from the main Rockies like forward positions of a great fortress. Still, on the west the limits of the Plains are defined far more precisely than elsewhere. On the north they gradually fade into the Canadian Subarctic, and on the south they blend into the Mexican desert. The common boundary with the Eastern Woodlands is, as we have seen, an indistinct frontier that runs parallel to and generally west of the Mississippi. The change takes place in a tier of five states: Minnesota, Iowa, Missouri, Arkansas, and Louisiana. Moving west through any one of these, a traveller eventually notices that somewhere he has passed out of the Woodlands and into the Plains. Westward, forest cover persists only in river valleys, and the spaces in between are huge rolling seas of grass.

Rivers generally flow eastward into the main channel of the Mississippi, following the land contours which slope in the same direction. Eastern sectors of the region are often called Prairies or Tall Grass Plains. Western sectors, which are drier and more elevated, are more usually referred to as the High Plains or Short Grass Plains.

The High Plains are carpeted with buffalo grass and grama, or pasture grass. Some areas are thick with yucca, cactus, and sagebrush as well. Juniper and pine trees grow in ridges, and in the valleys there are groves of cottonwood and willow trees. Where streams have cut down through recent unconsolidated deposits and into the underlying bedrock, springs occur. These nourish the small stands of trees, as well as thickets that often contain wild plums, berries, and other edible plants.

Since the disappearance of the last of the Ice Age mammals, the High Plains have been inhabited by bison, antelope, mule deer, coyote, and various smaller species. Bighorn sheep were once not as restricted to mountainous areas as they now are. Other game for prehistoric Indians included the prairie chicken and grouse.

In the western Dakotas there are dry, heavily eroded areas that are usually lumped together under the heading of 'Badlands'. The Black Hills provide an area of relief and forest cover in western South Dakota. To the southeast are the Sandhills of Nebraska, a vast area of stationary sand dunes held stable by a cover of bunchgrass, yucca, and cactus. The Sandhills are dotted with lakes and marshes, but trees are scarce; as elsewhere on the Great Plains, they may well have been more abundant before Indians developed the practice of driving game into traps by starting prairie fires. Some of the lakes supported stands of wild rice, as well as beaver, muskrat, and various waterfowl.

48 Map of the Great Plains, showing principal modern towns, regional subdivisions into High Plains and Prairies, and main topographical features.

The Missouri River flows through this region, and with its tributaries drains much of the northern Great Plains. The river is important to archaeologists for two primary reasons. The first is related to the construction of a series of dams in the Missouri valley during this century. The building work and flooding that took place over several years was preceded by intensive archaeological salvage excavation, supported by government funds, which has meant that the middle course of the Missouri valley is archaeologically the best known subdivision of the Great Plains.

The second reason for the Missouri's importance is its relationship to the physiography of the region. Where it veers southward through the Dakota states, the river channel marks the margin of glacial deposits left behind by one of the ice-sheet advances out of eastern Canada during the Pleistocene. As a result of this glacial history, the land east of the river is very different from that to the west of it. The eastern Dakotas, Iowa, and Minnesota are now largely farming areas that support staple crops. West of the river the unglaciated landscape is not suitable for farming, and instead is largely committed to cattle ranching. Thus the Missouri over much of its course provides us with a sharp boundary between the Midwest and the West.

As a boundary line, the Missouri was as meaningful prehistorically as it is today. In the northeast, where canoe travel was common, rivers were often public highways through the centers of tribal territories. But on the Plains boat travel was not well developed, and the Missouri proved a barrier to easy movement. Moreover, the rich Prairies with heavy soils east of the river were not exploitable in the absence of draft animals and plows, and the early agriculturalists of the Dakotas lived primarily on the river floodplain where the sod cover was thin and easily tilled. So it has happened that prehistory has provided an unusual concentration of sites along a single river valley, and recent American history has provided a reason and the funds to excavate them.

South of the Missouri River and the Nebraska Sandhills flows the Republican River, and south of that lies central Kansas. Splitting the state is a jagged series of ridges and escarpments where stream erosion has dramatically separated the western uplands from the lower eastern region. This is the Plains Border, where the westward traveler sees the High Plains loom ahead of him like a great crumbling wall. Most of the streams that flow from here eastward through the gently rolling Prairies are permanent, but this is not the case to the west.

The transition zone from High Plains to Prairies persists southward across Oklahoma and into Texas, where the High Plains have the name *Llano Estacado*, or 'Staked Plains', so called by the Spanish for the stockade-like wall of rock upon which this raised plateau rests. In southern Texas, however, the distinction between High Plains and Prairies fades, and the main topographic contrast here is between the interior Edwards Plateau and the coastal lowlands of the Gulf of Mexico. The Great Plains, as we have defined them, become something else in Mexico. From Texas south, prehistoric cultures were different too, at some point in space ceasing to be Plains cultures, becoming North Mexican instead.

Winter on the Great Plains can be bitterly cold, and the summer unbearably hot. Omaha, Nebraska, has experienced the not atypical extreme temperatures of minus 32 degrees and plus 114 degrees Fahrenheit. Summer rainfall is unpredictable. Rain often falls in torrents from a towering thunderhead, a cumulus cloud, while a few miles away the ground remains dry. Thus, the measured annual rainfall for a given locality can vary far above or below average from one year to the next. A few consecutive years of below average rainfall can destroy once prosperous farmland. This happened prehistorically, and it happened again in the first half of the twentieth century. Land stripped of its natural protective cover by modern plowing was turned into a dust bowl by drought.

As we have already seen, Pleistocene game and the old Paleo-Indian lifeway have been gone from the Great Plains for 7000 years. The change forced an economic shift away from big-game hunting toward a more generalized pattern of hunting and food-gathering. The trend was continent-wide, but on the Plains, the ecological forces that compelled it were so strong that the area became almost uninhabitable. Archaic period Indians here were few and scattered, reduced to a way of life very different from that of the historical Plains Indians.

Between the time that the last native horses were killed and eaten, and the first historical Spanish mustangs arrived on the Great Plains, the region was a marginal extension of the Eastern Woodlands. A few native peoples like the ancestors of the historical Kiowa remained through this period as pedestrian nomads, but more advanced developments tended to radiate out of the East as cultures there flourished and waned. They came as pioneering agriculturalists, moving westward up the tributary streams of the Mississippi during periods of favorable climate, and withdrawing again when conditions deteriorated and farming became impossible. The first big wave out of the East is called the 'Plains Woodland', which coincided roughly with the expansion of the Hopewell cult. Eventually, it was replaced by a 14 series of 'Plains Village' cultures that were distant expressions of the Mississippian tradition.

The Hopewell cult began to appear in sites around Kansas City in the early 48 centuries AD. From here, Plains Woodland cultures worked their way westward up the fertile river valleys. The expansion was apparently facilitated by agriculture, but these people were compelled to depend heavily upon hunting and gathering as well. Their communities were small and semipermanent. Houses were shallow pit dwellings with simple roofs of wooden poles and hide coverings. The dead were buried in small earth mounds that sometimes contained stone-lined chambers. Like the later and more familiar European pioneers the Plains Woodland people sacrificed most of the comforts and trappings of Eastern culture in order to travel westward in search of new territory.

Plains Woodland artifacts were utilitarian, but bear certain unmistakable Hopewell features. We find rocker-stamping and decoration in panels or 'zones' on pottery. Platform pipes were made from clay, based on the classic Hopewell stone 25 prototypes. In the northeastern part of the Great Plains, local Woodland tribes controlled and worked the famous catlinite quarries of Minnesota. From this material they made tubular pipes and incised tablets. They seem also to have traded the raw material eastward, where it was shaped into finished artifacts by Hopewell artisans. Objects made of exotic materials such as native copper and marine shell indicate that these Prairie communities were part of the vast trading network that spread outward from the main Hopewell centers.

Gradually, the Plains Woodland people began to move into the fertile valleys of the High Plains, reaching the Rockies by the third century A D. The westernmost of them may have been the first link in another of the long chains of Hopewell trade. As we have seen, obsidian from northwestern Wyoming reached the hands of Ohio artisans mostly during the second century A D, the very period when the Woodland cultures were pressing into the High Plains.

For reasons we still do not fully understand, the Plains Woodland cultures eventually began to wither. Perhaps their cultigens were only barely adequate in the first place. Perhaps one or more of the cyclical periods of drought made what was already a marginal adjustment an impossible one. Whatever the reason, the permanent establishment of agricultural communities on the Great Plains had to await the second great wave of migration out of the East.

After A D 900, the prehistory of the Great Plains entered what is known as the 'Plains Village' period. Its primary inspiration was the expanding Mississippian culture of the Eastern Woodlands, but it was not simply the product of colonialism by that great tradition. Plains Village communities left behind artifacts that seem to combine Mississippian traits with older ones of Plains Woodland origin. Economically, the new period was marked by the introduction of a tough strain of maize that could withstand frosts, and mature in the short space of 100 days. Specially resistant strains of bean were also emerging. The Great Northern bean, which is still grown in this region, is a hardy variety originally developed by these prehistoric farmers. 14

Plains Village farmers continued to depend upon hunting to some extent, but the new reliability of agriculture made their settlements more stable and permanent. Instead of the older semipermanent Plains Woodland houses, they now built permanent dwellings, large square pit houses with roofs of heavy timbers covered over with sod and earth. Houses of this sort appeared in increasing numbers in the decades following A D 1000, sometimes in loose clusters of up to twenty units, sometimes scattered randomly along the river bluffs of the Plains.

The houses themselves generally ranged from six to ten meters in diameter, large enough to house an extended family of three generations. The populations of these dispersed villages probably ranged up to 100. The homes were often abandoned for weeks at a time, when the farmers packed up and turned hunters. Major bison hunts were annual or semi-annual affairs that provided these sedentary people with meat for most of the year. The techniques were ancient ones. Long converging rows of men, women, and children would force the bison into an increasingly narrow path as others drove the whole herd along. In the end the animals found themselves trapped in a compound or toppling off a cliff. Unlike earlier Indians, these people could afford to butcher the largest kill completely. They were sedentary, and had the capacity to preserve and store the meat, an option not available to nomads who had to travel light. The meat was cut up, smoked, and dried, providing a year-round balance to cultivated crops. Food, particularly maize, was often stored in bell-shaped storage pits dug into the floors of most pit houses. With such storage facilities and the secure warmth of their earth lodges, the people could wait out the worst winter blizzards in relative comfort. Later, European settlers adapted sod construction to their own building styles, and were similarly successful. A few aboriginal prototypes and nineteenth-century adaptations still exist.

XII *The circular shield of shrunken bison hide was the 'canvas' of the Plains Indian artist. This magnificent Crow war-medicine shield, with magical crane's head and eagle feathers attached, depicts the Moon, which appeared before the owner during a vision and gave him the shield.*

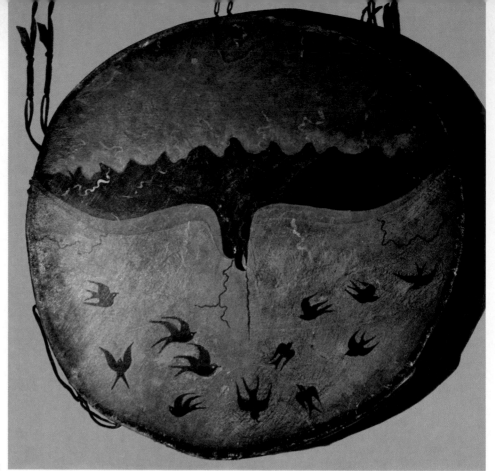

XIII

XIV

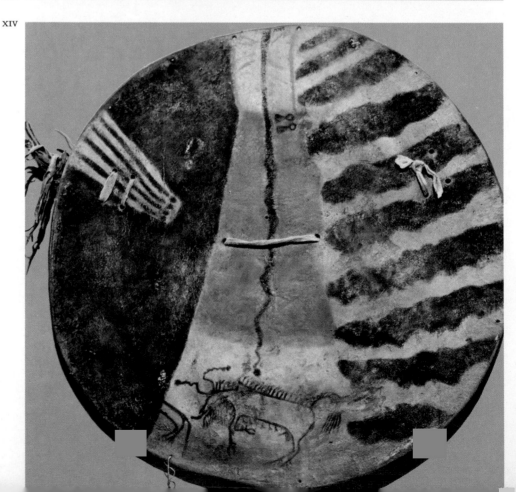

The Missouri River valley, with its large number of excavated sites, provides us with a case study of Plains Village prehistory. We have seen that the glaciation which diverted the river southward also laid down the agriculturally rich croplands of the eastern Dakota states. We have seen too that, without the plow, little of this land could be exploited by prehistoric Indian farmers. As a result, modern river towns tend to be situated on the left (east) bank of the Missouri, where they were most accessible to nineteenth-century farmers, while prehistoric Indian villages tend to be located on the right (west) bank, giving the Indians easy access to the great bison herds which were most numerous west of the river.

Plains Woodland sites along the middle reaches of the Missouri date to the period between 450 BC and AD 750. This development fades as it did elsewhere on the Great Plains, and was replaced by the first Plains Village settlements around AD 900. Some or all of the early villagers had migrated from an area around the Iowa-Minnesota border almost 400 kilometers to the east. Their houses were square pit dwellings dug down about a meter into the soil, typically measuring about ten by eight meters. There are a few structures of more than twice this size which may have served communal functions. Throughout the houses were found pots, celts, points, and bone tools. Most striking of the last category are the scapula hoes that occur scattered about in large numbers. Occasionally made from the scapulae of elk or deer, the hoes are more often bison scapulae, simple artifacts that in themselves clearly define the combined hunting and farming economy of these people.

Some early Plains Village settlers established themselves as far north as central North Dakota. After AD 900, these people moved down-river and began to compete for farmland already held by their neighbors in central South Dakota. The competition appears to have erupted into open warfare, and villagers on both sides fortified their settlements on natural hills with ditches and log palisades, defenses that resembled those of the fortified Mississippian villages of the Eastern Woodlands. The palisades were often strengthened with bastions at the corners and at fifty-meter intervals in between. The conflict did not last, however, because the marginally favorable climatic conditions of AD 900 became marginally unfavorable by AD 1250. For two centuries after that date, the settlers of the middle Missouri contracted into a handful of villages, outposts of people transformed from pioneers into temporary refugees.

The so-called 'Central Plains' tradition grew up in Nebraska and Kansas at about the same time as the initial Plains Village settlements were being built along the Missouri. The tribes of this tradition began moving up the Platte, Republican, and other rivers tributary to the Mississippi around AD 900. Although they were part of the same migration, these people sometimes had contrasting lifestyles. For example, the Upper Republican phase settlements were small villages made up of shallow pit houses. In the Nebraska phase, there is less indication of village settlement, and the isolated houses were large and deep, often excavated more than a meter. None of the groups of the Central Plains tradition fortified their villages, something that contrasts strikingly with the heavy fortifications around the villages of the middle Missouri at about the same time. The reason appears to be that all the early villagers of the Great Plains co-existed quite happily with the nomads who roamed the grasslands between the river valleys. Fortifications became necessary only where the

XIII *A thunderbird, mythical creator of Plains storms, swoops out of the sky, hurling lightning flashes at darting swallows on this graphic Pawnee ceremonial drum.*

XIV *A Crow shield from Montana bears the image of a galloping bison, medicine animal of the shield's owner, from which he got his power.*

villagers found themselves pitted against each other. Far from being hostile, ancestral Kiowa and other nomads probably traded bison meat and wild produce for maize and other domesticates. This trading relationship between villagers and nomads continued with various elaborations until the nineteenth century.

The Mississippian heritage in all the Plains Village developments is strong if not pervasive. The conical forms of Woodland pottery gave way to the globular Mississippian forms, and details like handles, rim-effigy adornments, and certain styles of incising developed. Occasionally, designs reminiscent of the Southern Cult appeared on Plains Village artifacts. At times these were in clay, at other times on bone or shell. Effigy pipes in both clay and stone have also been found.

Plains Village societies were tribal, politically unsophisticated compared with the highly structured chiefdoms of Eastern participants in the Mississippian tradition. Economically and politically they were not the sorts of societies that could support the construction and maintenance of temple mounds, or even the flamboyant portable art that went with them. Theirs was probably the sort of religion usually found in tribal societies, more private than public, and lacking full-time religious leaders. Plains Village economies, although highly developed, were nevertheless relatively unstable. The High Plains were and still are not congenial to farmers, even those with the most advanced domesticates and technology. As has happened to others since, adverse climatic cycles of the fifteenth century threw the Plains Village cultures into a convulsive struggle for survival.

After 1470, there were three long droughts spanning a combined total of forty years. At first only the farming communities that had penetrated the High Plains were affected. But as time went on, the climatic change began to produce a succession of crop failures in eastern sections as well. Gradually, the dispersed villages were abandoned, and new ones were established downstream to the east where the drought was not so severe. Previously scattered tribes became nucleated into tightly packed settlements, and the distances between tribes were reduced. As the agricultural peoples of the Plains coalesced along Prairie rivers, cultural differences began to fade, and a broader, more uniform cultural alloy began to emerge. This blending and leveling of previously divergent cultures led to what is called the 'Coalescent' tradition of the Great Plains.

The Coalescent tradition saw a general shift to circular houses, packed close together in large and often palisaded villages with deep external dry moats. Intervillage warfare, which had already emerged in the middle Missouri, was now part of the Central Plains way of life as well. Plains agriculture was still limited to the fertile river floodplains, where sod could not develop naturally. There was a struggle for control of the best fields. However, there was also a new threat. The Navajo and Apache were by now well established in the Desert West, and there are sites which show that the Apache were taking up residence in the central and southern High Plains. Some groups adopted agriculture, but they did not become full participants in the Plains Village economic pattern. The long dry years must have been hard on them as well, and it is likely that their raids combined with crop failures to force the villagers back eastward, and into compact fortified villages.

Gradually, the Plains Villagers learned to live with each other, and intervillage relations stabilized. Tribal groups that had once been relatively distinctive came to be quite similar. In the Missouri valley, the Siouan-speaking historical Mandan and Hidatsa, and the Caddoan-speaking Arikara remained linguistically distinct, but became culturally almost identical. There was some blending of burial customs, although this was an area of religious importance where old traditions died slowly. The Arikara usually practiced individual primary inhumation, individual burials grouped in cemeteries away from the village sites. In contrast, the Mandan and Hidatsa wrapped their dead in clothing and blankets, and placed them on pole scaffolds. The corpses were allowed to decay in the open air, held up to the sky on their flimsy biers. In time the weather and carrion animals picked the bones clean and scattered them about, and the Indians must have thought that the spirit thus released was better off than it would have been locked in an earthen tomb. As in the Eastern Woodlands, the scattered bones were sometimes gathered up and buried in bundles as the final step in this protracted rite.

House forms, on the other hand, became standardized. The interiors of the earth lodges had curtained beds around the walls. Special places were reserved for the storage of food, firewood, and ceremonial paraphernalia. The fire and cooking equipment was located at the center of the lodge under the smoke hole in the roof. In early historical times, the typical lodge had sleeping accommodation for elders near the fire, and even a corral for favorite horses by the door. Lodges were so large that none of this caused serious space restrictions. In the dead of winter, each household could survive for long periods as a self-contained unit. The occupants lived on stored food, and were warmed by the fire and the body heat of the horses. If one did not mind the attending odors, it was a comfortable existence.

When the first Europeans arrived on the Plains in the sixteenth century, they found most of the agricultural villages confined to the eastern margin of the area. The High Plains had reverted to the foot nomads such as the Kiowa who had been there for millennia, and to newcomers such as the Apache. The Arikara had found their niche alongside the Mandan and Hidatsa. The Pawnee had pulled back to their XIII, 49 compact villages nearer the Mississippi, as had the Ponca and Omaha. The northwestern branch of the Mississippian tradition that we have called 'Oneota' gradually became the historical Iowa, Missouri, Oto, and Winnebago tribes. To the south, the Kansa and Osage, late arrivals from the Eastern forests, joined the others on the Prairie fringe. Still farther south, another Plains Village culture was established by the people we know as the Wichita.

Coronado and his expedition of Spanish treasure-hunters reached Kansas in 1541. They visited villagers whom they called 'Quivira'. These people can be identified with the Wichita, speakers of a Caddoan language like the Pawnee and Arikara. The Wichita, however, were much closer to the Caddo proper, who were responsible for what we have called the 'Caddoan Mississippian'. The Wichita sometimes dug large circular ditches of about thirty meters diameter, which are analogues of the ceremonial council chambers built by the Caddo and other participants in the Mississippian tradition as far away as Etowah, Georgia. Human bones have been found in these structures, suggesting that human sacrifice was not an unknown practice even to these distant contemporaries of the Southern Cult. Indeed, even the more distant Pawnee retained some ritual human sacrifice until the nineteenth century. In one instance, a captured maiden was due to be sacrificed to Venus the

dried-up lakes. These are sometimes filled and even inundated by torrential flash floods when rain chances to fall on the hills above. The rainfall is sparse everywhere, rarely over 60 centimeters a year in any locality and usually less than half that. The soil, unaccustomed to rain, cannot absorb it if it comes in quantity, and most runs off.

The numerous small mountain ranges provide a diversity of environments even within a relatively small locality. Desert sagebrush and associated flora are found on valley floors, but higher up on the mountain flanks are forests of juniper, piñon (a kind of pine), and spruce trees. Still higher are alpine environments. This succession of local environments is repeated over and over again with each mountain range, producing for any band of hunter-gatherers a wide variety of plant foods as well as a wide range of animal species. The survival of Desert Culture has been largely a matter of establishing a seasonal round of movement from one microenvironment to another, exploiting each of the many special resources in its proper turn.

Probably the best known Desert Culture site is Danger Cave, which overlooks 55, 56 the Great Salt Desert in western Utah. The cave floor lies 34 meters above the present

level of the Great Salt Lake, at an altitude of about 1325 meters. A larger Ice Age lake cut the cave and laid down a floor of beach sand for its first human occupants. On this base human debris began to accumulate after about 9000 BC. The cave yielded 2500 chipped-stone artifacts, over 1000 grinding stones, and similar numbers of wood, bone, hide, and fiber artifacts that would have perished in a wet environment. Mixed in were the bones of game such as mountain sheep, deer, antelope, bison, jackrabbit, bobcat, dog, desert fox, and wood rat. There were no bones of extinct animals found with human remains in Danger Cave, although there were some in Etna Cave, a Desert Culture site near Las Vegas. Astonishingly, the mountain sheep was the commonest game animal. This wary creature now lives 57 only in the least accessible parts of the mountain West. Hunting it even in the days when the species was more numerous and widespread cannot have been a job for amateurs.

The plant species found in Danger Cave numbered over sixty-five. From these were made many of the artifacts that the people of the Great Basin Desert Culture required for survival. Wood was fashioned into arrows, knife handles, shafts, and traps. Vegetable fibers of various sorts were worked into cordage, nets, textiles, and basketry. All these were relatively simple functional items, but clearly great value was put on careful workmanship and in some cases elaborate decoration. Also found in both Danger and Etna Caves were small stick figures, made to resemble game

57 Shamans and sheep abound in the petroglyphs of the Colorado River's Glen Canyon. Sheep were among the most important prey of the Desert West Indians, but they were never domesticated in prehistoric times.

58 Worn-out moccasins preserved in the dry soil of Hogup Cave, Utah, had been patched before being discarded about 1500 years ago. Ingenious Indians often used deer-leg hide for the moccasins so that the animal's dew-claws might serve as hobnails on the soles.

animals. Typically, each was made from a single long twig, split into two elements except for the basal end. The two elements were folded and wrapped around the base and into the shape of some unspecified herbivore. Quite often these tiny figures were 'killed' with small spears that are still embedded in their chest cavities, a characteristic that seems to link them to hunting magic. Examples have been found in several other Great Basin sites and all seem to date to around 1500 BC.

Artistic impulses found their principal outlet in basketry. Around 7500 BC the baskets at Danger Cave were uniformly made by twining. This technique involved the use of vertical 'warp' elements either singly or in small bunches. The horizontal 'weft' elements were applied as pairs of elements, around and around the basket, with a half twist of each pair in the spaces between the warp elements. Twined matting was made in which the weft elements were spaced relatively far apart; the result was an open pattern. Alternatively, the weft elements could be packed closely together, producing a closed pattern that resembles coarse woven fabric. Generally speaking, this early technique produced porous baskets for which the decorative possibilities were rather limited. Different colored weft elements could be applied in bands, or two different colors used in each pair of weft elements. In the latter case, diagonal or herringbone patterns were achieved. Only rarely, however, did twining create designs that were not rigidly geometric.

By 2000 BC, preferences had shifted so that most of the baskets were less porous and allowed a greater variety of decoration. The newer technique is called 'coiling'. In this case, the horizontal weft element was a continuous spiral coil, sometimes a single shaft, but more often a long bunch of grass fibers. A long pliable fiber was used to wrap the long spiral coil and, at the same time, stitch each successive row in the coil to the preceding one just below. If the elements and the stitching were small enough, the result was a basket so tight that it was virtually waterproof. In the best examples, fibers of various colors were used to cover and stitch the coils so that fine geometric designs were created. Several colors could be used, either by selecting naturally colored fibers, or by making use of the wide range of natural vegetable dyes. If the coils were fine, the stitching was also fine, and designs could therefore depart from rigid geometry. Some of the world's most attractive basketry was made with this technique by the prehistoric Desert Cultures and their historical descendants. It was a remarkable achievement for people living in such a hostile environment.

Other specialized artifacts are found elsewhere in the Great Basin. In a few sites located near more or less permanent lakes, archaeologists have found composite fishhooks of bone, wood, and fiber. Such sites have also produced duck decoys made out of rushes, sometimes even equipped with duck feathers. The prehistoric Indians must have observed the tendency of waterfowl to splash down in the lakes next to their own kind. The decoys would have lured the ducks down into the reeds where the hunters lay hidden, ready to pounce. Elsewhere, sickles were made from mountain sheep horn, and used to harvest wild grasses. Lacking only the proper grass species and a little rainfall, these people never knew how close to the first stages of agriculture they really were.

The evidence from Danger Cave indicates that by 4000 BC Indians here had acquired many of the objects which we normally associate with the historical

59 Tiny fiber and bone figurines from Hogup Cave, 6–7 cm. high, bear magical horns, and may have been the embodiments of sickness that shamans pretended to suck from the bodies of their patients in purification rites about 1500 years ago.

cultures of the West. Deer-hoof rattles, bone dice, wooden gaming sticks, etched pebbles, mica discs, clay effigies, and bird-bone tubes all occur. The last of these were probably connected with the widespread practice of menstrual seclusion, when females were often required to drink through such tubes. Menstruating women were regarded as both physically and magically contaminated, and had to be kept away from other people and utensils used in common.

In most dry caves there is evidence of the manufacture of robes from feathers and strips of rabbit skin. Heavy fur-bearing animals were not often available, and local groups were sometimes forced to make do with rabbit hides. Such fur may be adequate for a jackrabbit, but in single layers provides little comfort for a human being. To compensate for the thin hide and light fur, the Indians cut the skins of small fur- and feather-bearing animals into long strips. These strips were then twisted and woven together like yarn. The result was a relatively warm covering.

In the Great Basin, Desert Culture remained largely unchanged for thousands of years. As a result, a careful examination of the historical tribes in the region can give us valuable insights into the non-material aspects of the Culture over that long period. The Shoshone, Ute, and Paiute Indians of AD 1800 carried on a way of life that was little changed from that of their ancestors. Groups were necessarily small, usually bands of one or two dozen related persons. One such band would move from place to place on a seasonal round, exploiting specific plant resources as each became ready for harvest. The need for protein was often satisfied with rabbit or antelope meat, but when these were not available, small rodents, reptiles, insects and even their larvae were eaten. The rumor of an especially productive food source might bring several families together in a single small locale for a brief period, but such a source would not be productive again for years. Rabbit populations, in particular, tended to fluctuate drastically.

Rumor of a valley full of rabbits attracted bands bent upon a communal hunt. Each male adult usually carried a net about the size and shape of a tennis net. Several of these nets were tied end to end and used to form a compound, or even block the end of a small valley. A dynamic and experienced man usually took charge of the operation, becoming the closest thing to a community leader these bands ever had. Typically, rabbits were driven down the long valley and into the nets. By the time the drive reached the nets, hundreds and even thousands of rabbits were snared. The hunters then waded into the panicky animals and clubbed or speared them to death.

The rabbit bosses divided the kill, usually giving a bit more to the net owners. The importance of the communal hunt was that there was food to sustain an un-usually large gathering until the meat spoiled or ran out. This allowed time for dancing, gambling, and visiting in a larger social context than was usually possible for these people. Local bands were exogamous, that is, young unmarried members had to look outside their own band for marriage mates. The socializing that followed communal hunts provided an opportunity for this and other important interactions to take place.

During a brief period of prehistory, around AD 1000, when climatic and other factors were favorable, a small part of the Great Basin yielded to the development of agriculture and settled life. 'Fremont' culture, as it is called, bloomed briefly in northern Utah. It is distinguished by a figurine cult. The figurines are up to fifteen 60

60 *Around* AD 1000
*Fremont culture, based
primarily on agriculture,
flourished briefly in
northern Utah, before
warfare and drought forced
a return to the more
primitive foraging pattern
of the Desert Culture.
Fremont figurines like this
one, 10 cm. high, suggest
links with Anasazi and
Hohokam farming
communities of the
Southwest.*

centimeters tall, limbless, and modeled from clay. They seem to be associated with stylistically similar petroglyphs in the same region. Despite these distinctive traits, however, Fremont culture was shortlived. Warfare and drought forced a return to the primitive but secure Desert Culture way of life. The carriers of Fremont culture may have departed entirely, in search of a more congenial habitat.

Some Desert Culture bands were in contact with Spanish outposts on the Rio Grande as early as 1609. The Spanish had horses, and the Indians proved to be natural riders. Horses were obtained by trade or theft, and it was not long before people like the Shoshone were themselves becoming agents of the introduction of the horse into the rest of the Desert West and even the Great Plains. Soon, French traders spotted young horses with Spanish brands in western Canada. Quickly assimilated by Indian cultures, the horses spread widely and proliferated. In the driest parts of the Great Basin the lack of suitable pasture kept the herds from becoming numerous, but elsewhere scattered Desert Culture bands gathered into larger and more permanent groups. The foot nomads became mounted predatory tribes. The new adjustment depended upon raids conducted against European outposts and other Indian communities, and it could not last. By 1850, most of the Great Basin nomads were mounted, but by 1870 they had been defeated and confined by the U.S. Army.

The Southwest

In its general appearance, the Southwest is just another province of the Desert West, different in detail, but otherwise similar to its neighbors. However, the agricultural potential of the province and its proximity to the heart of American civilization in Mexico led to profoundly different cultural developments. This area alone in the United States provides significant archaeological remains of standing domestic architecture. It is also the only part of the country where the archaeologist can really satisfy his appetite for fine painted ceramics. It is no surprise that it has received so much archaeological attention.

Generally, the entire Southwest can be classified as arid. However, average temperatures, rainfall, and the resulting vegetation types are controlled largely by altitude. In Arizona, Yuma is the lowest and driest point, with less than 8 centimeters of rainfall a year, and an average annual temperature of 72 degrees Fahrenheit. Flagstaff, Arizona, at 2150 meters, has an average temperature of 45 degrees Fahrenheit. High in the mountains the forests are dominated by spruce and fir. Lower down, yellow pine, piñon, and juniper take over. Below about 1850 meters is open country covered with sagebrush, grass, salt bush, and other plants, depending upon local conditions. Below about 1075 meters are found typical desert species of cactus, mesquite, and associated plants. The animal species that inhabit these varying environments are distributed according to altitude much as they are in the Great Basin. They remained important to at least some of the Southwestern cultures down to historical times.

Gradually, Mexican traits began to appear in the Southwest, grafted onto the indigenous variants of the Desert Culture. Excavations at Bat Cave, New Mexico, have uncovered the remains of primitive pod corn or maize. This is not wild corn, but an ancient variety that already showed some indications of domestication and improvement. It dates from about 3000 BC, indicating that at a time when little other influence from Mexico was finding its way into the Southwest, basic economic shifts were already beginning.

We may therefore imagine a small Desert Culture community, locked into the same seasonal round followed by its ancestors for thousands of years. Each move would bring the band to a traditional camping place where milling stones, used to grind vegetable foods, and other heavy implements had been left behind from a previous visit. When local wild plants were harvested and consumed, the band moved on. Semidomesticated corn was probably added to this kind of pattern without disrupting the larger system. Corn could be planted at a particular traditional campsite, and left to grow and mature unattended as the band moved on to forage elsewhere. The band would later arrange its movements so as to be back at the first site in time to harvest the corn, much as if it were just another wild resource. Thus, the evidence from Bat Cave might indicate that corn was playing an important economic role in at least part of the Southwest for centuries before settled life appeared there.

A semi-agricultural, sedentary way of life emerged about 2000 years ago, in the form of three major and several minor cultures. The 'Mogollon' tradition was located principally in the Mogollon Mountains that stretch from central Arizona southeastward into southern New Mexico and the Mexican state of Chihuahua. North of these mountains is a large upland plateau, heavily eroded on its margins, which for our purposes centers on the point at which the states of Arizona, New Mexico, Utah, and Colorado come together. This was the province of the 'Anasazi' tradition. Its eastern portions are drained by the upper Rio Grande and its tributaries, whereas the western portions are drained by the upper tributaries of the Colorado River. Finally, there is the hot dry desert of Southern Arizona and Mexican Sonora. Waters from the mountains to the north and east feed the Gila, Salt, and other tributaries of the Colorado that flow through this zone. They were crucial to the development of the 'Hohokam' tradition. Minor traditions such as the 'Sinagua' and the 'Salado' were marginal to the three major traditions.

Mogollon culture

The story of the Mogollon cultural tradition is one of human adaptation to a mountainous environment. The first villages of around 200 BC had fewer than twenty houses, and were built on the high ground of ridges and bluffs in the Mogollon Mountains. Dwellings were usually circular pit houses dug down knee- or waist-deep into the ground. Usually, the houses were arranged randomly, but with their entryways facing east, where they could catch the warm rays of the morning sun. Patterns of refilled postholes show that the houses had conical or ridged roofs of wood and earth, and special facilities for storage.

The picture of the early Mogollon is one of moderately successful part-time farmers, drawn together into small, easily defended tribal communities. The Mogollon were among the first agriculturalists of the Southwest, but they never evolved the strong commitment to it that we shall see elsewhere in the region. They continued to exploit the wild foods of the mountains and the transitional zone verging on the desert below. Their conservatism served them well in hard times still to come, but in the end it contributed to their loss of cultural leadership to the Anasazi tradition, which in these early centuries was an undeveloped variant of the Desert Culture.

The selection of defensible village sites might seem anachronistic in these early centuries of settled life in the Southwest. It was several hundred years before the peoples of the other major traditions were forced to take defense seriously. The reason for the early Mogollon pattern seems linked to their location. Below them in the desert, the settled villages of the Hohokam tradition were already thriving, while behind them to the east and north lived bands of hostile nomads. The Mogollon people found themselves in a tension zone where incompatible lifeways overlapped. But as time went on, the Anasazi tradition developed and spread north and east of the Mogollon, creating a buffer zone and pushing back the nomadic hunters. Gradually, tension relaxed, and Mogollon villages grew and spread into unprotected areas that would have been too insecure earlier.

The pottery of the earliest Mogollon phases can be divided into three basic types, of which 'San Francisco Red' was the finest. These pots have attractive, colored 'slips', that is, very thin layers of fine clay which were applied before firing to the outer faces of the pots. All Mogollon ceramics appear to have been inspired by Mexican types of the same period. Manufacturing techniques, vessel forms, and finish are all reminiscent of highland Mexico. Vessels were built into jar or bowl forms by coiling. Here, as elsewhere in America, the potters wheel was unknown until contact with Europeans. Mogollon vessels were always smoothed to final shape by scraping and then polished with a smooth pebble. The result was a dimpled surface finish that sets Mogollon pottery apart from the other early ceramics of the Southwest.

Cigar-shaped tubular pipes of clay or stone were smoked at this time, as apparently were reed cigarettes. Tiny human figurines were also sometimes made of clay. But the innovation of clay vessels did not necessarily lead to a reduction in basketry. In fact, flexible twined basketry was added to the older inventory.

By AD 300, Mogollon culture was expanding and exerting considerable influence on the Hohokam and Anasazi traditions. Internally, the Mogollon tradition was beginning to differentiate into several regional variants, a predictable development given the vigor of this culture. Improved pottery types, now often with painted decoration, were introduced. Pit houses tended to be more deeply excavated by this time, but apart from ceramic developments, Mogollon culture continued with much the same material inventory as before.

Villages increased in size as their populations flourished. But then disaster struck the Mogollon. Investigations have shown that there was a reversal in corn production in the two centuries following AD 500. A series of crop failures brought on a near collapse of Mogollon agriculture. It was a great depression in which people starved, and the survivors turned back to old patterns of hunting and gathering. Some appear to have left the homeland in search of new opportunities. Although the depression ended by AD 700, the cultural tradition had been weakened. As they resumed their former growth and vigor, the Mogollon tribes drew heavily upon the developing Anasazi.

The renewed geographic expansion of the Mogollon was such that by AD 900 they had intruded westward into territory that we usually define as belonging to communities of the Hohokam tradition. This trend continued over the following two centuries. Eventually there was such an intergrading of Mogollon and Hohokam communities in the south that in places the distinction between them is hard to define. Something like this was happening in the north as well. Here, the Anasazi tradition was coming into its own, and whereas earlier influences had flowed largely from Mogollon to Anasazi, the trend was now reversed. Some of the northernmost Mogollon communities came to be so heavily influenced by the Anasazi that they lost their cultural distinctiveness. As a whole, Mogollon culture was becoming increasingly diluted.

Before AD 1000, pit houses were the most common type of Mogollon architecture. After that date, however, there was an increasing preference for multiroom structures built above ground level. This trend began in the north where Anasazi influences were particularly strong. At the same time, there was a parallel trend toward smaller rooms. Some new pit houses were built alongside surface rooms, but in neither case were the rooms as large as they had once been. As the population grew, smaller and smaller rooms were built and the number of people per room was reduced. The most obvious consequence of these trends was a rapid proliferation of rooms in Mogollon villages. Socially, the new architectural styles probably reflected a shift from large extended families to smaller nuclear family groups. A young married couple would live apart in a newly constructed room rather than stay with either his or her parents. It is likely that the Mogollon had maintained a preference for post-marital residence with the man's parents through their early development and the great depression that almost destroyed them. The pattern is normal for people with a major dependence upon hunting, because in this way the men who hunt together live together as well. Among full-time agriculturalists, the residence pattern is the reverse; the primary work group is made up of female relatives, and it is advantageous for them to live together. Any shift from male-oriented residence to female-oriented residence will usually pass through an intermediate stage. This may be what the change in Mogollon architecture signifies. Female-oriented residence was strong among the Anasazi, and as their influence on the Mogollon increased, young Mogollon couples probably tended more and more toward separate residence and the organization of female work groups. In the end, Mogollon villages came to have an average of 275 rooms each.

There were other important shifts in Mogollon architecture. Before AD 1000, most pit houses were round, the most economical shape for subsurface dwellings. However, the best shape for contiguous surface rooms is square or rectangular, and as they increased in popularity, new pit houses took on similar four-sided shapes. The disappearance of male-dominated extended families led to the construction of subsurface 'kivas', ceremonial rooms modeled on the pit houses which served as meeting places for male clan members and perhaps their sisters and mothers as well. Like most cultures having clans, the Mogollon probably forbade marriage between members of the same clan. The ties between blood relatives would have been strong, and the need for kivas almost mandatory.

Most remarkable of all were the 'Great Kivas' that the Mogollon began building at about the same time. These were large subsurface rooms that sometimes measured more than ten meters across. Only one was built for each village, and they probably functioned as ceremonial centers for the entire community. Like so many other things in the later life of the Mogollon, this was an innovation borrowed from the 86 Anasazi. Unlike the Anasazi, however, the Mogollon extended the new square floor plan to their Great Kivas as well as to their smaller kivas.

It is clear that life for the Mogollon was much changed by AD 1000. Defense was no longer an important consideration in village site selection. Pit houses and storage pits were now largely replaced by surface dwellings with storage rooms. Nuclear families lived apart, and many everyday items were taking on an Anasazi style. The bow and arrow had been part of the Mogollon hunting kit from the beginning of the tradition, but by preference they had also retained the much more ancient spear-thrower. Now, after more than a thousand years, they gave it up. Like the Hohokam and Anasazi, the Mogollon found that the bow and arrow alone was more than adequate for their needs as the importance of hunting declined.

In the century preceding AD 1000, a new Mogollon pottery style emerged in the 61–6 Mimbres area in southwestern New Mexico. The pots were decorated in a series of black-on-white styles that had developed from earlier red-on-white designs, partly

as a result of Anasazi influence. Both jar and bowl forms were made, but the latter seem to have found their way more frequently into museum displays. Many are decorated with complex geometric designs that make use of elaborate triangles, scrolls, zigzags, and frets. These are usually done in white, solid black, or cross-hatching. More popular today, however, are other Mimbres vessels showing stylized human and animal forms. Rabbits, bears, insects, frogs, fish, deer, mountain sheep, humans, and other creatures are all depicted in a simple crisp style that is particularly delightful to twentieth-century eyes. Many of the vessels were originally intended as grave goods, and as a result are punctured by 'kill-holes', like some of the Weeden Island culture pots of the Eastern Woodlands. There is usually one such hole to a vessel, neatly perforating its base. The holes disappoint people who see them only as flaws in otherwise beautiful works of art. To those who understand their ritual purpose, however, the kill-holes provide an additional dimension of meaning to the Mimbres vessels. They were much more than works of art for the Indians. Each vessel had an essence which grew as the potter worked her craft, and which was released to join its dead owner's spirit when the kill-hole was struck.

61

62–64

61, 62 and 63, 64 (overleaf) In the 10th century AD a new Mogollon pottery style emerged in the Mimbres area of southwestern New Mexico. Bowls 30 cm. in diameter were decorated with black-on-white designs depicting insects (left) and other animals. Enigmatic human figures (right and overleaf) may represent the contrast between life and death or male and female; this bowl was part of a grave lot, and the hole puncturing the base, 'killing' the object, helped release the vessel's spirit into the next world.

65, 66 The originality and craftsmanship of Mimbres potters are fully displayed on these two bowls showing the guardians of the four directions (above) and figures on the back of a waterbird (below). Both vessels functioned as grave goods, which were ritually 'killed' or punctured before burial.

By AD 1100, the Mogollon were facing disaster again. This time, however, it was part of a general crisis that affected most of the peoples of the Southwest. It was the beginning of a phenomenon known as 'the abandonment'. There was a catastrophic drop in the number of rooms per village in Mogollon country without a balancing increase in the number of villages. Elsewhere in the Southwest, many villages were abandoned completely. The trend was reversed for a hundred years following AD 1250, but then it began again. There seems to be no single cause for the abandonment, but rather a number of factors. Linguistic evidence indicates that the Apache broke from their Athapascan relatives in Canada in about AD 825 and began drifting toward the Southwest. Their Navajo cousins followed them some 175 years later. These nomads were not always hostile, but their presence would almost certainly have led to a renewal of the feuding that had plagued the early Mogollon. Just as serious was a subtle change in the pattern of annual rainfall, which led to periods of severe erosion around AD 1100 and again around AD 1300. There are also clues suggesting crop failure due to drought in some areas and shortened growing seasons in others. Any of these factors occurring alone would have led to serious stresses; together they put an end to the florescence of Mogollon culture.

Isolated branches of the Mogollon persisted in some northern localities, but from this time on the culture as a whole appears to have retracted more and more toward the south. The site of Casas Grandes on the Mexican side of the modern border (not to be confused with Casa Grande, Arizona) persisted into the fifteenth century. But north of the border, the Mogollon dwindled into a minor Southwestern tradition. *55*

With their above-ground pueblo dwellings, and their black-on-white pottery, the later prehistoric remnants of the Mogollon tradition seem to have been engulfed by the Anasazi. Still, the Zuni, as Mogollon survivors, continue to maintain their own distinctive variation on the general theme of Southwestern culture. They, and the faceless Mimbres potters who preceded them, silently caution us not to measure a culture's worth by its population size.

Hohokam culture

The Hohokam tradition emerged west of the Mogollon in the desert of southern Arizona. The cultural name means 'those who have gone' in the language of the Pima Indians who now live in this part of Arizona. Throughout its long history the Hohokam tradition seems always to have shown more profound Mexican connections than the other Southwestern cultures. Linguistically, the Pima and Papago descendants of the Hohokam are part of the Azteco-Tanoan language phylum, as are so many other Indians of the Southwest and Mexico. There is some evidence that within this large phylum the Hohokam people were most closely related to Indians living in what is now northern Mexico. Thus, it is possible that the Hohokam tradition was intrusive into the Southwest, having moved northward out of Mexico. As immigrants, the earliest Hohokam might have been the primary agents for the transmission of Mexican traits into the Southwest. *55* *15*

The first of these people must have been extraordinarily perceptive to see much future in the barren desert of Arizona. Their agriculture depended from its beginning upon careful irrigation, an effort that even in its most rudimentary stages takes special skill and planning. Today, irrigation is about twice as costly as terracing, which is itself twice as costly as field contouring. This set of relationships gives us some idea of the investment Hohokam farmers were required to make in order to see their desert bloom. But costly as it was, the benefits were enormous. The irrigation canals and the rivers that fed them filled with clear water from March to April as the mountain snows melted far upstream. They filled again each August as summer rains fell in the same distant mountains. With two annual surges of irrigation water, the Hohokam were able to plant and harvest two crops each year. This abundance was supplemented further by the annual harvests of saguaro cactus, mesquite, and other wild foods. Hohokam towns of twenty-five or more inhabitants were in existence by 300 BC, and fully sedentary life was developing. As we shall see, the productivity of these man-made oases eventually led to the emergence of Hohokam chiefdoms.

Much of what we know about the Hohokam tradition has come from the site of Snaketown, a Hohokam town that existed for centuries on the banks of the Gila River. During the first few centuries of occupation following 200 BC, a few plain and red-slipped pottery types were produced. These early types are superficially very similar to the early Mogollon ceramics of the same period, but there are a few differences. 'Vahki Red', the red-slipped Hohokam type, glitters with small mica flecks that are never found in the Mogollon San Francisco Red pottery. Furthermore, Hohokam potters shaped their vessels by slapping the wet exteriors with a paddle while holding a stone 'anvil' inside with the other hand. The smoother exteriors of

55, 68–

67 *The harsh Arizona desert failed to destroy this 2000-year-old Hohokam clay figurine, 6 cm. high. The small female torso may have had Mexican origins, like many traits of the Hohokam people – literally 'those who have gone' in the language of the modern Pima.*

120

the finished vessels never show the dimpled surface that is so familiar on Mogollon vessels.

A type called 'Estrella Red-on-Gray' is the earliest two-color painted pottery in the Southwest. Also appearing early in the sequence are small human figurines. Sometimes whole torsos, sometimes only heads, these tiny figures appear to have been modeled on Mexican clay figurines. Their manufacture was already an ancient custom in Mexico. 67

Later Hohokam pottery was mostly a long series of red-on-buff types. One unusual shape stands out in this series. It is a hemispherical jar form, where the small mouth is located at the apex of the hemisphere, and the nearly flat side of the vessel is the base. Thus, the shoulders of vessels of this form are broad, but only just a bit higher than the base, leaving a broad curved surface between the low shoulder and high neck for painted decoration. A buff slip provided a background for the repetition of an almost infinite series of geometric and zoomorphic forms in red. 68–71

Early Hohokam houses are called pit houses, but typically they were very shallow in relation to their size. Some do not really qualify as pit houses at all. Excavation seems to have been carried out only to lower the floor to the hard layer of 'caliche', the rock-hard subsoil that underlies so much of the Arizona desert. On that foundation, the Hohokam built houses that were usually square in plan, and sometimes very large. Some were the size of Mogollon ceremonial structures, and perhaps had a similar function. Customarily, the interiors were broken by four roof supports and a fire pit, the latter being just inside the door. About 100 such dwellings formed the core of the Snaketown community at any given point in time.

Hohokam burials were cremations from the beginning almost to the very end of the sequence. Ashes and burnt bone were placed in jars, inverted bowls serving as covers, and interred in or near the home. Burial ceremonies appear to have been simple, enough to maintain links between the living and the dead.

Wild game was always less abundant in the Hohokam area than in the Mogollon area. By AD 500, the Hohokam economy was based almost exclusively upon agriculture. It was a commitment that the Mogollon never made, partly because they did not have to. Hohokam agriculture was in turn dependent upon irrigation. By this time, the people of this tradition were constructing extensive irrigation systems, some of which are still in use today. Looking at the ditch systems in the context of the twentieth century we find it difficult to imagine how Indians could construct canals up to twenty-five kilometres long without surveying tools and earth-moving equipment. But the Hohokam were a practical people, and they found a remarkably simple solution to the problem. All they did was to tap into streams at a convenient point, and then allow the habit of water to seek its own level to direct their digging. If in their digging they increased the downward gradient too rapidly, the excavators would see the water rising dangerously as the ditch progressed. Conversely, if they inadvertently reversed the gradient, they would see the water level drop. By digging the ditch ahead of them, and standing waist deep in water, the excavators had little need for surveying equipment. Moreover, the water helped to soften the hard desert soil, and made its removal with digging sticks and baskets a little less arduous. In this way, the Indians constructed long ditches that were sometimes as much as four meters deep.

1000-year-old red-on-buff pottery from Snaketown, an important Hohokam site on the Gila River, exemplifies vivid Hohokam ceramic styles.

68, 70 Masked Hohokam figures with distorted limbs interweave in ceremonial dance on a potsherd (above) and the exterior of a bowl (opposite). Agriculture and settled life encouraged an increasing concern with ritual.

69 This delightful bird (below) is found on sherds from several sites in the valleys of the Gila and Salt Rivers.

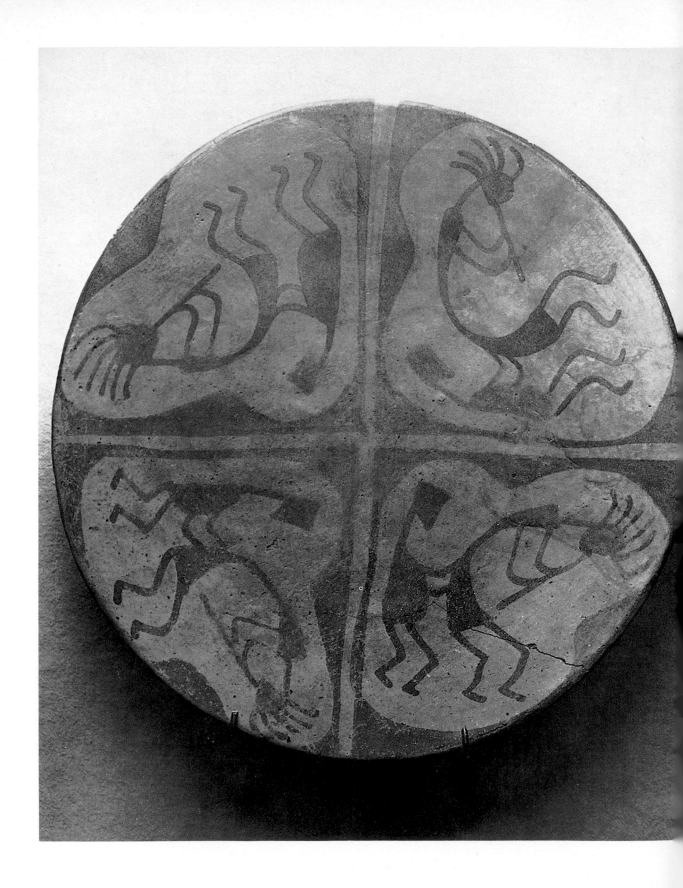

By AD 600, the Hohokam had developed the techniques to produce the beautiful carved shell and stone artifacts for which they are justifiably famous. Long-bitted stone axes with deep grooves for handles were pecked and polished from hard close-grained rock. Stone palettes were carved, sometimes with elaborately decorated relief frames, sometimes with human or animal appendages added to the basic rectangular shapes. These may have been used to grind pigments, or, with a thin coating of water, used as mirrors. Incense burners or medicine cups in the stylized forms of various animals were carved and then sometimes deposited in large caches. Long slivers of chert were chipped into delicate projectile points that often had serrations and other elaborations that went far beyond functional requirements.

Shells were imported from the Gulf of California, sometimes to be cut into beads and bracelets, sometimes to be treated in other ways. There are examples of single-valve shells used as backing for turquoise mosaics. More extraordinary, however, are shells upon which designs, usually animal motifs, were etched. The first step in this process was to coat the surface with pitch or wax where the artist did not want the design to appear. The shell was then soaked in the fermented juice of the fruit of the saguaro cactus, and the weak acid solution etched away the unprotected parts. The pleasing designs that resulted were thus made by a process not discovered by Europeans until several centuries later.

Perhaps the most outstanding Mexican trait found in large Hohokam sites is the ball court. The one excavated at Snaketown is typical. It is an elliptical structure almost 120 meters long and just over 33 meters wide. The actual playing surface was smaller, for these dimensions include the earthen embankments that flanked the court. The embankments were highest along the sides of the structure, perhaps as much as 6 meters high. Thus, the game was played on a sunken court, presumably

72

VII

71 A Hohokam flute-player is pursued or perhaps helped through the panels of a 10th-century bowl from Snaketown. Viewed as a whole, the vessel, 27 cm. in diameter, seems to revolve under their feet.

72 The horned toad, a harmless lizard of the Desert West, was the inspiration for this 12-cm.-long Hohokam pigment mortar carved at Snaketown 1100 years ago.

with the rubber balls that have been uncovered in some Hohokam sites. The latex to make such balls must have come from the Mexican lowlands, more evidence of continuing Mexican trade contacts. Probably the game had much the same composite social, political, and religious significance in the Southwest as it had in highland Mexico. There, often set in great urban centers, ball courts were large stone I-shaped edifices. The games were much more than simple entertainment, often forming part of an elaborate public ritual. In some cases teams attempted to score points by putting a rubber ball through a stone loop. In others, as in the Southwest, no loops have been found and we must assume that there was an alternative means of scoring. The rules appear to have forbidden the use of hands. Play was rough and the stakes sometimes high. Losing teams in Mexico often found themselves stripped of their finery, and in some rare instances the victims of human sacrifice. But the grand ball courts of Mexico had simpler counterparts in the Southwest, and we must assume that Hohokam games were less elaborate too.

By about the same time, AD 600, some Hohokam communities were building small platform mounds, modeled again on Mexican prototypes. At least some of these were apparently surmounted by temples, as was the case in Mexico. They were small structures, often only one meter and rarely much more than three meters high. They tended to be rectangular, sometimes as long as thirty meters. We know nothing of the ritual performed on these structures, but it must have paralleled the public ritual of the Mexican city states and the chiefdoms of the Eastern Woodlands.

Only large communities had major public structures like ball courts and platform mounds. Smaller communities, often strung out along communal irrigation systems, lacked these features. But archaeologically, the smaller communities that surround larger ones often share strong similarities in detail. At the peak of the tradition Hohokam settlements, especially along the Gila and Salt Rivers, seem to have been clustered politically in groups comprising a few communities. Each group would have had a principal center, a few smaller settlements, and a network of trade partnerships to link them all together. One very important center was the giant ruin now called 'Mesa Grande', which is preserved in a residential section of the modern city of Mesa. The implications of this kind of organization are profound, because they point to the emergence of political structures beyond the tribal level. The Hohokam culture of AD 1000 was probably made up of a series of small chiefdoms, each governed by a chief with the power to make and enforce regulations. In place of egalitarian tribal life with its set of part-time leaders and shamans, there emerged a formal élite, including both religious and secular leaders. With such an advanced organization, fragile irrigation canals and public ceremonial structures were built and maintained in an orderly fashion.

Not all Hohokam communities evolved into chiefdoms. South of the great towns along the Gila and Salt Rivers were dozens of villages that participated in the more general Hohokam lifeway, but remained rather rural by comparison. Some archaeologists refer to these marginal Hohokam as the 'Ootam', the word the modern Pima use to refer to themselves. They think that the desert branch of the Hohokam may be the real founders of the tradition (the Ootam) who were pushed out of the Gila and Salt River valleys around AD 1000 by Mexican invaders. The changes that occur later around 1300 could have been partly the result of a reassertion of the Ootam people.

Tiny Mexican copper bells found at Hohokam sites offer further proof of contacts with civilizations to the south, probably in this case by way of a trade network. Each bell is a teardrop shape, with an eyelet at the top for suspension. The lower part is a hollow resonator with a slit at the base. Inside is a small pebble or nodule of copper that acts as a loose clapper. All such bells were made by the 'lost-wax' method. Each was fashioned first in wax, then encased in clay. After the clay dried, the wax was melted out and replaced by molten copper, poured in from the top. Mexicans obtained copper in native nugget form; they had not developed techniques for extracting the metal from ore. Still, their use of molten copper, gold, and silver, along with the casting techniques they developed, all mean that they were becoming accomplished metallurgists. Each item was necessarily made from scratch with the lost-wax method, a unique work of art not duplicated either before or since.

Some more elaborate examples of cast copper are known from various parts of the Southwest. A bell from the Mogollon site of Casas Grandes, Chihuahua, is 55 made in the form of a highly decorated turtle. Still, the most exotic examples of cast metal known from highland Mexico are not found in the Southwest. The region was always in some ways a distant outpost of Mesoamerican civilization.

As we have seen, communities of the Mogollon tradition pressed westward in the centuries following AD 500, refugees from the great depression that hit their homeland at this time. This meant an intergrading of Hohokam and Mogollon culture in some areas, particularly in what is now southeastern Arizona. Still later, around AD 1200, groups of Anasazi Indians began intruding into traditionally Hohokam territory as well. In some cases, Hohokam and Anasazi communities were joined together as single communities, apparently living side by side in a kind of prehistoric peaceful coexistence. The immigrant groups seem to have been attracted by the security offered by Hohokam irrigation agriculture, with its apparent immunity from unpredictable changes in local rainfall. But the security was an illusion. The economic base of Hohokam life was under increasing stress. A careful analysis of seed remains at Snaketown has shown that each century brought crop failures in ever increasing frequency and severity to the Hohokam people.

Hohokam arts did not decline, even as the long tradition began to contract upon itself. Very fine cotton cloth was woven near the end of the sequence. Weaving was 73 an art at which all the Southwestern cultures excelled. Prehistoric American cotton is an unexplained cross between a wild American species and another species from the Old World. How the two species came to produce the domesticated hybrid is still unknown. Although it has excited the speculations of advocates of prehistoric transoceanic travel, it remains possible that the hybrid could have been produced by natural means. In any case, it is thousands of years old in the New World, and has been utilized for the production of textiles for much of that time. Little of the cloth has survived in the Southwest, but the examples available reflect considerable skill. Buttonholes, for example, were made as the cloth was woven, by using weft elements to pull warp elements apart. The looms upon which such cloth was made were not elaborate, probably not much more than simple vertical frames. Similarly, the spinning of thread was accomplished with simple spindles, each of which had a clay whorl to act as a fly wheel. Yet even with such basic equipment, the Indians of the Southwest, like others elsewhere in the New World, produced some of the finest textiles known.

Many of the groups that moved into Hohokam territory around AD 1300 carried what is now called 'Salado' culture. Migration was familiar to the people of this culture. Their story began in AD 500 with the advent of the disastrous depression of the Mogollon. Some of the Mogollon drifted westward out of their homeland and into the Verde Valley of central Arizona. Here they took up new lives as best they could, adopting ideas from the Anasazi just north of them, and perhaps residing with some outlying Anasazi communities. The resulting cultural amalgam is called 'Sinagua', the ancestor of Salado. From AD 500 to about 1050 the Sinagua people lived as an unimportant minority, surrounded by the dominant traditions of the Southwest. Their culture developed slowly, and then seemed to face certain destruction with the eruption of Sunset Crater volcano sometime between AD 1046 and 1070. The sky blackened with ash, and the Sinagua people fled. Where they went is still a mystery. The cinders and ash that covered the Verde Valley killed much of the low vegetation, turning it into fertilizer. The moisture and heat held beneath this fertilizer stimulated the development of a natural mulch that made farming potentially more productive than ever. New Sinagua towns sprang up as much of the population returned after AD 1100. For two centuries they rode a crest of agricultural bounty, reaching a cultural climax around AD 1300. Then the complex ingredients of the general Southwestern 'abandonment' reached them too. The cinder mulch dried and blew away, and the Sinagua people found themselves overextended in the face of shortage. They abandoned the Verde Valley again, this time forever, and fanned out in search of new lives. Many of them headed south, becoming immigrants into Hohokam settlements. There they adapted once again, becoming what we now call 'Salado', and forming dual societies with the Hohokam.

The Sinagua abandonment of the country around Flagstaff left dozens of towns deserted. One of these was Tuzigoot. Another was a cliff dwelling that now bears the colorful but inappropriate name 'Montezuma Castle'. Both are preserved as National Monuments, and visited by thousands of tourists each year. Fewer than 10,000 Sinagua people lived in this area before final abandonment. Of them, about a third moved south to take up residence with the Hohokam, reversing for a time the steady decline of Hohokam population in the southern desert. As we have seen, some archaeologists think that this was also a time that saw the revival of the Ootam, the desert branch of the Hohokam. Implicit in this view is the notion that grand sites like Snaketown were inhabited by Mexican invaders before 1300, and that their abandonment left the Hohokam country to the original founders of the tradition and the newly arrived Salado people. But the mystery remains unresolved.

Living together, the two cultures produced a composite archaeological record that reflects sometimes a compromise of differences, sometimes a careful maintenance of them. While the Hohokam continued to bury the ashes of their dead in red-on-buff vessels, the people of the Salado culture made red, black, and white polychrome forms to accompany (but not contain) their burials. Salado architecture consisted primarily of rectangular enclosures of above-ground caliche-adobe

73 *Prehistoric Indian cotton, a mysterious cross between American and Old World species, was used by Hohokam weavers of the late prehistoric period to produce fine cloth garments. The geometric decoration on this cotton fabric was painted on after the weaving was complete.*

55
II–VI
74–7

74

(mud-brick) structures. Within the enclosures were single- and multi-storied houses, some of them huge central 'Great Houses'.

One such enclosure complex is Casa Grande, now a National Monument south of Phoenix. The Great House at Casa Grande, like those elsewhere, was built by 'puddling' courses of wet adobe one on top of another, as each successive course dried. The walls are thin at the top, but massive at the bottom. At Casa Grande, the lower walls are one meter thick, but at other sites they have been known to be twice that. The interior walls are vertical, while their exterior faces slope inward. The floor plan of the Casa Grande Great House is of a single interior room surrounded by a ring of outer rooms. The ground floor interior room was completely filled with adobe during construction so that an additional three stories could be added above. The outer ring of rooms has only two additional stories above the ground floor. The resulting 'penthouse' that stands atop the house is perforated by holes, the functions of which are still unknown. They are too small to be doors, windows, or even ventilators. Current interest in astronomical alignments has led some archaeologists to look into the possibility that these were sighting holes, perhaps for solar or lunar observation.

The rectangular wall around Casa Grande was originally about three meters high. There were no doorways in it, and the Indians used ladders to enter the compound. Inside were about sixty rooms, including those of the Great House. Perhaps enclosures like Casa Grande were built for defensive purposes, with the Great Houses serving as citadels. It is more likely though that the Great Houses served a regular function. As we have seen, there is much to suggest that chiefdoms had emerged within the Hohokam tradition. This being the case, the Great Houses may well have been the residences of local élite groups.

By 1450, the ominous increase in crop failures caught up with the Hohokam and their Salado partners. Bands of hostile Apaches moved in and the elements of abandonment that had struck most other areas of the Southwest earlier finally reached the southern desert. The Salado contingents, and perhaps some Hohokam communities as well, quit the area around Phoenix. Some linked up with Anasazi communities, others moved eastward to join dwindling Mogollon groups. But most of the surviving Hohokam remained in their homeland. The tradition persisted in the form of the historical Pima around Phoenix, and the Papago to the south. By the time Father Kino, a Jesuit missionary and explorer, visited the area in 1694, the great towns and irrigation systems were things of the past. The complex social and political institutions necessary to maintain chiefdoms and irrigation systems had collapsed under the strain of crop failure and Apache competition. Those who remained fell back upon less elaborate tribal organization, and left the old ditches and ruins to 'those who have gone'.

Anasazi culture

Of the prehistoric traditions of the Southwest, the one that has attracted the most popular interest in modern times is the one created by the people called the Anasazi. The name means 'the old ones' in the language of the Navajo who now dominate the area. The Anasazi were responsible for well-known sites such as Pueblo Bonito in Chaco Canyon and the cliff dwellings of Mesa Verde. In the course of their early

Descended from migrant Mogollon and Anasazi groups, the Sinagua people of central Arizona (AD 500–1300) built towns and cliff dwellings (opposite), developing an attractive art style in shell and other materials (overleaf).

74 The Sinagua site of Montezuma Castle stands in a natural rock shelter in the Verde Valley. Not really a castle, and never known to the Aztecs of Mexico, the misnamed site is now a National Monument.

75 The symmetrical valves of Pacific Ocean brachiopods have been transformed into Sinagua toad ornaments.

76 Sinagua shell earrings of about AD 1200 take the form of miniature birds or animal effigies.

development, they centered upon the four-corners area of Arizona, New Mexico, Utah, and Colorado, but later they spread outward in almost every direction. Sometimes, as we have already seen, this expansion was at the expense of the other sedentary peoples of the Southwest. Near the end of prehistory, it became a tragic overextension that contributed to the collapse of the Anasazi tradition inward upon itself.

We have a better understanding of the chronology of the Anasazi culture than of other cultures in the Southwest, largely because of the heavy use of 'dendrochronology', or tree-ring dating, in the Anasazi area. The technique is possible because in the arid Southwest trees live a rather precarious existence. A good year will produce rapid growth, but conditions need only be slightly poorer for tree growth to be almost halted. The conditions that produce these dramatic changes in growth patterns are general over large areas, so similar patterns of growth can be observed from tree to tree over much of the Anasazi area. Beams from prehistoric structures have been compared with a master log, many centuries old when scientists cut it down. By careful comparison, the beams can be matched to the master log, and by counting the number of rings between the outer ring of the beam and that of the master log, the archaeologist can determine the year in which the beam was cut down. Of course, there are difficulties. Dressed beams sometimes lack their outer rings. Indians sometimes took beams from older ruins to use in more recent structures. But these difficulties aside, the technique of dendrochronology has allowed the development of an exceedingly accurate chronology for the Anasazi. The benefits of this technique have been extended to the other traditions by 'cross-dating' the pottery types traded across cultural lines. Thus, specific Mogollon pottery types that appear in Anasazi contexts can be used to date the Mogollon sites from which they were derived. Similarly, Anasazi trade pottery can be used to date the 'foreign' archaeological contexts in which it occurs.

In the centuries before 100 BC, the plateau area drained by the upper tributaries of the Colorado and Rio Grande was occupied by one of the many varieties of Desert Culture, called 'San Jose'. The Anasazi tradition, divided into 'Basketmaker' and 'Modified Basketmaker' for the period before AD 700, and 'Pueblo' for the period following, grew directly from this base.

At 100 BC, the Basketmaker people were less advanced than the Mogollon or Hohokam. They made no pottery – hence their name – and appear to have had little agriculture. They hunted with the atlatl, not the bow and arrow which the Mogollon used. Their houses were impermanent shelters in most locations, although there is some evidence that they occasionally built circular, domed dwellings with clay floors. These ranged up to eight meters in diameter, the floors being depressed in the middle, but not enough to qualify as pit houses. Upper walls were made with sticks and mud. Apart from these structures, the Basketmakers built only storage pits or 'cists' of stone slabs. They appear often to have lived in the mouths of caves, in rock shelters, and in the open. Their early villages usually consisted of three or four houses (although occasionally as many as twenty), representing band populations of about a dozen people.

The Basketmakers wore fiber sandals and robes of woven fur and feathers. Fibers of many sorts were used to make such things as bags and women's skirts. Basketry 77, 78

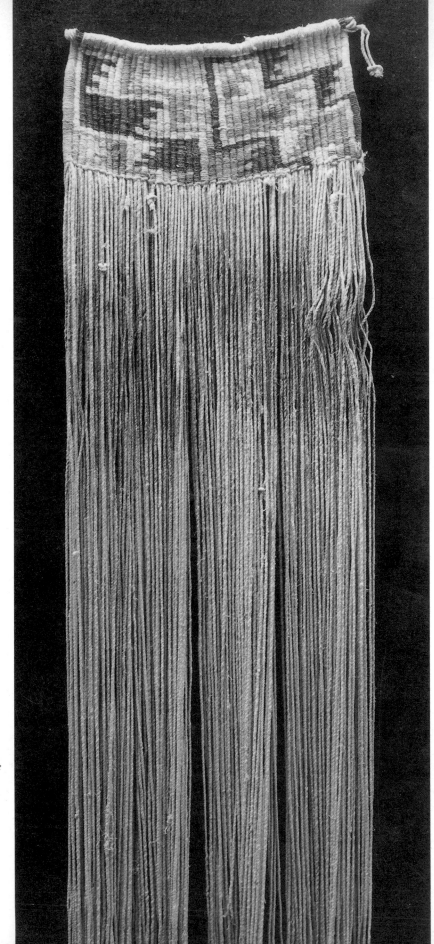

77, 78 *Early Anasazi
Indians (literally 'the old
ones' in the language of the
modern Navajo) are famed
for their elaborate coiled
baskets (opposite), hence the
name 'Basketmakers' given
them for the period up to
AD 700. Basketmaker
women wore small fiber
aprons (right) as pubic
coverings.*

was highly developed, and turns up in several forms. The most elaborate examples were made by coiling, wherein the coil was often composed of two stout rod-like fibers for stability, and several finer ones for bulk. Wrapping fibers were dyed black and red, then used to decorate on a white background. Some baskets were water-proofed with pitch.

In Modified Basketmaker times, around AD 400, what had started out as storage cists began to evolve into pit houses. Many of these later Basketmaker houses were quite shallow, and as small as three meters in diameter. However, larger structures also began to appear, sometimes with diameters of eight meters. These were not the clay-floored huts of earlier times, but permanent dwellings with walls of stone slabs

or clay plaster. Roofs were domed cribworks of logs, each with a fire or smoke hole at the apex.

As house pits got deeper and deeper, the difficulty of constructing entrances increased. The problem was finally solved when people began to enter and exit the houses through the central smoke holes. But the old-style entrances had also served the important function of allowing a circulation of air without which, smoke holes notwithstanding, the rooms would soon have filled up with smoke. So it was that as smoke holes became entrances, entrances became ventilator shafts. Later houses always had deflectors in front of ventilator shaft openings to prevent severe drafts.

Such houses also always had a small hole in the floor, a 'sipapu' to symbolize the hole in the earth from which in the beginning the human race emerged. The belief is an ancient one among Southwestern peoples, and there were several elaborations of the myth. According to one Hopi version, the primeval world was dark and lifeless. Below the earth were three cave worlds, one above the other, the lowest of which held the human race, which was living in the misery of its own filth. Two brothers, dual culture heroes, propagated plants upon which the people were able to climb to the middle and then to the uppermost cave. At this level they discovered fire, and finally pierced through to the surface of the earth, emerging from the hole along with the most sacred members of the animal world, Coyote, Spider, Locust, Swallow, and Vulture. Each of these creatures then made its contribution to the world we know. Coyote released the stars from a jar, Spider spun the moon, Vulture fanned the waters into the basins of the seas, and the others turned to lesser tasks. The people made the sun from the skin of a white deer, and the brothers made channels for the rivers and streams. The participants in this story continue on through a long cycle of adventures and creative acts, both large and small. They were part of the heritage of the Anasazi, and they remain today part of the living legacy of the Hopi people.

The people of the Modified Basketmaker phase were the first in their area to make pottery. The idea appears to have come to them from the Mogollon. The first examples were heavily tempered with coarse fibers. This was later changed to grass, then grass seed, and then finally eliminated altogether. With each step in the reduction of temper, finer pottery was achieved. Early examples also often contain quantities of coarse sand, which potters were not yet winnowing out of the clay. One form imitates gourd ladles. The handle, which is hollow and open at the end, is the closest thing to a spout ever made in the Southwest.

AD 700 is the official boundary between the Basketmaker and Pueblo sequences. In the light of present knowledge, the boundary seems to make too much of a not very extraordinary transition, but early archaeologists thought otherwise. They noted that there was a sharp change in the physical character of the Anasazi people at this time. The practice of inhumation and the dry conditions of the area had enabled physical anthropologists to reconstruct the prehistoric Anasazi physique with considerable accuracy. In particular they had observed the long-headedness of the Basketmakers as opposed to the round-headedness of the later Pueblo Indians. This, it seemed to many archaeologists, argued strongly in favor of a hypothesis that there was a major population replacement around AD 700, and therefore a major break between the two sequences. Later, however, it was discovered that the

change in cranial form occurred at a time when infant cradleboard styles were 79
changing. The Basketmaker people had developed a kind of cradle made out of soft
fibers, which was carried on the back. Their descendants used hard boards instead,
and thus inadvertently flattened their infants' malleable heads, a deformity which
was carried into adulthood. They would have been amused by the archaeological
consternation this later caused.

During the first of four Pueblo phases, the Anasazi developed their own ceramic
styles. They adopted ideas from the Mogollon and Hohokam to the south, but not
without making a few changes. The southern prototypes were vessels colored with
slips and paints that ranged through various reddish and buff colors, colors that 68–71
indicate firing in an oxidizing atmosphere. These vessels were baked under conditions that allowed air to circulate and the oxygen in it to combine with the iron-
bearing minerals in the clay and paint. In contrast, the Anasazi potters fired their
vessels in a reducing atmosphere (heating without oxygen), probably under heaps 80
of dried dung. The result is pottery with vivid black, gray, and white colors, colors
that do not imply oxidation. Thus, the Anasazi were already showing the almost
stubborn virtuosity that has ever since characterized their arts. Ignoring ceramic art
for centuries, they made its adoption contingent upon their own technological
innovation, producing from the beginning their own distinctive style.

79 *A Mojave infant of Southern Arizona was swaddled to its cradleboard when it was four days old, as this 25-cm.-long doll shows. Awake or asleep, the child spent most of his time there until he was old enough to walk.*

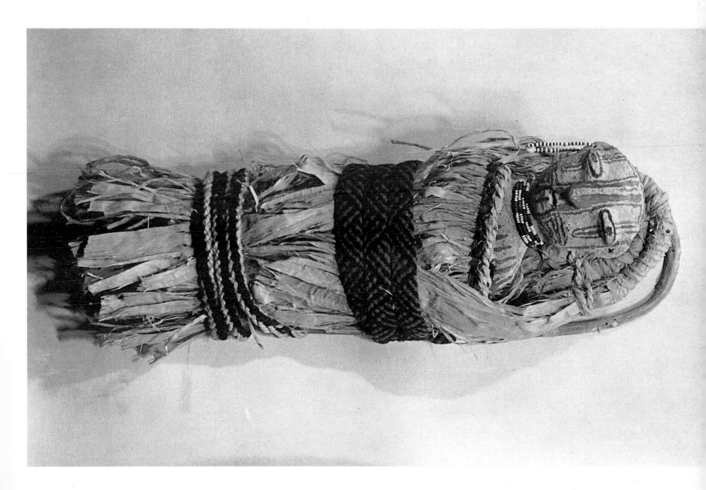

At about the same time, after AD 700, the Anasazi began to shift to above-ground dwellings. It appears that this was at least partly the result of the need to pack living quarters close together. Pit houses cannot be contiguous unless artificial walls are built between them, and if that is done, there is little sense in putting everything underground. Apartment-style quarters also put an end to round rooms, at least in the case of dwellings. Eventually, most structures were built above ground. Pit houses, however, were retained for ceremonial purposes, with all their carefully defined features intact. We have already seen how similar kivas emerged in Mogollon country. A few of these are found even today in Pueblo villages, surviving largely as meeting-places for male clan members. These survivals have provided us with much of what we need to know in order to interpret the parallel evolution of kivas and apartment dwellings among the Anasazi and Mogollon.

Generally speaking, Pueblo communities are organized socially and spatially along female lines. Clan membership is through one's mother, and for a man residence after marriage is with his wife and her family, people who are necessarily not of his own clan. Thus, the men of the community are scattered after marriage into the homes of persons who do not belong to the same clans. The kivas, therefore, provided a place in which men could maintain their clan identity, and prepare the public ritual for which Southwestern clans have been traditionally responsible.

The period around AD 1000 was one in which Anasazi culture expanded widely as many small villages proliferated. Over the next few centuries, the culture reached its highest total population and greatest areal extent. The most rapid development was in the eastern part of the plateau, in what is now the upper Rio Grande drainage of northern New Mexico. Much of this expansion was at the expense of the Mogollon, and much of it can be attributed to the onset of a period that saw an improvement in the annual rainfall pattern. Improved varieties of the primary crops may also have become available. The Anasazi were dry farmers, they never depended upon vast irrigation networks as the Hohokam did, or upon a mixed economy like that of the Mogollon. Their agricultural talents gave them an economic edge over the Mogollon, but their dependence upon springs and rainfall meant that they were not as free from climatic variations as the Hohokam. When times were good, as they were during this period, the Anasazi experienced an economic boom. Unfortunately, the reverse was also true, as we shall see.

Anasazi populations expanded rapidly in such well-known localities as Mesa Verde, Chaco Canyon, and Canyon de Chelly. Surface rooms appear on Mesa Verde by AD 700, with an average of eight rooms per village. Gradually the villages contracted into tight apartment complexes with a kiva for every twelve rooms on the average. At the same time, however, another trend was developing. Previously the Anasazi had spread into new areas through a proliferation of small communities. Now the situation was reversed as villages were abandoned and populations combined to form a smaller number of large towns. The trend toward aggregation began around AD 950 in Chaco Canyon and continued over the next two centuries here and elsewhere in Anasazi territory.

The new development was partly the result of an evolution toward chiefdoms, something that, as we have seen, occurred in the Hohokam tradition as well. Typically, the larger towns were D-shaped aggregates in which most of the domestic

80 What this hermaphroditic monster lacks in grace it gains in power. Anasazi potters fired their vessels in a reducing atmosphere (heating without oxygen) to obtain the rich black-on-white designs of bowls such as this one, 1000 years old, from Mesa Verde, Colorado.

86, 87,
81, 82,
XV
86

87

apartments were arranged along a high curved back wall. The apartments could be six or eight deep on the ground floor, and stacked to a depth of four or five stories, usually stepped so that the back row of apartments was also the highest. The lower rear rooms, buried in darkness under the others, were usually used for storage. Inside the arc of clustered apartments was a smaller arc of kivas, sometimes two dozen or more. Inside this was the central courtyard, sealed on one side by the long straight wall that formed the flat side of the 'D'.

Chaco Canyon contains twelve of these large towns, of which Pueblo Bonito is the best known. The flat side of the complex faces south toward the river. Northward, the curved side backs up against a cliff face, part of which has seemed ready to fall on the town for centuries. Pueblo Bonito covers three acres, and

87

contains over 800 apartments. Built gradually over 150 years, it probably had a population of about 1200 at its peak around AD 1100. Yet these internal features of Pueblo Bonito are only part of the significance of this and the other large towns of Chaco Canyon. The large towns are arranged north of the arroyo that splits the canyon. On the south side are 200–350 smaller towns, most of which appear to have been satellites of the main centers. Pueblo Bonito, with its large population and Great Kiva, was almost certainly the capital of an Anasazi chiefdom.

The circular Great Kivas of the Anasazi first appeared around AD 650, centuries before they were adopted by the Mogollon. Great Kivas at sites like Pueblo Bonito 87 range up to twenty meters in diameter, with roofs of earth and wood that weighed up to 100 tons after a heavy rain. One to a town, they probably served major community ceremonial functions. The smaller kivas in Pueblo Bonito and its satellite villages fulfilled the needs of individual clans. A wide masonry bench encircles the interior of each Great Kiva, and in the center there is usually a large raised fireplace. At Pueblo Bonito there are two sunken rooms on either side of the fireplace, probably anterooms used in a variety of public ceremonies. A thousand years have passed, and there are no records, but it seems likely that these ceremonies were similar to ones still performed in the Pueblo villages of the Southwest. Clansmen dress in the highly stylized costumes of one or more of the hundreds of 83 'kachina' ancestor gods that abound in the Pueblo cosmologies. The ceremonies are often concerned with fertility, rainfall, and other matters dealing with the maintenance of order and regularity in the universe. They are colorful rituals that even today are closed to outsiders.

Pueblo Bonito, and many of the other large towns like it, had no doors or windows in the outside walls. Entry to the town was by ladder over the wall. There appears to have been a main entrance at one time, but this and smaller openings were later sealed. All this suggests that both the size and the layout of the town were at least partly defensive features. The Apache and Navajo were drifting into Anasazi territory by this time, and crop failures among Anasazi villagers who had extended themselves too far into marginal areas may have turned Pueblo Indians against each other as well. The first symptoms of abandonment appear, and Anasazi culture began to contract in upon itself. Marginal communities were displaced, and larger communities at the core were put under increasing stress.

On Mesa Verde and a few other places, the open villages on top of the mesa were gradually abandoned, and to replace them the Indians built the famous cliff dwellings. Most Mesa Verde villages were located on top of the mesa up to about AD 950. A century later, half of the occupied villages were cliff dwellings, and by 1150 virtually all the Anasazi of Mesa Verde lived in cliff dwellings. The cliff faces produced by erosion of the plateau in this area are streaked with horizontal crevices. Natural erosion of the soft sedimentary beds has left crevices that are at times only tiny niches, at other times huge rock shelters. Many, even the smallest of these in Mesa Verde, have been used for the construction of dwellings and storage places. Perhaps the grandest of all is Cliff Palace, a massive complex containing more than 85, 200 rooms and 23 kivas. The original entrance to the structure was by an improbable series of hand- and footholds, difficult to negotiate and easy to defend. Such a community could withstand the longest sieges hostile nomads could muster, but

83 Modern Pueblo ceremonies, rooted in prehistory, are linked with over 250 kachinas, the living spirits of the dead personified in masked dancers or cottonwood dolls such as this one, with rain-cloud eyes as symbols of fertility.

84 The polychrome decoration on this rare 1000-year-old painted mortar, 20 cm. high, shows the influence of textile design on Anasazi craftsmen. The mortar comes from Pueblo Bonito, an impressive town covering 3 acres in Chaco Canyon, New Mexico.

85 *Security-conscious villagers of Cliff Palace, Mesa Verde, gained access to their cliff dwelling through a narrow, easily defensible defile. Fields cultivated on the plateau above (Plate 86) were reached by wooden ladders and footholds on the sheer rock face.*

there was another kind of siege that no community could withstand, as we shall see. The modern visitor has been provided with a more convenient access, but will find the courtyard pitted with unroofed kivas. In contrast, the kivas at nearby Spruce Tree House have been restored for the visitor's benefit. 88

Generally, there is a ratio of about twelve rooms for every kiva in the cliff villages of Mesa Verde. However, the ratio at Cliff Palace is fewer than nine rooms per kiva. In addition to being the largest of the cliff dwellings, then, this site also has an unexpectedly large number of kivas. Because of this, it seems likely that the village of Cliff Palace functioned like that of Pueblo Bonito. It was probably a regional 86 87

144

center to which other Mesa Verde villagers came for special ceremonies and to exchange goods. Cliff Palace appears to have been an organizational center, like Pueblo Bonito the hub of a centralized political structure.

The masonry at places like Pueblo Bonito and Cliff Palace was quite simple. Rough natural stones were used, and the irregular gaps were filled with mud mortar. Sometimes smaller stone fragments were used to close up the large gaps between courses, and mud plaster was often used to cover the results. Such walls would not last long in a wet environment, but in the Southwest, and particularly where sheltered by cliffs, they were sturdy and permanent.

There are some interesting differences of architectural detail between Mesa Verde and the Chaco Canyon sites. Some of these at least are probably the result of differing local materials. Walls at Pueblo Bonito, for example, were often built of tabular rocks and packed with cores of rubble. There are no rubble-filled walls at Mesa Verde, and the stones used there had to be roughly dressed. Mesa Verde is also known for its towers, which appeared after AD 950. These are structures of two or three stories that are usually associated with kivas. Sometimes they are incorporated into larger structural complexes like the one called 'Tower House'. The association with kivas suggests that they had a ceremonial function. However, towers are sometimes isolated circular structures that may well have served defensive purposes. Whatever their function, they seem to indicate continuing Mexican influence in the Anasazi area. 87 86

Anasazi pottery became varied and specialized after AD 1100. Black-on-white types continued to be produced, but in a wider variety of forms, some of which were made in small localities and distributed elsewhere by trade. Perhaps the most famous product of this time was the Mesa Verde mug, which has been repeatedly copied by modern potters for a twentieth-century market. Just as important as the diversification of older styles, however, was the introduction of polychrome pottery. These types are often decorated with black, orange, and yellow paints, colors that imply oxidation during firing, and therefore some change in firing technique. In the upper Rio Grande district, one polychrome type involved the use of a true glaze paint. Application over whole vessels would have produced fully waterproof pots, but the potters who discovered the glaze appear never to have seen this potential. 84

Opposite:
88 The top of ladders poke out of the entrances to ceremonial kivas built into the courtyard of Spruce Tree House, Mesa Verde. Typical 'keyhole' doors give access to darkened interior rooms.

87 Pueblo Bonito in Chaco Canyon, a town of over 800 rooms and 1200 inhabitants at its peak 900 years ago, was built as a D-shaped enclosure, with rubble-filled walls covered in mud plaster.

Pots which bear this unusual paint are prototypes of ones made by the historical Zuni, people who by this time had diverged from their Mogollon heritage and entered the Anasazi cultural sphere.

This period is also known for fine cotton cloth, woven into complex designs that sometimes look like lace. At the same time, ornaments of turquoise and other materials were made in large quantities. 90

But all this soon ended. The cultural crest of the Anasazi was halted, if not reversed, around AD 1300 and their communities began a long retreat from the limits of their vast territory. As we have seen with the Hohokam, the arrival of the Apache and Navajo may have had something to do with the contraction. Some archaeologists think that under this pressure internecine fighting between Pueblo groups would also have been likely. Still, neither of these facts alone can explain the disruptive events of about AD 1300. A more potent explanation is needed. 91 92

89 *A black-on-white Anasazi pitcher, 20 cm. high, shows the vessel form popular at this time, about AD 1000. The geometric design can be traced back to earlier coiled basketry.*

90 *A late-prehistoric shirt demonstrates the skill Pueblo Indians achieved in weaving native cotton. Unlike later Navajo weaving, Pueblo weaving was done by men.*

149

In addition to providing us with precise dates, tree-ring analysis in the Anasazi area has allowed the reconstruction of a long climatic record. Prominent in that record is evidence of a disastrous drought between AD 1276 and 1299. Already threatened by warfare, Anasazi communities watched their 'permanent' springs dry up. Year after year, ancient ritual failed to make the rains appear. Without the large irrigation networks of the Hohokam, the Anasazi could do little more than retreat before the effects of a decade of crop failure. Many villagers must have starved, but the remains of burned villages and the unburied skeletons of their unlucky defenders indicate a bloodier end for some.

Under the impact of so many calamities, the Anasazi contracted into smaller and smaller areas. Mesa Verde and many other parts of the plateau were abandoned 92

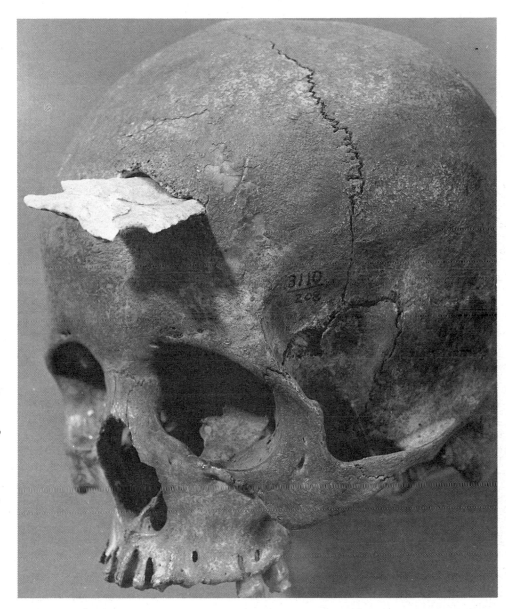

Around AD 1300 *Anasazi culture began to retreat under the combined pressures of warfare, drought, and famine.*

91 Betatakin, a cliff dwelling with 135 rooms in northeastern Arizona, was an Anasazi stronghold against invasion by Navajo and Apache Athapascan nomads. It fell and was abandoned by AD 1300.

92 The skull of a 20-year-old woman from Mesa Verde still holds the point that killed her, a grizzly reminder of the conflict that beset the Pueblo Indians in the closing centuries of prehistory.

forever. Pueblo towns after AD 1300 clustered on the Little Colorado River and on the upper Rio Grande. In these areas there was enough water for survival, and some security from Athapascan attack. Despite the hardships it was not a period of cultural deterioration. Indeed, the consolidation of artisans into a few compact communities appears to have stimulated even more experimentation and innovation. Ceramic production was as vigorous as ever, and the textiles that have survived also show remarkable quality. In northern Arizona, a series of polychrome types were produced that have been revived in modern times by Hopi potters. In many places, there were loom holes in the flagstone floors of kivas, which indicate a steady production of cloth by men. On the Rio Grande, styles shifted quickly as communities absorbed Anasazi refugees from the west. Here as elsewhere the Pueblo Indians made the best of their new situation, reaching what some anthropologists think was their peak of cultural development.

The retrenchment of the Anasazi was followed by yet another threat. In 1540–42, Francisco Vasquez de Coronado led an expedition through the Southwest, looking for the legendary 'seven cities of gold'. His three hundred and seventy soldiers each hoped to repeat the exploits of Cortés. They never found their cities of gold, but their exploration opened the Rio Grande region to Spanish colonization. In the following century, the Pueblo Indians were compelled to struggle against enslavement by the Spanish, who made strong efforts to profit as much as possible from the production of Pueblo crafts. In 1680, the Indians revolted and threw the Spanish out entirely. Colonial control was not re-established until 1692.

The episode had some happy results. The marauding Navajo adopted pastoralism from the Spanish and took a kinder attitude toward the Pueblos. The latter sometimes took refuge with the Navajo during the wars with the Spanish, and in the course of this contact the Navajo took on Southwestern weaving techniques. Done by women, not men, in Navajo culture, weaving combined with sheep-herding to begin the long tradition of wool blanket production that still thrives. At the same XVI time, all the peoples of the Southwest were learning to work silver. Combining this new technique with older design motifs and materials such as turquoise, the Indians began another series of artistic traditions, one that continues today.

The communities of the Anasazi still persist as introspective cultural enclaves that have resisted capitulation to dominant European cultures. The Navajo and Apache are now pacific, and the Spanish are gone. Anglo-American culture seems to be everywhere, but the Pueblo Indians exist on their own terms, terms rooted in a tradition that is 2000 years old.

The Athapascans

xv *Now a National Monument, Arizona's Canyon de Chelly was once a natural Anasazi fortress against marauding Navajo. For a while it was a haven for refugees from Mesa Verde and Chaco Canyon, but the nomads overran it soon after AD 1300.*

Most Athapascan languages are found not in the Southwest, but scattered through the interior portions of Alaska and western Canada. Athapascan-speakers are the descendants of the second-to-last major prehistoric influx of people into the New World. They were followed only by the Eskimos and Aleuts.

Why some Athapascan-speaking bands broke off from the main body and started drifting south is not yet understood. Ancestral Apache bands began their journey around AD 825. Ancestral Navajo followed them southward about 175 years later. Their movement took them along the flanks of the Rockies. The traces of the first

XVI

bands to enter the Southwest are understandably scanty, and archaeologists are still not sure that they have really found them. At first these Athapascans probably just exploited the large unoccupied spaces between agricultural settlements. Later, as their numbers grew, the settlements themselves probably came to be viewed as resources to be exploited, and the long period of warfare began.

We have no good archaeological evidence for the Athapascans in the Southwest almost until the historical period. There are scattered sites from AD 1500 and later that are clearly Athapascan. These sites contain the remains of structures that look very much like later Navajo dwellings (hogans), and distinctive ceramics. With the Spanish intrusion, their cultures changed quickly. From the Spanish they acquired horses, sheep, and cattle. From Pueblo refugees they learned advanced techniques of pottery-making and weaving. These contacts even led to some changes in social structure. The development of matrilocal clans among the Navajo, for example, is attributed to imitation of Pueblo social structure.

Old Athapascan religious practices appear to have centered around curing and other activities by shamans. Contacts with the Pueblo Indians, however, generated interest in public ceremonies conducted by priests. Curing remained primary, but the Navajo and Western Apache took on much of the indigenous Southwestern symbolism.

The modern descendants of these later prehistoric invaders are the Navajo, Western Apache, and other Apache tribes called Chiricahua, Jicarilla, Mescalero, Lipan, and Kiowa. They survive today. Among them, the Navajo stand out as a vigorous and expanding nation. They own large and growing tracts of Arizona and New Mexico, and their unique crafts flourish in a seller's market. Like the Pueblo   XVI Indians, they persist on their own terms in the contemporary world.

XVI *Two supernatural 'holy people' flank the sacred maize plant, which was their gift to mortals, within a rainbow arc on this 19th-century Navajo blanket. Similar scenes appear in the sand paintings for which the Navajo are famous.*

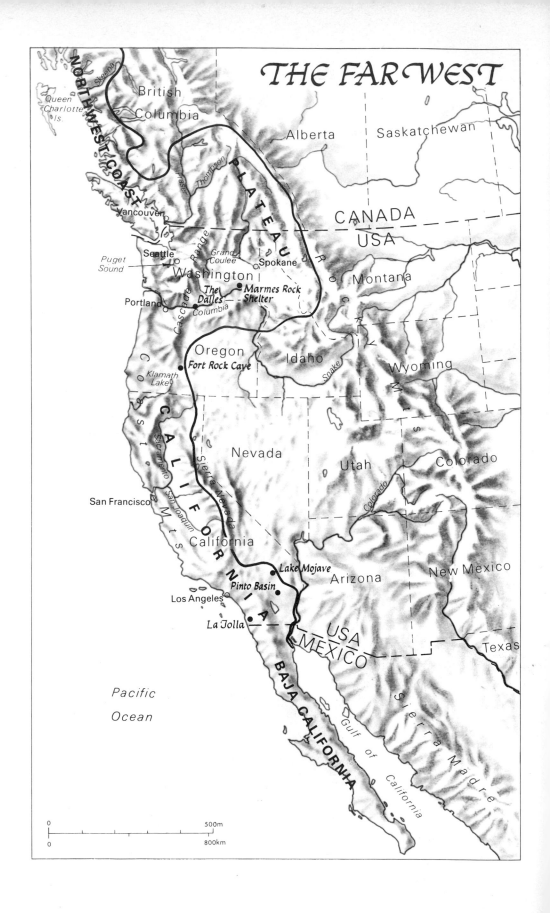

THE FAR WEST

British Columbia

Queen Charlotte Is.

NORTHWEST COAST

Skeena

Fraser

Thompson

PLATEAU

Alberta

Saskatchewan

Vancouver

CANADA

USA

Puget Sound

Seattle

Grand Coulee

Spokane

Cascade Range

Washington

Montana

The Dalles

Marmes Rock Shelter

Portland

Columbia

Rocky

Coast Mts

Oregon

Fort Rock Cave

Idaho

Snake

Klamath Lake

Wyoming

Sacramento

CALIFORNIA

Sierra Nevada

Nevada

Mts

Utah

Colorado

San Francisco

San Joaquin

Colorado

California

Lake Mojave

Arizona

New Mexico

Pinto Basin

Los Angeles

La Jolla

USA

MEXICO

Texas

Pacific

Ocean

BAJA CALIFORNIA

Gulf of California

Sierra Madre

0		500m
0		800km

The Far West

The western margin of North America is a long coastal strip that is concealed from the rest of the continent by rugged mountain ranges. The Coast Range of the Alaskan panhandle and British Columbia is linked to the Cascade Range, which runs down through Washington and Oregon into northern California, where it becomes the Sierra Nevada. Baja California, politically part of Mexico, is a long peninsula separated from the rest of the continent by the Gulf of California. There is easy passage from the Southwest to the California coast between the northern end of the Gulf of California and the modern city of Los Angeles, a distance of about 250 kilometers. Similarly, 4000 kilometers farther north, there is fairly easy passage from the Alaskan interior to Prince William Sound on the Pacific coast. In between, travel to the coast from the interior ranges is difficult, sometimes nearly impossible. Not many rivers puncture the relatively low coastal mountains, and fewer still have tributaries east of the larger ranges. Only the Columbia and Fraser Rivers have substantial drainage basins east of the mountains. They drain the Plateau, which spreads over the eastern parts of Oregon and Washington, as well as much of Idaho. Physically the Plateau is part of the Desert West, but its rivers drew the local prehistoric Indians into closer contact with coastal cultures.

Climate and environment along the coastal strip of the Far West vary primarily with latitude, but also with altitude and distance from the sea. Much of Baja California is parched desert, which would have restricted the Indians there to a Desert Culture way of life were it not for the availability of marine resources. To the north, the climate moderates, so much so that the environment of California has often been called 'Mediterranean'.

North of San Francisco stand towering forests of redwoods, and still farther up the coast begin the thick forests of moisture-loving conifers. Average annual rainfall is progressively greater toward the north. Average temperatures are progressively lower, but are always moderated by the warm currents of the Pacific, even as far north as southern Alaska. The coastal forests from Oregon northward can be properly called rain forests, even though they are not characterized by the intense heat of tropical rain forests. The floors of these forests are often so clogged with brush and fallen trees that they are virtually impassable. They alone would have stopped most prehistoric travelers. Although modern machinery can handle the dense forests, the mountains still form an impenetrable barrier in certain places. Many of the modern southern Alaskan communities can be reached only by boat or airplane.

There is little conclusive evidence to indicate that Indians were present on the coastal plain of the Far West during the long period when Paleo-Indians dominated

93 *Map of the Far West, showing principal modern cities and ancient sites, regional subdivisions into Northwest Coast, Plateau, California, and Baja California, and topographical features mentioned in the text.*

the vast hunting grounds east of the Rockies. That is not to say that no one has found possible evidence, only that much of the evidence discovered so far is unreliable. For example, ancient bone fragments with breaks and polish not unlike similar patterns on man-made tools have been found in dry caves. Zoological research has shown that large carnivores can produce such bone 'tools' with their jaws, even to the extent of manufacturing bone tubes by biting off the ends of long bones. The same kind of research has also uncovered instances of supposed bone 'awls', well polished in transit through the bowels of the same carnivores.

Excavations on Santa Rosa Island, off Santa Barbara, have revealed the skeletons of dwarf mammoths, in 'association' with man-made artifacts and possible hearths. The relationship of the tools and hearths to the mammoths is not yet clear. They may all be very old, but we have seen nothing to support the claim that together they indicate the presence of man on the island 30,000 years ago. The dwarf animals were probably descended from mammoths that had been marooned on the island during the gradual rise in sea level which accompanied the retreat of the last Canadian glacier. The dwarf species must have taken some time to evolve, and it may well have outlived its larger relative on the mainland.

For the present it seems likely that most of the Far West was populated within the last 10,000 years by small bands which had traveled from the east through mountain passes and down coastal rivers. As we shall see, this is consistent with early historical ethnographic data. The Far West has always been marginal, but it has also always been a trap. The journey was difficult, and once there, small immigrant communities had little reason to leave. The regions of the Far West were so much more favorable than adjacent areas to the east across the mountains that large-scale human movement was always westward. It is a characteristic of the west coast that still persists.

If the geography of the Far West encouraged the immigration of many diverse bands, the environment encouraged the perpetuation of that diversity. In some places mountainous terrain isolated local groups. Elsewhere, more subtle factors led Indian bands to settle into varying microenvironments. Dozens of native languages can be classified into no fewer than six major stocks, a linguistic mosaic unequaled elsewhere in North America. Communities of people speaking unrelated languages sometimes shared common cultures, while communities speaking closely related tongues carried on ways of life that contrasted dramatically. Moreover, the population density of the region was the highest on the continent north of Mexico, even though there was no agriculture. Everywhere the pattern was a variation on the theme of hunting, fishing, and gathering. In many places the natural resources were so bountiful that what we normally regard as a bare subsistence economy allowed sedentary life, occasionally in villages with populations in the hundreds. It is a complex and paradoxical region that fascinates and puzzles us.

Baja California

Few points in the New World were more remote from the prehistoric mainstream than the southern tip of the Baja California peninsula. It is not a distant and hostile land like Tierra del Fuego or Baffin Island. In fact, there is an abundance of maritime resources, and the exotic civilizations of Mexico flourished just across the Gulf of California. Still, the slender peninsula is over 1000 kilometers long, and the southern end is separated from the mainland of Mexico by more than 150 kilometers. Thus, it has always been a natural cul-de-sac for Indian populations. Prehistoric groups entered from the north, rarely if ever by sea from Mexico, and there they persisted as an extension of the cultural pattern of the Far West. Although politically now part of Mexico, Baja California was never connected with prehistoric Mexican culture.

The peninsula averages less than 100 kilometers in width and has a rugged mountain spine. There are many small valleys in the interior, and many small bays along both coasts. For the most part, it is a semiarid land, but there is enough rainfall to support wild plant and animal resources. Rainfall is relatively higher in the south, and wild foods were abundant there prehistorically. Throughout the peninsula there was enough to eat if maritime resources were combined with land resources. As a result, the aboriginal population density was quite high here, exceeded in only a few other areas north of Mexico. It was a marginal region, an almost forgotten appendix to the continent, and an area untouched in prehistoric times by agriculture and the trappings of civilization. Yet, because of these peculiarities, it was an area that supported and protected relic populations of people who thrived on one of America's most ancient subsistence systems.

The Hokaltecan language phylum, which many regard as the most ancient of the western language groups of North America, was the only phylum known to have been represented in aboriginal Baja California. Speakers of these languages included the California Yumans in the north of the peninsula, and the Peninsular Yumans in the center. The Guaicuran languages, spoken in the southern third of the peninsula, are still not securely classified, but they probably belong to the Hokaltecan phylum too. They were isolated for so long that their natural evolution made them almost unrelatable to the other languages of the phylum.

The linguistic distributions in the peninsula have led anthropologists to conclude that there were waves of migrants drifting into Baja California through the long prehistoric sequence. Three major waves are indicated, each one pressing its predecessor farther south, with perhaps a certain amount of overlapping between new immigrants and the older population. Archaeological evidence supports the idea of migratory waves. We are led to the conclusion that the historical Guaicurans at the southern end of the peninsula were the descendants of the first influx, and that the Peninsular and California Yumans were the descendants of the second and third influxes respectively.

Physical anthropologists may be able to supply additional clues. Long-headedness has been regarded for some time as an ancient characteristic in the Americas. There appears to have been a steady shift toward round-headedness in Indian populations through the prehistoric period. Perhaps this means that more recent arrivals to the New World had physical characteristics rather different from those of the very oldest populations. The discovery of long-headed skulls from the southern tip of Baja California, the Guaicuran region, seems to support this idea.

The ancestors of the Guaicurans probably arrived in the guise of a Desert Culture variant called 'Pinto Basin'. This archaeological complex dominated both the desert of southern California and the peninsula south of it during the millennia preceding

1000 BC. The time of arrival is still unknown, but may have been 10,000 years ago or more. The Pinto Basin people adapted themselves to local subsistence resources, including fish and shellfish. It was a successful adjustment that continued undisturbed by disruption from the outside, and changed little until the shock of Spanish colonization.

The next wave of migrants, the Peninsular Yumans, perhaps arrived as a variant of the so-called 'Amargosa' tradition. Amargosa culture was apparently shared by other Yumans living in the California desert and along the Colorado River. But unlike the Yumans of the peninsula, these relatives later adopted pottery, agriculture, and other advances that came from Mexico by way of the Southwest. The Peninsular Yumans had probably arrived in Baja California before these innovations were added to the Amargosa tradition, perhaps as early as 1000 BC.

On the peninsula, the Amargosa tradition culminated in an archaeological phase known as 'Comondu'. Basically, it was a kind of Desert Culture to which fishing and shellfish collection had been added as major parts of the subsistence pattern. Thus we find coiled basketry and seed-grinding implements in dry cave sites, but we also find net and hook remains, as well as coastal shell middens. In the north, there is evidence that the Peninsular Yumans may have adopted pottery just before the historical period, but most ceramic remains come from historical sites.

Isolated as they were, the Peninsular Yumans did not have the stimulus of a constant flow of exotic foreign ideas. Nevertheless, they managed a minor fluorescence on their own. Both engraved petroglyphs and colorful painted pictographs were made by these people, sometimes in rock shelters and caves where they are still well preserved.

The culture of the late prehistoric Guaicurans is called 'Las Palmas'. Basketry was rare, and in its place these people made simple containers from sewn palm bark. The bow and arrow appear to have been a relatively late addition, and the spear-thrower probably continued in use until the historical period. Despite the availability of fish, no hooks or net remains have been found, and the historical Guaicurans are known to have used only spears to take fish. Shellfish provided an important food source, and the streams, bays and beaches of the southern peninsula were congenial settings for hunter-gatherers. This was one of the few areas of the world where marginality did not carry the onus of endemic famine. The remote idyl ended abruptly, however, when European diseases were introduced. Conversion by Spanish missionaries proceeded smoothly, but so did the decimation of the population by pestilence. There were few survivors.

California

Archaeologically, the California area lies mostly within the modern state boundaries. As we have seen, a few California Yumans resided in the northern part of Baja California. The desert country of eastern and southeastern California lies on the Great Basin side of the Sierra Nevada, and is therefore part of that great province. Far to the northwest, the corner of coastal California that borders on Oregon is properly thought of as part of the Northwest Coast area. What is left is most of coastal California and valleys inland, notably the Sacramento and the San Joaquin.

Although the various subareas of California are bound together by their common favorable climate, there is still great environmental diversity. Rainfall, even apart from the desert areas, can be less than twenty-five centimeters annually in certain districts, while other places are drenched by more than ten times that much. Towering redwood forests on the northern coast give way to oak-shaded parklands in the inland valleys. Hills of the interior are often covered by the low dense scrub called 'chaparral'. Generally, the rainfall is greater in the north than in the south. But local environments are also determined by distance from the sea, elevation ranging from sea level to 4400 meters, and local topography. The result is a multiplicity of distinctive microenvironments that encouraged the cultural diversity of prehistoric California.

There was also a confusion of tongues. At the end of prehistory, California was populated by speakers of dozens of languages belonging to no fewer than five separate phyla. Some were part of the ancient Hokaltecan phylum with distant relatives scattered as far away as Central America. Others were related to the Athapascans of Canada, the Algonquians of the East, or other closer language blocks.

The number of native California cultures depends upon the criteria used to define them, but most anthropologists agree that there were no fewer than two dozen major groupings. Within each of these there were usually several independent tribelets. Thus there was even less political than linguistic unity, and the boundaries within the two mosaics did not usually coincide.

Eliminating the highly questionable evidence for very early human populations in California, we are left with remains that are assignable to the post-glacial period. There is no evidence for a major Paleo-Indian development on this side of the Rockies, but a California version of Desert Culture may well date back to before 5000 BC. Remains of this age from Lake Mojave in the southeastern California desert country and San Dieguito nearer the coast seem to have Desert Culture affiliations even though few food-grinding implements have been found.

Food-grinding implements appear clearly in the California sequence after 5000 BC. In the south 'La Jolla' culture developed. The remains of this culture have been unearthed at several sites, and all seem to speak for a relatively uncomplicated adjustment to a hunting, gathering, and fishing way of life. There is no pottery and none of the C-shaped fishhooks that were popular later on. Thus, the exploitation of maritime resources was still only poorly developed, and secondary to other subsistence techniques. Cremation was not yet the preferred mortuary practice. The dead were buried in flexed positions or prone. Sometimes there are secondary burials of persons whose bones were disarticulated before interment. At some sites there are large cairns of milling stones covering burials. Often the stones have had their bottoms knocked out, as if the purpose was to 'kill' the implements. Equally unusual is the appearance of tubular pipes at some sites. Just what, if anything, was being smoked at this early time is still not known.

Remains from central California provide another variation on the common theme. The best-known sequence comes from the Sacramento Valley. Here the remains include grinding tools, twined (but not coiled) basketry, clay balls, and a variety of shell beads and ornaments. The clay balls were probably used instead of heated stones for boiling liquids in flammable containers. Burials were extended, but always face down, an unusual practice. They were often accompanied by charm stones, which appear in a variety of forms, usually perforated near one end, and sometimes phallic. Burial goods are evenly distributed among the graves and the general picture is one of an egalitarian society without much emphasis on wealth. It is a picture that changed dramatically in later centuries.

There is some evidence to indicate that around 2000 BC there was a great population replacement in parts of California. Burials before 2000 BC tend to be of long-headed individuals, not unlike the long-headed skulls from Baja California; many archaeologists suspect that California was inhabited almost entirely by Hokaltecan-speakers at this time. Then, around 2000–1500 BC, there was an influx of people with rounder heads. Perhaps these were Penutian-speakers whose arrival disrupted the older cultures. Modern speakers of these languages in California resemble the invaders in their physical characteristics. 15

The primary weapon of the Hokaltecans had been the spear-thrower, but the new arrivals carried bows and arrows. Individuals in central California were now almost always buried tightly flexed, and not infrequently with imbedded projectile points. The obvious implication is that this was a period of increased violence. Coiled basketry was introduced and the manufacture of shell ornaments and charm stones broadened. Still, fewer of these things found their way into burials, suggesting that emphasis on wealth was increasing and inheritance was now the preferred means of dealing with the accumulated goods of the deceased. A few cremations also occur, usually with lavish offerings. This appears to have been a burial practice reserved for persons of high rank, another indicator of increasing wealth and status consciousness. Everywhere the sites are larger than in previous periods, and the population presumably larger also.

The period after 2000 BC is characterized by the introduction of several new types of shell bead, small obsidian arrow points, and a beautiful and diverse series of abalone shell ornaments. Obsidian is an attractive and easily worked stone, and many of the arrow points are exquisitely formed, often with jagged but precisely serrated edges. In addition to arrow points, these craftsmen also turned out asymmetrical crescents of obsidian, again usually with edge serration. We know from the ethnographic record that these were tied to the fingers of dancers in certain ceremonies to imitate bear claws. When new, they would have been as sharp as razors. 94

The changes following 2000 BC do not seem to have been so dramatic in southern California, possibly because the Penutians did not penetrate this far. Instead, here the new pattern was an elaboration and intensification of the old one. Villages grew larger and tools were adapted for the exploitation of special resources. The basket- or hopper-mortar was a particularly important development. It was a special stone mortar, provided with a conical basket hopper stuck to the rim with asphalt. Apparently it was used in the processing of acorns. These nuts are high in tannic acid, and to be made edible, they must be hulled, ground, winnowed, leached in warm water, and cooked. It is a complicated technique, but one that once perfected spread throughout the oak parklands of California. In places the oak became a virtual domesticate, fueling the growth of sedentary communities and the population as a whole. Acorn exploitation was supplemented by hunting and shellfish collection.

Along the coast, particularly in the vicinity of Santa Barbara and the Channel

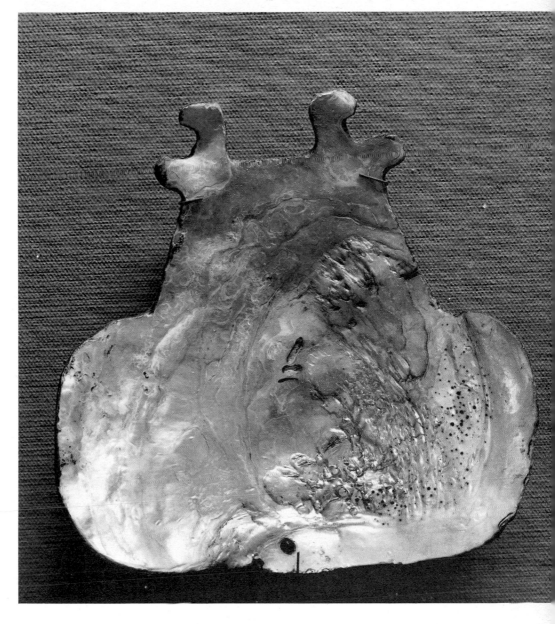

94 *Many California Indians gathered abalone shells to convert into jewelry, small containers, and inlays for larger pieces. This item, about 13 cm. wide, was used as a broach, a ladle, or both.*

Islands, a strongly maritime subsistence pattern emerged at a later date, after AD 250. The coastal zone did not provide an abundance of edible seeds and nuts. Instead the emphasis was on mussels, abalone, and marine mammals. A few deer and other land animal bones have been found, but most bone remains uncovered belong to dolphins, porpoises, and seals. These animals were probably speared from plank boats, a technique used by the historical Chumash in the same area.

Contemporaneous cultures along the flanks of the Sierra Nevada left behind petroglyphs, mortars cut into bedrock, as well as campsite remains. In one locality deep limestone shafts in the mountains have been discovered that were used as burial places. The bodies of the dead and various burial offerings were simply thrown

95

95 *The basketry of prehistoric California was the finest in native North America, and Pomo baskets like this one, 20 cm. long, with decorations of hummingbird, woodpecker, and quail feathers, may well have been the finest of all.*

into the natural shafts, rock formations that must have seemed like routes to the underworld to the Indians. Some of the bones discovered have thick crusts of travertine, and at first they were thought to be very old. Radiocarbon dating has shown, however, that the fossilization of the bones took place within the last 1400 years.

The hopper-mortar became even more common after about AD 300, indicating the widespread exploitation of acorns. Some of the finest examples of coiled basketry to be found anywhere in the world were also produced at this time. Archaeological sites are full of the sharp bone awls used in the manufacture of these baskets, some of which were so finely and tightly coiled that they were watertight. The historical Pomo are well known for their coiled baskets, decorated with intricately interwoven bird feathers. Some examples are completely clothed with the feathers of tiny birds.

Steatite became the common material for the manufacture of bowls as well as smoking pipes in southern California. The exception to this trend was in the southeastern corner of the area where pottery was introduced from the Southwest in late prehistoric times. Long bone tubes with extremely fine and detailed incised decorations were also made, but these appear not to have been connected with smoking. More likely they were drinking tubes used in connection with the ritual restrictions imposed on menstruating women.

96 *Associations of shamans grew into the Kuksu cult of the historical central California Pomo, Patwin and Maidu tribes. Elaborate paraphernalia, such as these shell disk-bead necklaces with stone and abalone pendants, was used for the ritual impersonation of mythical characters.*

Mortuary practices also changed after AD 300. Cremation was more popular, as was the custom of burning grave offerings in the burial pit, and then burying the corpse uncremated after the fire went out. These elaborate practices can be traced through the archaeological record to the rites of the historical period.

In the last centuries of California prehistory, we see a trend toward the production of small arrow points and fancy shell ornaments. A C-shaped shell fishhook is especially well known in southern California. This artifact is quite similar to hooks used by the Polynesians of the Pacific, a trait that along with a common maritime adaptation has led some anthropologists to suspect prehistoric contacts between Polynesia and the California coast. There may have been contacts, but both physical anthropologists and linguists assure us that there were no Indians on the Pacific Islands, and no Polynesians in California at the beginning of the historical period.

The best-known archaeological phase of southern California is the Canaliño, the people of which appear to be ancestral to the historical Chumash of the Santa Barbara coast. These communities built their villages in the bottoms of the small canyons found along this section of coastline. Their subsistence was based upon maritime resources and the birds and game they could harvest from nearby brackish lagoons. Wild plant foods were also gathered from thickets of scrub. Archaeological data and historical sources have combined to give us an unusually clear picture of these communities. Houses were domed circular structures from about four to

seven meters in diameter. There was a central fire area and a smoke hole in the roof. In addition to the dwellings there was usually a communal sweat house in each village. These were semisubterranean structures roofed with heavy timbers and earth. They were probably as important to these communities as kivas were to the villagers of the Southwest. Hot rocks filled the chambers with dry heat, and bathers sat about sweating and scraping themselves clean. It was as effective as using soap, and the relaxed atmosphere provided an opportunity for older people to pass along the knowledge and lore the younger ones needed to preserve their culture. Often a session in the sweat house ended with an invigorating plunge in a nearby stream.

Each village usually had a hard-packed oval depression in the ground. Most were twenty meters or more in length, and probably served as communal dance floors. Circular stone enclosures were often also located nearby. These structures, which are composed of boulders set in a ring six or seven meters in diameter, sometimes contain caches of charm stones and stone effigies. At least one historical source describes such an enclosure with totemic wooden posts, but their specific use remains a mystery.

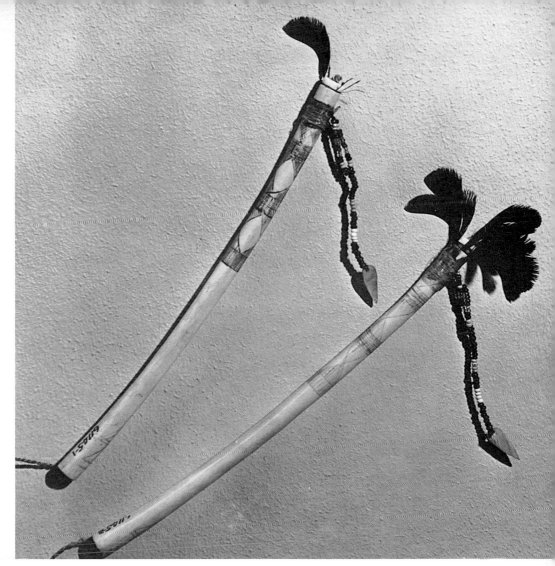

97, 98 *The initiation of boys into manhood was one of the functions of the Kuksu cult, a ritual that might include the piercing of ears so that ornaments (right) could be hung from them. Hairpins (opposite) were another of the Kuksu trappings.*

The Canaliño people were fine stone-carvers. They produced bowls in a wide range of forms made out of sandstone and steatite. Some of these bear shell inlay and other embellishments. Some of the shallow bowls show traces of carbon around their rims, which suggests that they were used as oil lamps. This is quite possible given the maritime orientation of these people and their access to a steady supply of sea-mammal oil. Stone was also fashioned into tubular pipes, as it had been for centuries, and into charming animal effigies. All of these objects have turned up in house excavations and as grave goods. Burials were usually tightly flexed, and the materials with them were frequently 'killed' before the pit was filled in. Again here we find the practice of burning the burial pit before the corpse was placed in it and covered.

The historical Chumash, direct descendants of the Canaliño people, are known for their plank boats, found also in Polynesia, but nowhere else in North America. The ocean currents that sweep past the California coast run toward Polynesia, but the superb Polynesian sailors may well have come ashore in southern California and inspired the plank canoes and shell fishhooks that puzzle us today.

The Chumash are also known for the complex multicolored pictographs they left behind on the rocky outcrops of the Santa Barbara coast. These drawings, perhaps more exotic than any others known on the continent, are now being slowly destroyed by erosion.

None of the prehistoric peoples of California ever adopted agriculture, even though it was easily available in the neighboring Southwest area. It is true that maize and some of the other available domesticates were not well suited to the California climate. But it is also true that California had considerable potential as an agricultural area even with the limited number of crops and cultivation techniques available. The explanation appears to be that the congenial and productive hunter-gatherer adjustment of the prehistoric Californians discouraged experimentation with foreign modes of food production. In AD 1600, the California area held about one percent of the total land area but ten percent of the total population of America north of Mexico. Such a successful way of life hardly encouraged people to risk a shift to a new and unfamiliar subsistence pattern.

So the Californians stuck to their special ways in their separate microenvironments. Somewhere in the long sequence small groups of Athapascans, Algonquians, and Azteco-Tanoans also drifted into the region, adding new complications to an already elaborate cultural mosaic. In the end, the place became a magnet for Europeans as well, and the Indian cultures were swamped, exterminated, or pushed into tiny enclaves. There a few of them still persist, now sharing the richness of the land with a sprawling civilization. Through it all, California still stands in a special relationship to the rest of the continent.

It is at the same time both ironic and fitting that of all the prehistoric Indians of North America, the last one to survive should be a member of a small California Hokaltecan tribe, the Yahi. He survived into the twentieth century, living most of his life as his ancestors had done for thousands of years, and never learning more than a few words of English.

The Yahi were one of four divisions of the Yana, a small aboriginal population living in the dry foothills of the Sierra Nevada. They were hunter-gatherers without the permanent villages of the more sedentary Indians in the valleys west of them. They moved about through the endless chaparral thickets in small bands, and were widely feared as accomplished guerrilla fighters. Raiding other Indians was part of their customary way of life, and it was a practice that they shifted to European settlements at the time of colonization. Domesticated cattle were hunted and ranches raided as a practical solution to subsistence needs. Of course, the ranchers did not see it in the same light.

White settlers set about trying to exterminate their Indian antagonists, a conflict in which the Yahi became more bitterly involved than the other Yana. The Europeans found it very difficult to flush the Yahi out of the rugged chaparral. Eventually, in 1865, a party of armed settlers found the Yahi camp and murdered virtually every man, woman, and child there. A few escaped, but from this point on the conflict was for practical purposes over. The Yahi were forgotten.

Later, in 1872, there was the reported sighting of two men, two women, and a child. Then there was another period of no contact that lasted more than thirty years. In 1908 a survey party ran into a hidden camp in the chaparral quite by accident. They found the entire range of aboriginal equipment, but not a single item of European or modern American manufacture. The baskets, arrows, hunting decoys, and other tools were entirely of native Indian origin. The thoughtless surveyors carried off most of what they found, leaving the owners to survive without their precious possessions.

The Indians had managed to survive for so long because their land was undesirable to the farmers, ranchers, and developers of California. But the raid by the surveyors broke up the last band, and one by one its old members died. Finally, in 1911, a lone starving man was found huddled by a ranch corral. His face was blackened and his hair singed short to show that he was in mourning. He was the last of his band, and he turned himself over to the settlers with the fatalism of someone who had nothing left to lose.

He was housed in the local jail, and the sheriff called in A. L. Kroeber and Edward Sapir, anthropologists at the University of California, Berkeley. Sapir, a linguist, arrived with his word-lists of California Indian languages. He tried one after another, getting only dull stares in return. Finally, he tried a word or two in Yana, and the 'wild man' came to life. First was the word for 'wood', then 'man', and then a flood of others. He was moved to the museum at Berkeley for lack of a better place, and Sapir set about learning the language. A few speakers of other related Yana dialects came by as well, and in time the man gained back his weight and will to live. He even grew strong enough to become assistant janitor at the museum.

He had lived for half a century never suspecting that there was another world outside the chaparral. Still, he adapted to San Francisco better than one might have expected. He learned a few words in English, but only a few, and took long rides on the famous trolleys. He could not face reservation life, and he refused to go home alone. He stayed in Berkeley and wore American clothes, even though it was clear that the urban diseases for which he had little natural resistance were eroding his health.

Sapir and Kroeber worked with him endlessly. He taught them all his skills of knapping, tool-making, and trap-setting. They made trips into the chaparral, where he led them through the routine of life in prehistoric America. He showed them hundreds of plants, each with its own name and its own special use. Some were for medicine, others for fiber, still others for food. He turned weeds into cordage, twisting the fibers on his thigh with the palm of his hand. He used the same technique to make much tougher cordage of sinew, and with these he lashed together the components of the tools of prehistoric California. For bows he chose the finest mountain juniper trees, and for arrows the branches of the hazel. He chipped arrow points from obsidian quarried on volcanic mountain slopes. It took him only a few minutes to chip the point into rough shape, and then finish off a perfect razor-sharp specimen. He showed his students how to cure and work these bits and pieces, and to assemble them into a powerful weapon. He showed them much more as well, the fire drill of soft dry wood, the harpoon point of bone, nets, nooses, lines, hooks, and dozens of other things. And with it all he showed them the protocol, the requirements and taboos that went along with the life of an Indian hunter. There were songs, stories, traditions, and the languages of dozens of wild animal species, the intangibles of prehistory that without this Indian we might never have known.

The 'wild man' was the last American to command his environment so totally, or to depend so totally upon it. His students learned the structure of Yahi society complete with many of its nuances. But his band had been too small to allow many of the conventions that had characterized Yahi culture in better times to flourish. Even sadder, discussion of many of these things was simply too painful for him to endure. He spoke of his family only with the greatest difficulty, and much of what we know of Yahi society is limited to general statements about proper behavior.

Perhaps most poignant of all was that a person in Yahi society was forbidden by custom to utter his own name. All the people who might have given us this man's name were dead, and he could not be made to speak it. They called him 'Ishi', which simply means 'man'. In 1916, at the age of 50 or 55, the last Yahi died of tuberculosis. He was the last of an ancient tradition. He had seen his society and his family die, but in the end he held on to the one important thing that could not be taken from him. He kept his name.

XVII *A Tlingit owl man, 50 cm. high, with human hair, perches on a raven. This image was carved to commemorate the death of a man at Yakutat, Alaska, in 1891; his clan crests were the owl and raven.*

Overleaf:
XVIII *The hand was a powerful shamanistic symbol for prehistoric North American Indians. This is a detail of the 19th-century Tlingit chest shown in Plate 113.*

XIX *A historical Haida mask of painted wood from the Queen Charlotte Islands represents the moon.*

100

99

XVII

XVIII

The Northwest Coast and Plateau

On the ocean side of the Cascade and Coastal mountain ranges lie the great rain forests of the Northwest Coast. Behind the mountain wall is the interior Plateau area, drained by the great Columbia and Fraser River systems. The environment of the Plateau is very different from that of the Northwest Coast, drier and subject to more extreme temperatures. Despite the environmental contrasts, however, the prehistoric sequences of the two areas are linked by the great rivers, and they are best considered together.

Much of the Plateau was overridden by ice and glacial lakes during the Pleistocene, and much of the landscape to which prehistoric Indians adapted was the product of geologically very recent events. For example, only 18,000 years ago parts of northeastern Washington and adjacent Idaho and Montana were covered by a glacial ice dam and a huge lake contained behind it. The lake held over 3000 cubic kilometers of water. The accumulation of the water was slow, of course, but once it rose over the top of the ice dam, erosion of the ice and loose soil was almost instantaneous. The water gushed out in a flash-flood, a wall of water sweeping everything before it for 550 kilometers to the Pacific. The rate of flow as the lake drained was over ten million cubic meters per second, ten times the combined present flow of all the rivers of the world. The water plunged westward, tearing away older deposits and stripping the land down to bedrock. At the site of modern Spokane, the flow split into three streams, each as much as 30 kilometers wide in places. One scoured what is now Grand Coulee, 80 kilometers long and 275 meters deep. The three streams rejoined and emptied into the Pacific by way of what is now the Columbia River gorge. The Spokane flood was all over in thirty days or so, but it set the scene for Plateau prehistory.

Contacts between inland and coastal communities were strongest from northern Oregon to southern British Columbia. Within this area, the Columbia and Fraser breach the mountains and provide convenient natural highways. In northwestern California and southwestern Oregon the ocean is fed only by relatively small river systems, which do not provide the same easy access to the interior. The same is true for the coastal regions of central British Columbia and southern Alaska. Thus, cultural interaction with the Plateau was a prehistoric feature more of the central part of the Northwest Coast than of its northern and southern subareas.

The Northwest Coast was a place of incredible natural wealth for the hunter-gatherer. Salmon runs provided enough fish for an entire year for a relatively small amount of effort on the part of fishermen. Sea mammals provided meat and oil. Candlefish could be converted to oil, or simply dried and burned as natural candles. Meadows provided game and berries in the summer, and shellfish abounded all year. The weather was mild, and the richness of the land allowed the artistic impulses of the Indians to flourish along with the societies that supported them.

The prehistory of the strip of coast from northern California to southern Oregon is not well known. Most surveys and excavations have produced evidence of human occupation for only the last thousand years, and much of that comes from only the last few centuries before historical contacts. Thus, much of what we know seems to be directly related to the historical cultures of the area. In prehistoric times these

xx A 19th-century Kwakiutl mask of painted wood and human hair depicts the mythical female Tsonoqoa ogre, a powerful but stupid creature said to live in inland forests, where only the meat of land animals was available. Occasionally the ogre would raid a Kwakiutl village for fish, and carry off misbehaving children as well. The appearance in public ceremonies of Tsonoqoa masks made the threat a real one to Kwakiutl children.

peoples were relatively small groups speaking languages belonging to four very different phyla, the kind of complexity we have already seen for California. The Karok, for example, speak a Hokaltecan language. The Wiyot and Yurok are Pacific outposts of Algonquian speech. The Hupa and Tolowa are among a few small Athapascan groups that appear to have moved into this area by AD 700–1000 while the main body of migrating Athapascans continued on to the Southwest. Just to the interior live the Klamath and other Penutian-speaking groups. Despite their linguistic diversity, the communities of the southern subarea of the Northwest Coast had a common lifestyle. They held social customs and the finer points of etiquette in common, and even such intangibles as myths and ritual cycles were shared. The Yurok, Karok, and Hupa all performed stylized deer dances as part of a shared ceremonial round, which featured the elaborate costumes and spectacular performances that were important in all the cultures of the Northwest Coast.

The houses and villages of the different tribes were nearly identical. Wedges and mauls were used to split giant cedar logs into planks, and the planks were sewn and pegged together on log house frames. The houses were substantial pitch-roofed structures, built to last in villages which were permanently occupied. There was no food production as we know it, but a wealth of natural foods allowed even the largest villages to thrive all the year round. Shellfish were plentiful, as were salmon, halibut, and other fish. Hunters took marine mammals offshore, and deer, elk, bear, and others in the interior. Berries, acorns, and other wild plant foods were abundant in season.

The diagnostic traits of the Northwest Coast area were least developed in the southern subarea, a feature that has led many to assume that this was some sort of cultural backwater. However, groups like the Hupa blended Northwest Coast and California traits to create a special and very successful adjustment to local conditions. Of the California features, perhaps acorn-leaching and elaborate basketry are most notable. In addition to this blending of cultures, there was some specialization as well, and villages traded for things they could not obtain themselves. Thus the Hupa supplied the Yurok with acorns and inland game in exchange for salt, canoes, and marine foods. This pattern of redistribution was combined with efficient food preservation and storage. Periods of hunger were rare, famine almost unheard of.

The ancestors of the Wiyot lived on Gunther Island off northern California. A site here has produced a radiocarbon date of about AD 900, and a whole range of Northwest Coast artifacts. We find bone and antler wedges and the stone mauls used in the splitting of cedar planks. We also find the zoomorphic 'slave-killer' clubs that were used by wealthy men in historical times to kill servants in ostentatious displays of rank and power. Carved-stone artifacts show Northwest Coast connections, along with harpoon heads and even a fired-clay figurine. Early burials on the island appear to have been placed in pits on the ashes of previously burned offerings. Later burials were interments without offerings of any kind, presumably as people shifted to keeping and accumulating huge stores of inherited wealth. Thus the wealth consciousness that swept the prehistoric Northwest Coast touched even the people of Gunther Island.

Klamath Lake lies 175 kilometers from the coast, farther if one follows the river. It is, in fact, in a part of Oregon that is transitional between the California, Great

Basin, Northwest Coast, and Plateau areas. Thus, it is no surprise that excavations here have produced evidence of prehistoric blending of several traditions. The historical Penutian-speaking Klamath Indians and their ancestors depended heavily upon the local 'wocas' (water lily) seeds for subsistence, as well as upon freshwater mussels and fish from the lake. For about the last 2000 years of prehistory here, the Plateau earth lodge was the primary dwelling form. Klamath Lake is too far removed from the cedar forests of the coast to allow plank construction. Such houses were semisubterranean, with roofs of cribbed logs and earth. The central smoke hole was also the entrance, and with the low conical shape of the roof, this gave the house the appearance of a giant ant hill. Unlike the Plains earth lodge with its ground-level door, or the Southwest kiva with its ventilator shaft, this house form did not normally have good provision for a draft of air to carry smoke up and out of the interior. Houses of this common type must have been smokey places.

The Columbia River system

As we have seen, the Paleo-Indian adjustment probably never achieved its full expression west of the Rockies. Like the rest of the Desert West to the south of it, the Plateau was not suitable for such a specialized way of life. During the Paleo-Indian period, people here practiced a more diversified subsistence pattern, one that emphasized a broad range of plant and animal resources. Fluted points are missing, and so are the open kill sites of the Plains. Instead, we have cave sites like the Marmes Rock Shelter and Fort Rock Cave, and the diagnostic artifact is the leaf-shaped biface called the 'Cascade point'.

IX, 102

There was an early shift toward the resources of the great rivers of the Plateau by its Indian inhabitants. One of the most crucial sites to our understanding of this and later developments is The Dalles on the Columbia. Here, where the river cuts through the Cascade mountains, waterfalls and rapids have served as a minor obstacle and a major resource for millennia. Travelers on the river must portage at this point, but the same obstacle has made this a prime place for catching vast numbers of salmon. It became a natural camping site, and historical Indians even collected tolls here. This long tradition at The Dalles may go back to 9000 BC. The cultural sequence thus begins at a date that makes the site antecedent to later developments both on the Plateau and on the Northwest Coast.

93

The late prehistoric inhabitants of the Columbia River and its tributaries were mostly speakers of Sahaptin languages, a division of Penutian. Linguistically, these communities contrasted with the Salishan-speaking communities in the basin of the Fraser River, the other major subdivision of the Plateau. But the two river systems shared huge annual salmon migrations which drew the earliest prehistoric Indians of the Plateau into a common riverine adaptation. On the Columbia, however, the salmon runs ceased around 6000 BC. We are not sure of the reason why this happened, although there may have been some progressive downcutting of the lower Columbia River, and perhaps increasingly arid conditions on the Plateau as well. Together, these shifts could have produced a drop at Celilo Falls that was simply too high for the salmon to ascend. After 6000 BC, we find only scanty evidence of fishing. At some sites the people appear to have turned more and more to the gathering of mussels as partial compensation for this loss. But a strong riverine orientation was no

15

101 Clubs made from the bones of whales, like this 17th-century Tsimshian specimen, 44 cm. long, were sometimes used to kill slaves in historical times in ostentatious displays of wealth and power.

102 *Fort Rock dominates the dry plateau of central Oregon. 10,000 years ago Ice Age Paleo-Indians hunted plentiful big-game animals from a cave in an outlying rock formation.*

longer possible on the upper Columbia. Here, the communities reverted to a way of life resembling that of the Desert Culture in the Great Basin, although on the Plateau there was more large game and there were a few productive plants, such as camas, the tuberous root of a kind of lily, which became almost a staple in some areas.

Sahaptin-speakers near the mouth of the Columbia were not cut off from migratory fish runs, and were thus able to continue their combined maritime-riverine adaptation. The contrast between these people and their relatives upstream,

178

for whom the riverine option was no longer open, grew steadily. By 4000 BC they had little in common apart from a shared linguistic heritage.

In about AD 1265, there was a small landslide which had important consequences for Plateau ecology, although it was insignificant compared with the earlier Spokane flood. This was the Cascade Landslide, a sudden event that has been duplicated occasionally elsewhere in North America in the last few centuries. The landslide appears to have reduced the drop at Celilo Falls, thereby allowing salmon to migrate upstream once again. Within a few decades, the salmon runs were restored to the upper Columbia basin, and the Sahaptin-speakers of the southern Plateau reverted to catching the bountiful fish. Knowledge of the original riverine adaptation had been lost from memory thousands of years earlier, so the Sahaptin-speakers looked to the Indians of the northern Plateau and the maritime communities of the lower Columbia for the necessary technology and the means to apply it. Thus the ancient links between the various Plateau communities which had lapsed after 6000 BC were renewed.

The arrival of trading ships off the mouth of the Columbia in the historical period strengthened these bonds even more. The Chinook of the lower Columbia soon came to dominate trade on the river, acting as middlemen and exacting tolls at The Dalles portage.

The Fraser River system

We know a little more about the prehistoric Indians of the northern part of the Plateau. This is the subarea that is drained by the Fraser-Thompson River system. There have been several important excavations at the mouth of the Fraser as well as several others upstream in the interior. The archaeology of the region shows the same tendency toward an upstream-downstream differentiation over time that we have already seen for the Columbia River. Here, however, the principal participants were Salishan-speakers, a linguistic division that is not yet known to be linked to any of the major language phyla of North America.

Northern influences were already being felt in the Fraser basin by about 5000 BC. They are too old to be attributed to the ancestral Eskimos, and probably represent intrusions by Athapascan-speakers, the second-to-last prehistoric group to migrate to North America from Asia. The Athapascans dominated western Canada and are discussed in the next chapter. Their importance here is that they introduced northern traits into the northern Plateau and the Northwest Coast, beginning a long series of contacts that appears to have persisted in one form or another until the historical period.

The long sequence known from sites on the Fraser delta is also very important. It documents the maritime adjustment of the Coast Salish, whose culture was the focal point for the Northwest Coast tradition. Earliest remains date to the first millennium BC. Bone refuse and primitive tools indicate that sea mammals were already being intensively hunted with weapons well suited to this marine economy. Harpoon heads were carefully fashioned from elk (wapiti) antler, often with slots on the ends for the insertion of cutting edges. Most were designed to 'toggle', that is, to detach from the harpoon shaft and turn sideways inside the animal. A stout line tied to the center of the harpoon head kept the animal from escaping. Bone points were

15

103 *Labrets, ornaments
inserted into a hole in the
lower lip, were marks of
beauty for some Northwest
Coast women, as this
19th-century Tlingit
painted cedar mask shows.*

sometimes fixed onto spear shafts, and were often barbed. Most of the necessary blade edges were made from ground slate. Knife and spear blades, some of them very long and slender, are numerous, and frequently have symmetrical beveling.

Slate was also used in the manufacture of small adzes and chisels, as well as ear-spools and 'labrets' (ornaments designed to be worn as plugs in holes made near the lower lip). 'Ulus', semidiscoidal knives with their curved edges sharpened, were also made from ground slate. The ulu, labrets, and indeed the whole use of ground slate, are often associated with Eskimo culture. These similarities, not to mention the presence of toggling harpoons, have led many to assume important prehistoric contacts between the Northwest Coast and the Arctic. The origins of the toggling harpoon are still obscure, but most scientists agree that ground slate was developed independently on the Northwest Coast, and was later diffused to the Eskimos. Before archaeological sites were adequately dated, there was also some suspicion that the Eskimos had influenced the development of ground slate on the east coast of North America during the Archaic period. That too now appears to have been an independent development. Thus, we have two prehistoric centers of origin for ground slate.

The maritime lifeway of the Fraser delta people evolved rapidly toward the historical Northwest Coast pattern after about 2000 years ago. Chipped-stone implements became more important, but apparently not at the expense of ground-slate objects, which were more finely finished than ever. Perhaps most significant is the increasing use of heavy woodworking tools. Large adzes, antler wedges, and stone mauls or hammers (without which the wedges would have been useless) were produced for the first time. Together they are strong evidence that cedar logs were being split into long planks for houses and canoes. The Fraser delta was the area in which cedar-log carving eventually developed into a monumental art form.

Small stone bowls were sculpted in anthropomorphic and zoomorphic forms. Often these are not so much bowls as small figures holding receptacles in their hands

103

104

106

110

105

Opposite:
104 *Stone mauls, such as this Haida example with magical incised decorations, drove the antler wedges that split cedar logs into planks for houses and canoes.*

105 *The seated human sculptures of steatite for which Fraser River sites are famous were the products of a tradition at least 2500 years old. The figures represented guardian spirits, and were still used by some shamans in recent times.*

106 This early historical headdress is one of the oldest surviving examples of Northwest Coast wood-carving. The bird beak was probably worn protruding from the forehead by a Kwakiutl dancer.

107 The long tradition of wood carving uncovered by archaeologists along the Fraser River culminated in the monuments and house posts of the historical Salish Indians. This house post (below) from Quamichan, British Columbia, stands about 2.1 m. high.

or between their legs. They were usually carved from steatite, although sandstone 105
examples are known too. The prototypes may date to as early as 800 BC on the
upper Fraser. Also popular were stone and shell beads, items that may indicate
increasing wealth consciousness.

By AD 500, the famous Northwest Coast emphasis on wealth and social stratification was well established. The increasing frequency of various kinds of luxury
goods in the prehistoric sequence seems to parallel the emergence of wealth as an 108–9
indicator of rank. The appearance of burial mounds may also indicate increasing
social stratification over time. Several of these mounds are known for the area
around Puget Sound, but few have been adequately excavated. Typically, they
consist of piles of earth and rock about a meter high covering a single interment and
ringed with boulders. Such a mound may indicate the importance of the deceased,
but the general absence of grave goods suggests that wealth was too important to the
living to be buried with the dead.

Work in ground slate and stone sculpture was gradually abandoned. We still do
not fully understand the reasons for this apparent lapse. Perhaps the Indians were just
shifting from one preferred medium to another. Bone was still carved, and it may
be that many objects were carved in wood and have since perished. The beautiful
abstract sculpture and low relief in wood, for which the historical Indians of the
Northwest Coast are so justly famous, must have taken centuries to evolve. Future 107
archaeological research will undoubtedly fill out our understanding of the long and
complex development of these styles.

Most of the stone carvings of the Fraser River and its tributaries were made of steatite, the others of sandstone.

108, 109 The native tabacco used in these steatite pipes (opposite below), 12 cm. and 5 cm. long, was cultivated in prehistoric times by a few Northwest Coast tribes, but most did not begin to use it until the 19th century.

110 A steatite screech owl effigy bowl, 13.5 cm. long, was found along the Upper Skagit River, British Columbia.

111 *The Skeena River of British Columbia has been the domain of the Tsimshian Indians for 2000 years. Carvers still work cedar here, and totem poles still stand before Tsimshian houses.*

Northern Northwest Coast

The southern part of the Northwest Coast was probably occupied by 4000 BC, but north of the Fraser delta glaciers and the lack of easy access to the interior held up colonization until much later. The ancestors of the historical Tsimshian arrived on the lower Skeena River about 1000 BC. They were Penutian-speakers who appear to have worked their way northward along the coast to their present location. About 2000 years ago some of them began to press upstream along the Skeena River, eventually splitting into two groups. Perhaps at about the same time as the initial arrival of the ancestral Tsimshian, the ancestors of the historical Tlingit and Haida broke off from the main body of Athapascan-speakers and took up residence

111

112 *Carved from tough basalt, this 19th-century Tsimshian burial mask is one of only two such masks in existence, and equals the finest stone sculpture of Mexico.*

on the coast. The Tlingit expanded primarily northward, eventually as far north as Yakutat Bay, Alaska. The Haida moved into the Queen Charlotte Islands. Between them and the Salishan groups lived the Kwakiutl and other tribes whose languages still defy exact classification.

The northern subarea of the Northwest Coast was the center for the most flamboyant expression of the regional culture in historical times. This, as some ethnologists have suggested, may have been the result of the close proximity of the Eskimos, who provided a certain cultural stimulus. Mound burial was not practiced here. Instead, the dead were buried or placed in wooden boxes in caves or rock shelters. Cremation was more common in historical times.

137

The manufacture of boxes and other items out of cedar planks was something for which these people were justly famous during the historical period. Artistic development in this medium was certainly spurred by the introduction of iron tools obtained from the Europeans, but many of the motifs carved with these tools were already very ancient. It is even possible that the necessary tools were being made in late prehistoric times from iron found in flotsam from the western Pacific, deposited on the shores of the Northwest Coast by ocean currents. Thus, the exotic totem poles for which the area is known may not be the products of just the historical period.

XVIII,
113, I

114, I

XXIII

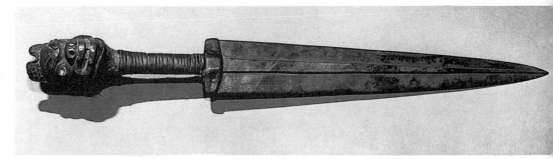

114, 115 *A 19th-century Tlingit copper fighting knife, 50 cm. long, with rawhide grip and ox-horn hilt, is similar to knives made of iron, and has a wig of bear fur, eyebrows, nostrils and lips of copper, and eyes and teeth of abalone shell.*

188

116 *This late 19th-century two-piece yellow cedar rattle, 14 cm. across, represents a face peering out from a bear's paw. The rattle once belonged to Chief Shakes, a famous Tlingit leader in southern Alaska.*

117 *The Western Grebe swims, even dives, with its young riding safely on its back. It was probably this curious trait that led a shaman (perhaps Tlingit) to select it as the model for his magical rattle, 37 cm. long, of unpainted wood.*

118 *This shaman's rattle of unknown Northwest Coast origin is made from two pieces of unpainted, polished wood lashed together by leather thongs. The face, 15 cm. across, may represent the sun or moon.*

119 *A fine-grained black stone called 'argillite' was usually the medium of Haida carvers, but this 13-cm.-long grease dish, depicting a frog with a human face on its forehead, comes from Tsimshian country.*

120 *Masks served to link Northwest Coast Indian dancers with the supernatural beings prominent in clan myths and secret-society rituals. This Tsimshian mask of a girl with human hair and red facial paint has winged-bird hair pendants that can hinge open as shown.*

Opposite:
Certain Tlingit ceremonial objects were traditionally worn only by chiefs or shamans at potlatches – extravagant gift-giving rituals which enhanced the donor's prestige.

XXI *This 19th-century Tlingit ceremonial copper headdress is inlaid with shell, and has feathers and sea-lion bristles attached.*

XXII *A stylized face woven in mountain goat wool represents a Tlingit woman. The design is a detail from the 19th-century ceremonial robe shown in Plate 134.*

Virtually everything made by the Indians of the Northwest Coast was the subject of painstaking decoration. Spoons, dishes, house posts, walls, canoes, boxes, and many other items were provided with low relief or fully three-dimensional carved designs according to the preferences of the artisan and the nature of the artifact. The designs were usually zoomorphic or less frequently anthropomorphic, warped and stylized in the interests of geometric symmetry and tradition to the point where they often defy quick identification. When the medium was essentially two-dimensional, like the side of a box, the figure shown was often distorted and made to fit the available space. Even three-dimensional renditions were subject to the exaggeration of some features and the suppression of others. Bears, wolves, beavers, killer whales, humans, and many others appear frequently. One of the

124
107

113

134
123

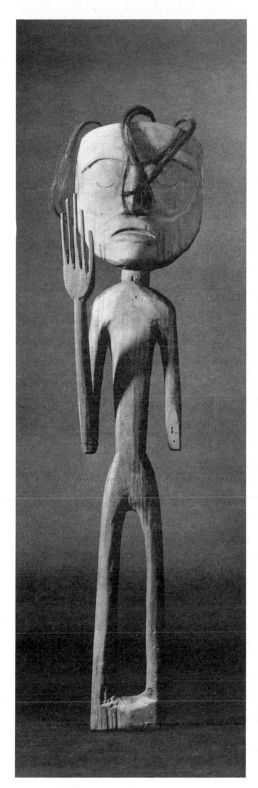
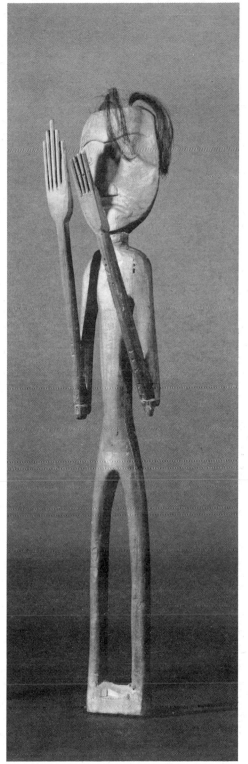

XXIII *Totem poles once forested the Northwest Coast, serving as heraldic devices or memorials to dead chiefs. This cedarwood head is a detail from a Tsimshian pole at Hazelton on the Skeena River, British Columbia.*

121, 122 *These 60-cm.-high cedarwood figures with human hair from British Columbia were once used as props in Bella Coola dances, and may have guarded their shaman owner in sleep and death.*

123 *This historical argillite and shell ornament from the Northwest Coast depicts a killer whale biting its own tail.*

124 *Raven, the mythical Northwest Coast creator and trickster, is represented in this 19th-century Tsimshian goat-horn ceremonial spoon, 25 cm. long, inlaid with abalone shell.*

125 *Trapezoidal Chilkat blankets were braided, not woven on a loom, by women of the Chilkat subtribe of the Tlingit. This masterpiece in dyed cedar fibers and mountain goat hair, one of the oldest surviving Chilkat blankets, bears a school of killer whales.*

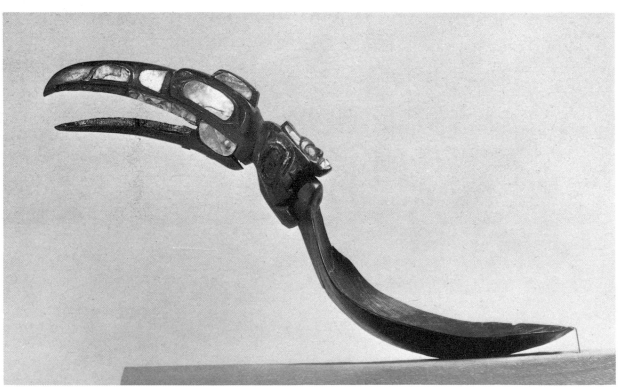

most important is the raven, because on the Northwest Coast Raven is a culture hero, trickster, and creator all at the same time. It was Raven who created the sun, moon, and stars, and released the forces of the world. But it was also Raven who engaged in crude jokes, and often saw them backfire. In one such story, Raven loses his white coat to Petrel, an immortal man. Raven tricks Petrel into thinking there is filth in his bed. Raven's purpose is to distract Petrel while he drinks his fill of a store of water kept by the man in a small box. The outraged Petrel chases Raven into a tree, then lights a fire that turns Raven's feathers black. Raven has been black ever since.

7, 124

126 *Haida mortuary poles commemorated high-ranking deceased. Smooth and plain for most of their length, these special poles were typically topped by a single impressive figure, here an eagle.*

127 *Haida houses had towering totem poles at their doors. A hole at the base of the pole, often the mouth of the lowermost figure, served as the entrance.*

Such designs were also employed in the manufacture of pentagonal Chilkat 125 blankets, which were woven from various plant and animal fibers by members of the Chilkat subtribe of the Tlingit. They were also applied to large sheets of native copper, beaten into shape and decorated for use as status items. Of all media, however, the relatively late monumental totem poles are the most visible. These were xx carved as heraldic devices, as memorials, as mortuary poles, to commemorate an 126 important event, or even to bring shame on an enemy. Most of these artifacts, both large and small, were connected with the functioning of the complex and highly stratified social systems of the Northwest Coast. The 'potlatch', in which property of all sorts was given away or destroyed as a means of 'buying' higher rank, may be the most famous expression of these systems. Much of the artistic output of the area was in fact fuel for the social machinery that clan leaders used to gain and hold rank.

The surest route to high
prestige for a man or
woman born to low rank
was to become a shaman.
Shamans were curers and a
few practiced witchcraft.
Animal claws, teeth, horns
rattles, masks and amulets
were all the paraphernalia
of their trade.

128 The horns of
mountain goats, inlaid with
abalone, were a 19th-
century Tsimshian
shaman's crown, a crucial
part of his curing regalia.

129 Linked Tsimshian
shaman's charms include a
human leg and sea
creatures.

Opposite:
130 A Haida shaman's
necklace was loaded down
with bone and ivory
amulets, and was designed
to clatter when he danced.

131 Whipped through the
air by a Tsimshian
shaman, the soul-catcher,
teeth bared, snatched the
wandering soul of the
patient and restored it and
health to its owner.

132, 133 Tiny Tsimshian
shaman's charms carved
from bear canines represent
fetal humans.

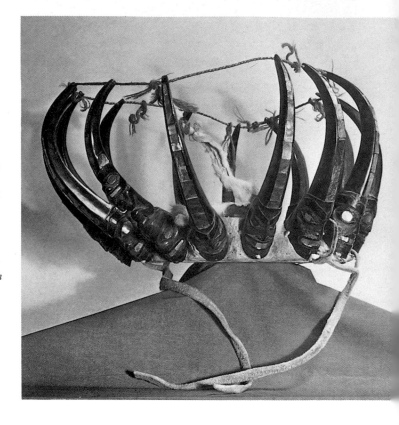

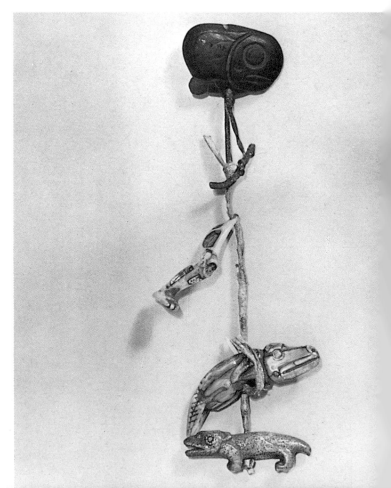

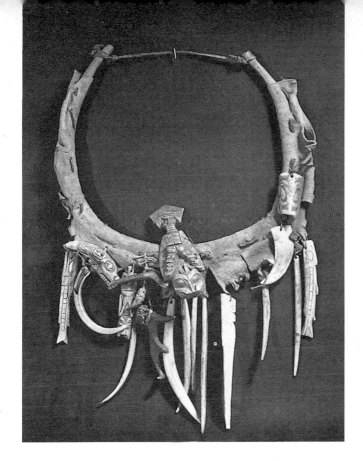

134, 135 *Northwest Coast men made and painted the pattern boards that women weavers copied. An early historical Tlingit board (right) was used as the pattern for the 19th-century robe (above) worn at potlatches by an Alaskan man of high rank. The robe was woven from mountain goat wool dyed black, blue and yellow and trimmed with otter fur. The design as a whole represents the Brown Bear, the most important crest or identifying symbol of the Tekwedi clan. The three central faces are those of the Bear, of the Tlingit woman who married the Bear (Plate XXII), and, below, their cub child.*

At times, a potlatch would involve extravagant gift-giving. Piles of goods would XXI, XXII, 134 be accumulated by clan members to be given away to invited guests from another clan by the clan leader. The distribution validated the rank of the leader and the clan as a whole. At a more subtle level, it functioned to redistribute the surplus of material wealth that was accumulated with such gusto. In its most extreme form, the potlatch became a competition between rival clans and their leaders. The ceremony would focus on each side trying to outdo the other in lavish gift-giving. At times this turned into bouts involving the wholesale destruction of valuable goods. Mounds of Chilkat blankets were drenched in candlefish oil and burned to demonstrate their unimportance to their owners. Slaves were clubbed to death with special 'slave- 136 killers' to validate and enhance the rank of their masters. Probably the most extreme form of the potlatch was practiced by the Kwakiutl, who placed an interest rate of 100 percent on the ceremony. Each recipient of goods had to respond with gifts worth double the value of those received. The ceremony never reached such extremes along the southern reaches of the Northwest Coast, and in northern California wealth was merely displayed. In the end, the historical fur trade and the economic dislocations that attended it turned the potlatch into a social aberration. Along with much of the rest of Northwest Coast culture it flashed brilliantly upon contact with the Old World, and then died.

There can be no doubt that contact with Eskimo culture stimulated the Indians of the Northwest Coast, but the reverse was also true. Some of the Alaskan Eskimos took on Northwest Coast traits, and archaeology has shown that many other shared traits are in fact older on the Northwest Coast than they are in the Eskimo area. We cannot view Northwest Coast culture as the product of late diffusion from Asia by way of the Eskimos. Instead, it must be seen as an indigenous development, yet another extraordinary facet of the American Indian.

136 *This meter-high cedar plank drum, with its x-rayed killer-whale design painted in red and black, once belonged to a 19th-century Tlingit chief from Wrangell Island, Alaska. He gave it up in a potlatch in exchange for slaves.*

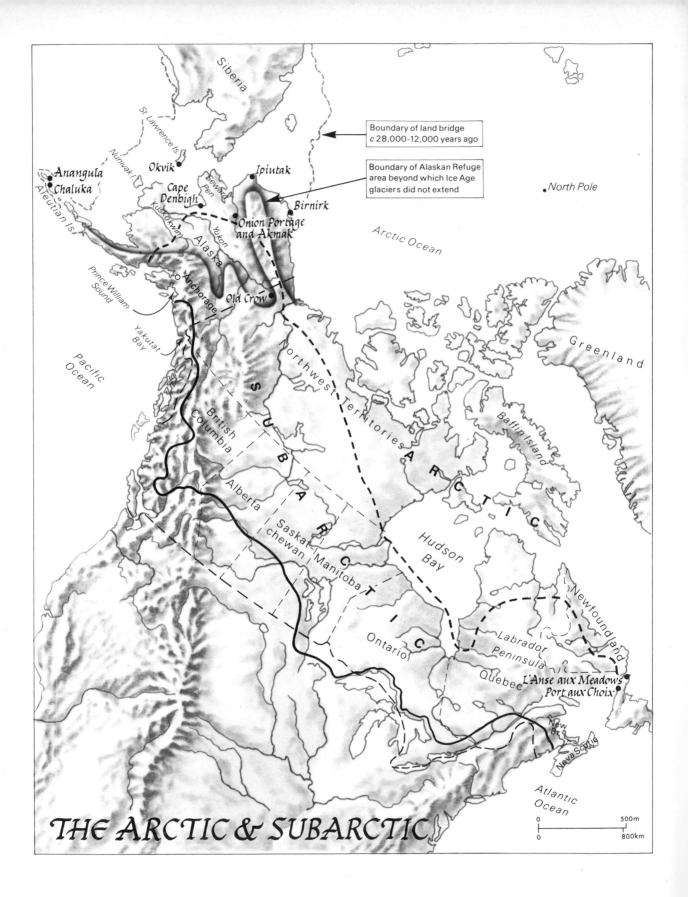

Siberia

St Lawrence Is.

Nunivak I.

Okvik

Ipiutak

Boundary of land bridge
c 28,000-12,000 years ago

Boundary of Alaskan Refuge
area beyond which Ice Age
glaciers did not extend

North Pole

Anangula
Chaluka

Aleutian Is.

Cape
Denbigh

Seward Pen.

Birnirk

Arctic Ocean

Onion Portage
and Akmak

Kuskokwim

Yukon

Alaska

Old Crow

Anchorage

Prince William
Sound

Yakutat
Bay

Pacific
Ocean

Greenland

S U B

Northwest Territories

A R C T I C

Baffin Island

British
Columbia

Alberta

Saskat-
chewan

Manitoba

A

R

C

Ontario

T

Hudson
Bay

I

C

Newfoundland

Labrador
Peninsula

Quebec

L'Anse aux Meadows
Port aux Choix

New
Br

Nova Scotia

Atlantic
Ocean

0   500m

0   800km

THE ARCTIC & SUBARCTIC

The Arctic and Subarctic

We come at last to the vast northern expanse of North America that was the prehistoric home of the late-arriving Eskimos, and waves of earlier Indian populations. Alaska, which lies at the western end of the area, was particularly important because it was the gateway to North America for prehistoric immigrants. It is conceivable that a comparative handful of people might have reached North America by some other route, but there is no convincing evidence of this. Both the earliest discoverers of America and the most recent aboriginal newcomers seem to have entered the New World by way of Alaska and western Canada.

Most of us fail to realize just how enormous the Arctic and Subarctic areas really are. As schoolchildren we notice that the island of Greenland is curiously larger than the continent of Australia, but this is quickly explained to us as a gross distortion caused by Mercator's projection of the globe onto a flat map surface. Even without the distortion of maps, however, Greenland is far larger than Alaska, which in turn is the largest of the fifty United States. Canada is one of the two largest countries in the world, second only to the Soviet Union. Canada, Alaska, and Greenland contain the area covered by this chapter, an area that is nearly twice the size of all the other areas discussed so far taken together. Relatively few archaeologists have carried out full-scale research in this vast region, but despite this disadvantage, its prehistoric sequences are quite well known.

In earlier chapters, we have looked at prehistoric Indian adaptations to a variety of more southerly environments. Communities of plants and animals generally cut across those environments. In the north, plant, animal, and prehistoric human communities fit more neatly into the major environmental divisions. The Subarctic is a region still dominated by spruce trees and caribou (the American reindeer). The Arctic is a zone of tundra where somewhat different plants and animals predominate. Prehistoric Eskimos and Indians had to adjust themselves carefully to one or the other, for each is harsh in its own way.

The northern tundra is often a desolate place. In the summer the upper strata of tundra soil melt to produce plains of shallow ponds and mushy heath, which in turn support a gray-green cover of grass and sedges. Under it all is a stratum of permafrost, a layer of frozen earth that never thaws. Most parts of the zone receive little precipitation, only twenty-five to fifty centimeters, and most of that falls in the winter as snow. But even with such low precipitation the topsoil is permeated with moisture because the permafrost keeps it from soaking in, and because the usually flat terrain has retarded the development of major streams. In a few places along the southern fringe of the tundra zone and along the west coast of Alaska, the permafrost

137 *Map of the Arctic and Subarctic, showing modern towns and ancient sites mentioned in the text, regional subdivisions, and the Alaskan Refuge area, where Ice Age Indians, crossing from Siberia into Alaska over the dry floor of the Bering Strait, were trapped until Canadian glaciers melted sufficiently 27,000 years ago to allow migration southward.*

is spotty, and spruce and other trees are able to take root here and there. Such an environment is park tundra as opposed to the barren tundra that dominates most of the northern margin of the continent.

Most of what is now tundra was heavily glaciated during the Pleistocene. However, one of the ecological ironies of North America is that western Alaska, which is now park tundra, was not glaciated. Along with most of the Yukon River drainage of central Alaska which was also not glaciated, it was occasionally sealed off from the rest of the New World by western Canadian ice. For this reason, we refer to it as the 'Alaskan Refuge'. Because the low water that produced the Bering land bridge 137 occurred at a time of maximum glaciation elsewhere, the Alaskan Refuge acted as a huge holding area or lock for early human populations. At low water, early Indians were attracted into the area by plentiful game, but were blocked by the ice from further movement east and south. Later, as the ice melted and the seas rose, the Indians were simultaneously blocked from movement back to Siberia and released into the central heartland of North America. The oldest convincing evidence for this process is a 27,000-year-old artifact – a bone scraper – from the Yukon. The next oldest remains come from the site of Onion Portage on the Kobuk River, and it is here that the story of Subarctic prehistory begins.

The Subarctic

Onion Portage is a well-known caribou crossing site, and Indians and Eskimos have 137 camped here for centuries in order to harvest animals from the migrating herds. The oldest stratum or layer at the site is 10,000 years old. The distinctive 'Akmak' tool assemblage found in the stratum must have been the work of early Indians, because it predates the earliest Eskimo remains by several thousand years. The implements consist of microblades – slivers of chipped stone – and larger stone tools. Together, they point to a hunting economy which utilized a kit of specialized tool types, many of which were composites of bone, stone, fiber, and other materials. The Pleistocene was coming to an end in North America 10,000 years ago, and it seems likely that as the ice melted back and the conifer forests of the Subarctic were established, hunting bands like those at Onion Portage began to occupy them.

Another important early site, dating to 6000 BC, is located on Anangula Island in 137 the Aleutian chain. Here again we have the artifacts of hunters, but this time in a marine context. Although there are no skeletal remains, human or otherwise, the location and tools all suggest that these people exploited sea mammals: whales, seals, sea lions, and sea otters. Eight thousand years ago Anangula would have been connected to its neighbor, Umnak Island. Indeed, the lower sea level would have made travel along the chain much easier for its entire distance, and we can reasonably suppose that much of the archaeological evidence of early hunters was later destroyed by rising water.

The archaeological sequence that begins at Anangula is picked up and continued at the nearby site of Chaluka. Chaluka is a deeply stratified site that has about 4000 137 years of prehistory preserved within it. Together, the two sites seem to point the way back to Siberia. The stone blade tools found at Anangula and the lowest levels of Chaluka resemble 7000-year-old implements found in Siberia and Japan more than anything that appears later in Alaska. Later Alaskan tools are clearly of Eskimo origin as we shall see, and while technologically parallel to them, the Anangula-Chaluka remains are stylistically more Asian. Another important contrast is in skeletal material, which although not preserved at Anangula has survived at Chaluka. The human remains are of long-headed individuals. Clearly these people were not the ancestors of the round-headed Eskimos or their Aleut cousins. Perhaps they were other Asians who were later absorbed, or pushed out by the Aleuts. Another possibility is that they should be more properly referred to as Indians. Perhaps they and the first hunters to visit Onion Portage were early Athapascans, the last wave of Indians to enter the New World before the Eskimos arrived and blocked further immigration by taking up permanent residence on the Alaskan tundra.

The western Subarctic

The western Subarctic was and still is the homeland of Indians whose unity and internal diversity are both best expressed in linguistic terms. The main block is made up of bands of people who speak a variety of Athapascan languages. They go by various names, but ethnic identity within the large block has been of more concern to anthropologists than to the Indians themselves. As a consequence, lines are not easily drawn. Languages and other cultural variables grade into one another almost imperceptibly. For most purposes, we can think of them as a single population with internal variations but few sharp contrasts.

We have seen that some linguistic relatives of the Athapascans split from them rather early and moved to the coast of Alaska and British Columbia. These were the ancestors of the Haida, Tlingit, and others, who are now linguistically far removed from the Athapascans. More recently some of the southern Athapascan bands split off from the main body to move into the Southwest as the Navajo and Apache. One tiny group even made its way to California. Finally, we have seen that the Sarsi split with the Athapascans to join the Blackfoot on the Great Plains.

The main block of Athapascans remained in the western Subarctic, and it is the prehistory of this area both before and after some of them departed to live elsewhere that concerns us most here. The Athapascan population began to expand southward out of Alaska and northwestern Canada some time before 5000 BC. At present, only the southern edge and the southeastern corner of British Columbia are grasslands. Seven thousand years ago the interface of grasslands and conifer forests was about 500 kilometers farther north. As the climate changed, the forests expanded southward onto the grasslands, and the Athapascans expanded with them. The tools they carried may have developed from the kind of blade implements we have noted at Onion Portage and elsewhere in Alaska. By 5000 BC the early Athapascans were in contact with people living on the Plateau and the Great Plains. From them they adopted side-notched spear points and the specialized weapons those points represent. The innovation spread northward through the medium of the Athapascan population. We see it at the Onion Portage site by 4000 BC.

The Athapascans, therefore, had arrived in the Subarctic by 5000 BC. Using the tools they brought with them and the innovations they adopted from farther south, they evolved a hunting-fishing-gathering way of life that was well suited to their interior Canadian environment. Eventually their culture developed into the late prehistoric 'Denetasiro' tradition, which is clearly associated with the early historical Athapascans.

The historical Athapascans are the products of a multitude of parallel developments over several thousands of years. Hundreds of Athapascan bands, each units unto themselves, roamed the western Subarctic forests. The total population was not large, and the population density was therefore under 2 persons per 100 square kilometers over most of the area. Typically, family bands came together now and again to form groups of around 200. Few individuals ventured outside these groups, whose members constituted the speakers of an Athapascan dialect. So-called Athapascan 'tribes' consisted of four or five such groups, although they were not corporate tribes at all, but rather convenient divisions defined by anthropologists primarily on linguistic grounds. Tribal names such as Dogrib, Slave, and Yellow-knife should not be taken too seriously lest they obscure the real basis of Athapascan ethnicity. In fact, members of Athapascan bands were able to understand members of adjacent bands quite easily. Mutual intelligibility was less likely with bands farther removed, and became impossible with distant bands. Thus, we must view the Subarctic Athapascans as a single block, internal ethnic differences being largely a matter of degree rather than kind. This is precisely what we should expect under the circumstances of their environment and lifeway.

Prehistoric Athapascan bands needed to be mobile in order to survive, and they confined their material arts to a few portable items, most of which have long since perished. The historical record, however, can tell us something about these crafts. Birchbark was bent into containers, tipis, and canoes. The interior of the bark was made to face outward, and its red surface was decorated by scraping away the red skin and exposing the white layer underneath. The designs were usually geometric, as was the case when painting was used to decorate the same items. Such decorations

138 *Trade with the Russians and other traders brought glass beads as substitutes for the porcupine quills that Indians of the western Subarctic traditionally used as decoration. This 18th-century cedar-bark pouch combines the two.*

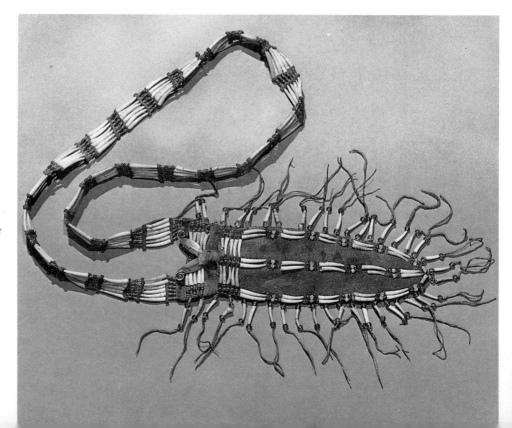

were added to wooden paddles, leather moccasins, and other everyday objects to raise them above the level of the ordinary. Perhaps the most pleasing of their crafts was decoration with porcupine quills. The Plains Indians and others south of them 138 had this skill as well. The effect was often striking. The quills were soaked and flattened. They were dyed with pigments derived from berries and fungi. After that, they were usually embroidered onto skin garments or small birchbark containers. Again the designs were usually geometric, but sometimes entirely covering the decorated object. In the historical period fur trading became important, and one of the side benefits was the availability of colored glass beads. The larger early beads have now been replaced by tiny seed beads, which are used by the thousands to decorate garments in colorful and elaborate designs.

Socially, the primary focus among the Athapascans was upon family relations between immediate relatives. Small band sizes and long distances between bands meant that large formal kin groupings were out of the question. Indeed, the exigencies of such a life required the practice of polygamy in two forms. Polygyny, where a man has two or more wives, was common. Polyandry, where a woman has two or more husbands, was much less frequent, but far from unknown. Mortality among males was high for a variety of reasons, including hunting accidents and fighting. But this was often balanced by female mortality in childbirth, and the occasional practice of female infanticide, the killing of young girls by their mothers. Thus fate often dictated marriage patterns by creating a numerical imbalance between the sexes within bands, thereby severely limiting the options.

Given their low population density and their amorphous ethnicity, it would be easy to miss the significance of the Canadian Athapascans to North American prehistory. All American Indians descend from ancestors who were at some stage Subarctic hunter-gatherers, and the stamp of that experience has remained embedded in their myths and their shamanism, where an archaeologist can never reach them. We need the Athapascan example to show us what life was like for earlier migrants passing through the Subarctic. With readapted representatives in such diverse regions as California, the Southwest, and the Great Plains, the Athapascans constitute a microcosm of American Indian prehistory.

The eastern Subarctic

The initial movement of Indian bands into the eastern Subarctic contrasts with that into the western Subarctic. In the west, receding ice released early Athapascans from the Alaskan Refuge and allowed them to move southeastward into the emerging conifer forests. In the east, conifer forests were similarly established by slow succession, but in this case human movement into the deglaciated Subarctic was generally from the northern Eastern Woodlands. The historical Indian residents of the eastern Subarctic are all speakers of Algonquian languages, a family of languages 15 that is ancient in eastern North America. Linguistic contrasts are stronger here than within the Athapascan block, which suggests that the prehistory of this area may well prove to be more complex. Only with the widely scattered small bands of Cree-Montagnais-Naskapi in the northeastern Subarctic do we have the kind of language grouping described for the Athapascans. South of them lived the more organized and distinctive tribes of the Beothuk, Micmac, Ojibwa, Ottawa and Algonquin.

The last of these is the tribe that has lent its name in modified form to all the related Algonquian languages.

The ancestors of the Subarctic Algonquians are even more elusive than those of the Athapascans. Bone and antler were easily available materials, and they were often used in place of stone. The acidic soils of the northern forests did not preserve these items any better than they preserved wood, bark, or fiber. As a result, the archaeologist is left with little to find, and it is to the historian that we must turn in order to gain some idea of the lives these northern Algonquians probably led. In summer they traveled in birchbark canoes, and in winter on snowshoes with their belongings pulled along behind on toboggans, all of which were innovations that Europeans later adopted. They lived in conical tipis and wore clothing that was sometimes well tailored, depending upon the degree of Eskimo influence. Where tailoring was not well developed, Algonquian women were inclined to decorate clothes with porcupine quill embroidery, much as in the Athapascan area.

In prehistoric times the Algonquians survived by hunting, gathering, trapping, and fishing. European colonization changed all this rapidly, however. Fur trapping became very important as demand for furs rose in Europe. The prehistoric pattern had emphasized a fluid nomadism, but the fur trade encouraged a rigid scheduling of activities within well-defined trapping territories. The concept of territory shifted from the notion of core areas and a kind of vague public domain to that of bounded territories owned by family bands. The speed at which these changes took place in any given area depended upon trade incentives, the rate of introduction of steel traps, the proximity of trading posts, the severity of European diseases, and the availability of beaver. Eventually the new pattern permeated the entire Subarctic, affecting Algonquians and Athapascans alike. We have already seen how the fire-arms and other goods obtained by the Ojibwa in exchange for their furs affected their relations with the Dakota, and influenced historical shifts on the northern Great Plains generally. The same sorts of ramifications had occurred in earlier decades in the woodlands of the northeast. Indeed, much of the protohistoric intertribal warfare of northern North America developed out of the dislocations and competition brought on by the fur trade.

The first European visitors to North America were not fur traders or explorers with royal charters. They were Norse settlers, and their first contacts with native Americans were with the Eskimos of Greenland and the Beothuk of Newfoundland. So little is known of these voyages from European records that we can probably expect to learn much more from archaeological research at the sites of their settlements. Iceland was settled by the Norse around AD 870. They displaced Irish monks who had been sailing there for perhaps as many as four centuries, but it is unlikely that any of these ecclesiastical refugees reached the New World. That 'discovery' was left to Eric the Red and a band of colonists who settled Greenland in 985. The great North Atlantic was under the influence of a climatic improvement at the time, and tiny Norse villages began to flourish on Greenland. Eventually, two settlement clusters were established, an eastern and a western group. Gardar, a village in the eastern settlement, rose to a population of about 3000, and became the seat of the bishopric of Greenland. In 1001, Lief, second son of Eric the Red, coasted along Labrador and stopped near the northern tip of Newfoundland. Here he established a small settlement at what is now called L'Anse aux Meadows. This was the Vinland of the Norse sagas. It was abandoned a short time later, but was used temporarily as a settlement twice again over the following dozen years.

The Black Death of the fourteenth century decimated Norse villages in Iceland and elsewhere. Worse, the climate deteriorated once again, and grain could no longer be grown on Greenland. Trade with Scandinavia ended, and by AD 1400 the Norse settlements in America were deserted. The Eskimos and the Beothuk of Greenland and Newfoundland (both called 'Skraellings' by the Norse) seem to have been hostile to the European intruders, for there is no clear indication of Scandinavian influence on the archaeology of either culture.

Little is known of the Newfoundland Beothuk. Only fragments of their language have survived, and not all linguists are sure that we can regard them as Algonquians. They were Subarctic hunters much like the others we have seen, who scheduled their annual round to include both marine and inland resources. Particularly important were the woodland caribou that also lived on the island, which were shot with arrows or stabbed with long spears from behind specially constructed fences. If the Beothuk were ancient residents of Newfoundland, they had survived isolation by the Dorset Eskimos, who moved onto the coast of the island around AD 100 and stayed for 500 years. We know that Indians did live here before the Dorset arrived. However, it is possible that the Eskimos displaced the Indians, and that the Beothuk were the descendants of people who moved onto the island after the Dorset withdrew northward around AD 600. If this was the case, the Beothuk can only have been on Newfoundland for 400 years when the Norse arrived. The historical Beothuk used harpoons made like those of the Eskimos, so we can conclude that there was some contact between them.

The Beothuk appear not to have been well treated by the Eskimos, the Norse, and the other Europeans who began settling Newfoundland in the sixteenth century. The English called them 'Red Indians' after the paint they used to cover their clothing and skin. In the following centuries, both English and French settlers took to shooting them for sport. Just as bad was the confinement of the Beothuk to the interior where they could not harvest vital marine foods. By 1800, the Beothuk population was down to a few hundred. It was extinct thirty years later.

The Arctic

Apart from the Alaskan Refuge, the North American Arctic appears never to have been the permanent homeland of anyone until the Eskimos arrived and claimed it as their own. The common ancestors of the Eskimos and Aleuts moved into western Alaska from Siberia no earlier than 3000 BC. They spoke a language that for convenience is usually referred to as Eskaleut. All the languages that developed from Eskaleut have clear linguistic connections in Siberia. The ancestral Aleuts split from the Eskimos very early, perhaps even before they crossed the Bering Strait. The Aleuts settled in what are now called the Aleutian Islands, where they turned to marine hunting and fishing for their livelihood. They remained there in relative isolation, their language and culture evolving further and further away from the Eskimos, until both groups were too dissimilar to share a common name.

139 *Sea hunters of the Aleutian Islands and west coast of Alaska sat low upon the water in their kayaks, and had to wear wooden hats to protect their eyes against the glare of the Arctic sun. This 40-cm.-long Aleut hat, painted and decorated with ivory, sea-lion whiskers and glass beads, was collected in the late 18th century from Unalaska in the Aleutian Islands.*

The Aleuts

After about 2000 BC the Aleuts became marine specialists. They concentrated upon sea mammals: whales, walrus, sea lions, seals, and sea otters. They also harvested large numbers of sea birds from the huge rookeries that dot the island chain. The sea mammals were harpooned from skin boats in the Eskimo fashion. Like the Eskimos, the Aleuts had harpoon heads that detached within the animal, after which the victim weakened and died tethered to floats. This type of harpoon took centuries to perfect, and it has frequently been said that it cannot be further improved. Like so much of Eskimo and Aleut material culture, the weapon is a masterpiece of both technology and artistry. Each harpoon is constructed like a modern three-stage rocket. The lower main shaft is the largest component. The upper foreshaft is about a half or a third the length of the lower shaft. Between them is a small shaft head that is socketed on either end in order to hold and join the two main shafts together. The

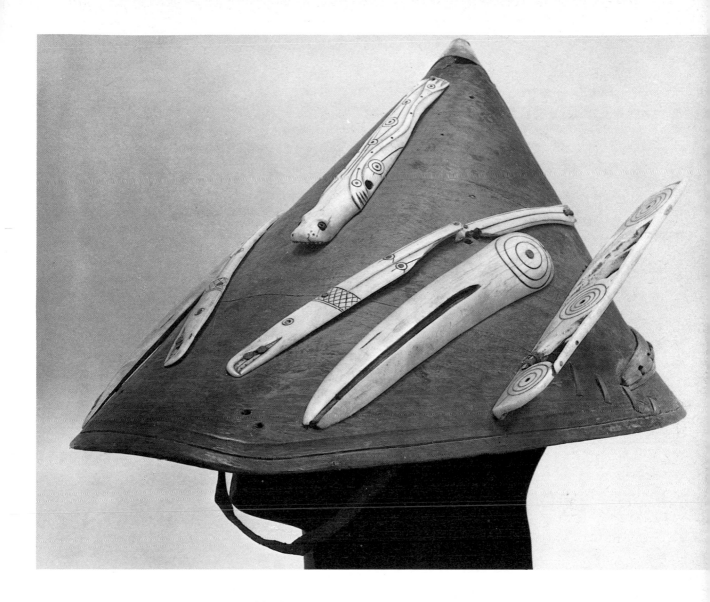

140 *This 19th-century Eskimo hat from west Alaska, 35 cm. long, with magical ivory ornaments, was made from one piece of birch bark scraped thin, bent, and sewed together at the back with fiber.*

joint is secured by lashing through holes in the foreshaft and the lower shaft so that there is a tough but flexible union. At the top of the weapon is the harpoon head, which is socketed to receive the foreshaft, and has a spur that extends down one side of the foreshaft. The spur is important, because this is what catches inside a harpooned animal and causes the head to turn sideways (toggle) so that it cannot be pulled loose. The tip of the harpoon head has a slot within which is mounted a stone or metal point, and there is a hole at the midpoint of the head through which the tether line is tied. The line also serves to hold the harpoon head tightly on the foreshaft before and while being plunged into an animal. A meter or so back from the head, a bone washer is tied to the line, and this in turn is slipped over a peg on the lower shaft to keep the line taut. Sealskin floats, drags, wound plugs and other highly specialized gadgetry complete what may well be the most sophisticated weapon system ever devised for a prehistoric hunter.

Later Aleut bands had stone lamps for burning the oil extracted from sea-mammal blubber. Usually these were shallow stone bowls with small mounds of moss for wicks around the edges. They also made stone dishes and bowls, and carved labrets for personal adornment. But for the most part, Aleut art was rather austere, not 141 equaling the flamboyance of Eskimo art, and it was expressed largely in the form of technological excellence.

Influences from the Northwest Coast became prominent in later Aleut pre-history. There was some concern for wealth, a reflection of the strong emphasis

141, 142 *These two 19th-century wooden Aleut death masks, 35 cm. high, come from Unalaska and Unga Islands respectively, in the Aleutian Island chain.*

upon wealth in Northwest Coast cultures. There was also some shift in the direction of unilineal descent, the reckoning of descent through one as opposed to both parental lines. Such influences, which were also strong among south Alaskan Eskimo communities in the historical period, might eventually have led to far-reaching changes in the cultures of the southwestern Arctic, if it had not been for the colonization of the region by the Russians in the eighteenth century. Few Aleuts survived the hundred-year Russian occupation and the disruption that accompanied the purchase of Alaska by the United States in 1867.

213

The Eskimos

Eskimo prehistory is much better known than that of the Aleut. It begins about 3000 BC with the appearance of a series of tool assemblages in Alaska that are referred to collectively as the 'Arctic Small Tool' tradition. The label is appropriate, because microblades and other microlithic tools dominate assemblages from these early Eskimo sites. To later Eskimos who found them, these miniature tools seemed to prove the existence of a race of little people. To us, however, they are evidence of connections with advanced Asiatic tool industries called 'Mesolithic' in the Old World. The tiny blades were set in bone to serve as cutting edges on tools which were often made out of three or four different materials. To produce these composite weapons, the early Eskimos first had to manufacture stone burins (engraving tools) and other specialized bone- and ivory-working implements. Finished products were assembled with glue, fiber cordage, and gut.

The Arctic Small Tool tradition was first identified at Cape Denbigh, on the west coast of Alaska. Since then, it has been discovered at several other sites, including inland ones such as Onion Portage. The expansion of early Eskimo bands carrying

143

143, 144 About 3000 BC Asian Eskimos crossed for the first time into Alaska, carrying weapons tipped with miniature tools or 'microliths' such as these 5-cm.-long chert blades (right). The Eskimos of this 'Arctic Small Tool' tradition built pit houses, 5 cm. in diameter, covered by low conical roofs of timber. This reconstruction (opposite) in Katmai National Park in the Aleutian Range shows a late prehistoric pit house, similar in size and construction to the first such houses brought from Asia.

this tool tradition appears to have been facilitated by a period of improved (probably warmer) climate. They moved through the park tundra and the fringes of spruce forests in Alaska, splitting their time between caribou hunting and sea-mammal hunting. They did not yet have pottery or stone lamps for burning oil, and their expansion was consequently restricted. Food had to be boiled with hot stones, or in bark or skin containers over open hearths, hearths that also provided heat and light. Without oil lamps to substitute for hearth fires, they could not venture onto the treeless tundra for long. They brought the bow and arrow with them from Asia, and they were probably the agents for the introduction of this innovation to the Indians of North America. They also brought a form of pit house, but whether Indian pit houses were copied from these or independently developed we cannot be sure. In southwestern Alaska, early Eskimo pit houses were excavated to a depth of about a meter. A typical house had a covered entryway about two meters long with 144 an excavated footpath. The house was round, about five meters in diameter, and covered by a low conical roof of timbers. There was a central smoke hole with a hearth on the floor beneath it.

Early Eskimo harpoons had little of the technological sophistication of later models. Walrus was apparently a favorite target, but the harpoons were used for thrusting, and the points were not designed to toggle within the animal, nor were they barbed. Instead, they were 'end-bladed', the cutting edges fixed at right angles to the shafts like chisels so that they would do the greatest damage before being retracted. No doubt many walrus were mortally wounded in this way, but without tether lines, a large percentage of them must have been lost to the hunters.

The Small Tool tradition was the first truly successful technological adaptation to the North American Arctic. However, it was still a fragile adjustment, and climatic deterioration about 1000 BC caused the Eskimo bands to fragment into a series of separate and relatively isolated groups. The onset of cooler conditions may have ended the annual migrations of caribou and fish in some areas. Expanding sea ice probably eliminated sea mammal populations in others. Those Eskimo bands that were caught in marginal areas were sometimes overtaken by the swift changes, and whole communities starved. Examples of this kind of band extinction are known for even the historical Eskimos, who are much better equipped to cope with the Arctic than were their ancestors of 3500 years ago.

The process of fragmentation and regional specialization in Eskimo technology led to the appearance of a variety of new archaeological traditions. On the Alaskan west coast, 'Choris' culture grew out of the small Tool tradition, while in the Canadian Arctic, 'Sarqaq' culture emerged from the same base. There were regional adjustments as well, particularly on the Pacific coast of southern Alaska, where local communities diverged from the cultural mainstream relatively early. Modern Eskimo speech in this area reflects the long separation by being substantially different from other Eskimo languages. In fact, the Eskimo languages of the Pacific coast, southern Alaska, Nunivak Island, and Siberia all show fairly strong contrasts with each other, contrasts that seem to indicate separate developments over the last 2000 years. Together, they are referred to as Yupic languages. The archaeology of these four regions is also distinctive, each area differing from the others and from the rest of the Arctic. The rediscovery of these regional variations on the more general theme of Eskimo cultural evolution is one of the most interesting of current archaeological research efforts.

The prehistory of the Siberian Eskimo is relatively well known as a result of research on St Lawrence Island. The island lies south of the Bering Strait, politically part of Alaska, but geographically closer to Siberia. Here 'Okvik' culture emerged from a Small Tool tradition base about 2000 years ago. This gradually evolved through 'Old Bering Sea' culture to become 'Punuk' culture. The long tradition was eventually altered and displaced by expanding 'Thule' culture in the last 1000 years, but not before it had created a remarkable archaeological record. Bone and ivory implements of all three phases were elaborately decorated with incising and even low relief by Eskimo craftsmen. Harpoon heads, for example, were always much more beautiful than they needed to be. Those of the first two phases can be distinguished by style, but in both cases examples are complicated and intricate. In the Punuk phase examples are more numerous, and more simply decorated.

Another fascinating series of artifacts from St Lawrence Island are the 'winged' objects, whose function is unknown but which vaguely resemble the bannerstones

145
147

216

of the Eastern Woodlands. They begin at the Okvik level as small winged artifacts. In the Old Bering Sea phase the standard width increases to about 21 cm., incised 150 decoration becomes more elaborate, and the objects come to resemble birds. In the early Punuk phase the wings change shape and grow reminiscent of butterfly wings 151 about 16 cm. wide. During the middle Punuk phase the artifacts become elongated, 152 and look like tridents. Finally in the late Punuk phase widths decrease to about 7 cm., 153 and the objects come to look first like small crowns, then dog whistles. The last of them are undecorated.

Taken together, the styles of the Okvik, Old Bering Sea, and Punuk phases are usually called 'Old Bering Sea art'. It was a sophisticated style. Decorative incising began with rather complex linear motifs, which gradually became even more complex and curvilinear, a significant accomplishment where the medium was tough ivory or bone. In the end, artifacts tended to have clean economical lines without much decoration. This general evolutionary trend can be traced in several artifact classes in addition to the winged objects already discussed. Harpoon heads, needle cases, harpoon shafts, adze handles, and pail handles were all part of this 156–57 distinctive tradition.

Farther east, two major new cultures eventually emerged from the fragmented Small Tool technological base. One of these is called 'Norton', the other 'Dorset'. Dorset culture arose from Sarqaq which as we have seen had earlier developed from the Small Tool tradition in the Canadian Arctic. Norton culture arose independently in Alaska, along a coastal strip extending all the way from the Alaskan Peninsula near the Aleutians to the northern Alaskan border with the Canadian Yukon. This is a distance of 3500 kilometers, much farther if the coastline is followed carefully. By about 500 BC, the Norton lifeway was established over the whole of this huge coastal zone. A few microblades in the Norton tool kits point back to the culture's Small Tool heritage, but many of the implements were relatively new innovations. Togglehead harpoons, for instance, are rare, but present. Another important addition is a coarse kind of pottery, which appears to have been introduced from the Lena valley area of Siberia.

The period of Norton culture also brought a shift from open fires to stone lamps that was crucial to later Eskimo cultural evolution. Early Norton sites contain evidence of both open hearths and stone lamps. Later sites contain only stone lamps, indicating that the technique of burning sea-mammal oil for heating, lighting, and cooking had been mastered. The late Norton Eskimos and their descendants no longer needed to stay near supplies of wood, and the expansion of bands far into the treeless tundra of the High Arctic became possible for the first time.

Houses tended to be less permanent than previously, with walls of driftwood set vertically. The well-known Eskimo single-seater kayak was by this time important, but the larger open skin boat called the 'umiak', which could carry whole families, was not yet developed. We can conclude that the Norton Eskimos were able to hunt small sea mammals through the ice or from kayaks, but in the absence of umiaks, whales and walrus may well have been too large to be hunted. These formidable game animals also required the use of the kind of sophisticated toggleheaded harpoon already described for the late prehistoric Aleut, but still largely missing from Norton culture 2000 years ago.

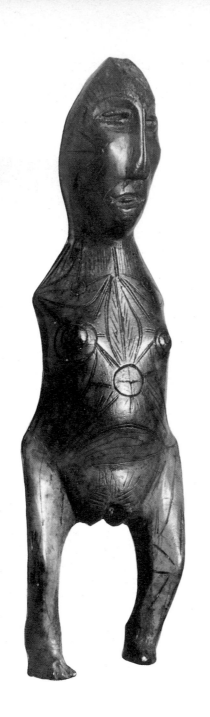

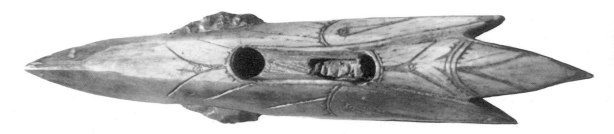

Eskimos of the St
Lawrence and Punuk
Islands, south of the Bering
Strait, created a remarkable
art style known as 'Old
Bering Sea' art, which
evolved through Okvik,
Old Bering Sea, and
Punuk phases between
2000 and 1300 years ago.

145, 146 Two walrus-
ivory Okvik figurines
(opposite), 17 cm. high,
represent fertility goddesses.
The one with prominent
vulva (left) may depict the
bear mother, connected with
the common Eskimo belief
in a powerful bear spirit.

Right:
148 Masculine facial
features are superimposed
upon a penis of walrus
ivory in this Punuk
shaman's fertility charm.

Below:
147, 149 The Old Bering
Sea harpoon is constructed
like a modern multi-stage
rocket, with a lower main
shaft, an upper foreshaft,
and, linking them, a shaft
head (below, of ivory)
socketed at either end.
Lashed onto the foreshaft is
the harpoon head (opposite
below, 12 cm. long, of
ivory with inset chert
blades) which detaches
within the animal but
which remains tethered to
floats until the victim
weakens and dies.

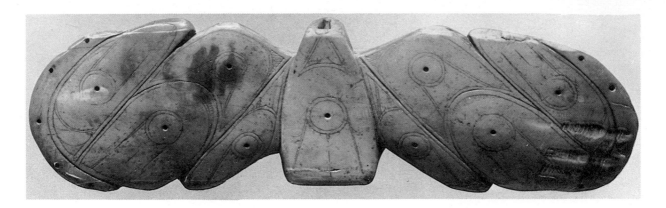

An extraordinary series of prehistoric Eskimo artifacts from St Lawrence Island are the walrus-ivory 'winged' objects, whose true function is unknown but which may have been attached to the butt ends of harpoons as 'wings', counterweights for heavy harpoon heads.

150 *Beginning 2000 years ago in the Okvik phase as small artifacts, winged objects gradually evolved during the Old Bering Sea phase, after* AD 200, *into bird shapes like this 21-cm.-wide piece.*

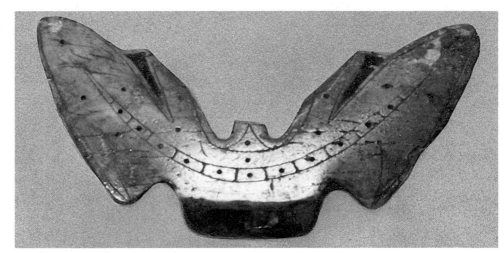

151 *In the early Punuk phase following* AD 700 *winged objects narrowed into 'butterflies', 16 cm. wide.*

152 *By the middle Punuk phase winged objects had become 10-cm.-wide tridents.*

153 *Late Punuk winged objects, 7 cm. wide, hardly had wings at all, and resembled small coronets.*

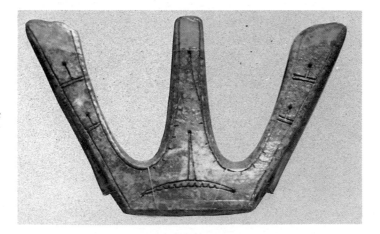

Old Bering Sea art is
characterized by intricate
curvilinear incised
decoration on objects of
bone and ivory.

154 An ivory animal
head, 7 cm. long, may
represent a wolf.

155 Ivory ornaments are
common in Old Bering Sea
art, and some, such as this
10-cm.-long animal head,
may have been shamanistic
charms.

156 Curvilinear designs
ornament an ivory box or
pail handle.

157 A stone or slate blade
was once fastened with
thongs to this ivory adze
handle, 31 cm. long. The
butt of the tool ends in a
wolf's head.

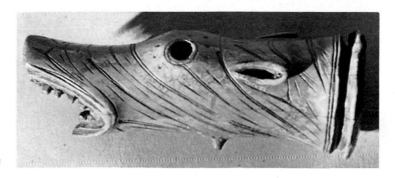

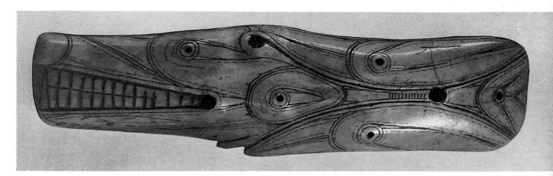

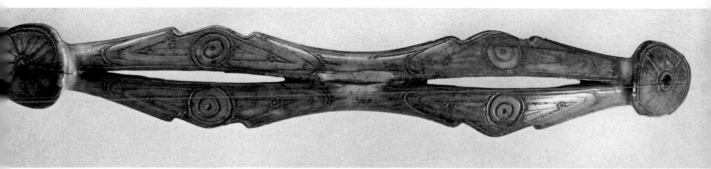

With Norton culture we see a bit more of the gadgetry and decorative art that eventually came to be so characteristic of the Eskimos. Polished-stone labrets were made in various sizes, tiny 'training' sizes for children and large plugs for adults. Both pointed 'men's knives' and semilunar 'women's knives' were being manufactured by this time. The latter, which go by the modern Eskimo name 'ulu', were used with a rocking rather than a thrusting motion. They were often made from slate, but 2000 years ago the Eskimo slate industry was not yet fully developed, and these early examples were not well made compared with later ones. Walrus and walrus ivory being in short supply, engraving and carving in this medium was not yet widely practiced.

Norton Eskimos dominated the western and northern coasts of Alaska, and were ancestral to the modern Yupic-speaking people of southwestern Alaska. In northern Alaska, other Norton Eskimos were the ancestors of modern speakers of Inupic dialects. As we shall see, these were the people who eventually came to dominate most of the Arctic. They spread eastward all the way to Greenland, and confined Yupic-speaking communities to their present homes south of the Seward Peninsula in southwestern Alaska. But before examining this late Eskimo development, we must turn to the Dorset bands, mysterious contemporaries of the Norton Eskimos, who lived in the Canadian Arctic.

158 Descendants of the Arctic Small Tool tradition Eskimos of Alaska were the Norton Eskimos, who colonized much of the Alaskan coastal strip about 500 BC. They introduced many of the tools that came to be so characteristic of historical Eskimos, including this ivory-handled slate 'woman's knife' or 'ulu', 10 cm. long, which was used with a rocking rather than thrusting motion.

Dorset culture was the second major development out of the Arctic Small Tool tradition. It emerged by way of the intermediate Sarqaq cultural stage almost 3000 years ago. In their initial expansion, Dorset bands spread widely across the Canadian Arctic penetrating new areas opened up to them by a general improvement in the climate. Like the Norton Eskimo bands west of them, they adapted earlier and more permanent pit-house forms to their new situation. Usually they lived near the seashore in relatively small circular houses that were not deeply excavated into the frozen tundra. Some of the houses had paved stone floors and sleeping platforms around the sides. A few had short entrance passages. But although there was a standard range of house styles, the materials from which houses were constructed varied widely, depending upon what was available. Some were hollow cairns of stone, others were made from driftwood. Still others were skin tents supported by the rib bones of beached whales, and if none of these materials could be found, blocks of thick sod were used.

The Dorset were hunters of both sea and land animals, and like the Norton Eskimos probably took migrating caribou in large numbers. They had both kayaks and umiaks to aid them in their hunting and traveling. Unlike the Norton people, they were far removed from Asiatic influences, and did not have pottery. Their cooking pots and the oil lamps that made life on the tundra possible were all made of

159 *Lip plugs or 'labrets' were popular personal adornments for many Eskimo men from Norton times onward, either worn singly in the middle of the lower lip or in pairs near the corners of the mouth. Wearers graduated from slender 'training' sizes to full-sized plugs, up to 5 cm. long.*

stone. Despite the absence of some Norton innovations, the Dorset Eskimos experimented with rare raw materials. Meteoric iron was sometimes found and fashioned into durable men's knives. Native copper nuggets were also used, usually to make wire for binding the components of tools made from other materials.

Some of the specialized Eskimo tools designed for survival in the Arctic were beginning to appear in numbers. Snow knives for cutting blocks to build winter snow igloos were made of bone or ivory. Ice creepers which attached to feet for traction, and goggles to prevent snow blindness, were made from the same materials. Small sleds were built from wood, bone, frozen leather, and other common materials depending upon what was available. But these were drawn by hand, dogsleds being a later development.

Most utilitarian objects were decorated with skill and care. Harpoon heads, for example, were made in a unique Dorset style. But these outlets appear not to have

160

160 *An archer stands over a prostrate man and a variety of animals on this incised bone comb of the Dorset culture, mysterious contemporary of Norton in the Canadian Arctic about 500 BC. Early Eskimo bands brought the bow and arrow with them from Asia, and were probably the agents for the introduction of this innovation into North America.*

161 *This 9-cm.-high figurine was carved by a Yupic Eskimo craftsman in Southwestern Alaskan, whose culture was one of several to evolve from the Norton tradition in the centuries following AD 1100.*

been sufficient to satisfy the impulses of Dorset artists, or to fill the hours of the long winter night north of the Arctic Circle. Their house sites are filled as well with pendants, amulets, and ornaments made from the whole range of available materials.   162

The Dorset were the first Eskimos to penetrate the eastern part of the American Arctic. For almost 2000 years they expanded and contracted with the waxing and waning of favorable climate. There was no single center of Dorset culture, but there were localities that were more suitable as refuges when conditions were bad. After one period of expansion, part of the Dorset retreated ahead of deteriorating conditions to the coast of Labrador and the island of Newfoundland. The Newfoundland Dorset remained for about 500 years following their appearance around AD 100, and displaced the earlier Indian inhabitants as we have already seen. With conditions once again more favorable to the north of them, and renewed expansion of Indian populations south of them, they abandoned Newfoundland around AD 600.

The ultimate fate of Dorset culture remains something of a mystery to archaeologists. It came to an end amidst the widespread changes that accompanied the climatic optimum, or peak period of warm climate, that occurred around AD 1000. In northern Alaska, Norton culture had evolved through stages called 'Ipiutak' and 'Birnirk' to become late prehistoric 'Thule' culture. The Thule Eskimos were charged with the collective products of their own innovation and elements adopted from Asiatic sources. With their efficient adaptations, they moved eastward, eventually swamping the Dorset Eskimos. At the same time, Norse long ships were setting sail westward from Scandinavia. Pockets of Dorset communities persisted even after the main Thule expansion, but eventually these were absorbed or died out, and neither Dorset culture nor the language these Eskimos spoke has survived. After AD 1000 all the Arctic save southwestern Alaska belonged to the Thule Eskimos.

Ipiutak culture, which evolved in northern Alaska about AD 350, is famous for carvings executed in ivory, bone, and antler. The Eskimos responsible for this   163 culture did much to lay the groundwork for their Thule descendants. There are chains, double and even triple helixes of ivory. There are daggers, beautifully shaped and engraved snow goggles, ingenious swivels to take the twists out of taut lines, human and animal effigies, and artifacts we can illustrate but not explain. There are   163 also a few exquisite masks of ivory mosaic, which are usually associated with burials.   166

Birnirk culture followed Ipiutak between AD 500 and 1000, and eventually gave rise to Thule culture. Bands of Thule Eskimos multiplied and spread rapidly eastward. Their villages were situated along the seashore, and whether made of bone, stone, sod, or snow, their igloos were built in a standard form. The basic house was circular, with a raised sleeping bench on the back and sides. The front of the circular room gave way to a covered passageway. The winter snow house is the most famous of the various igloos, and required the most skill to build. Special probes and snow knives were used to find and quarry snow of the proper consistency. Blocks were cut and then laid in a spiral that arched around and inward at the same time. A central keystone block was the last one to be set in place. A hole was usually cut for the insertion of a block of clear ice that would allow the feeble winter light to supplement light from oil lamps. Snow houses had cold air traps in their passageways, curtain doors, skin linings for insulation, and a wealth of other devices to make life more comfortable.

162 *Perhaps a powerful shamans device or a prop for winter entertainment, the precise function of this 3.3-cm.-high Dorset ivory mask from Sugluk, Quebec, remains unknown.*

Eskimos of the Ipiutak culture, descendants of Norton in northern Alaska, evolved a distinctive art style about 1500 years ago, executing carvings in ivory, bone, and antler.

163 *A bone carving, 14 cm. long, could represent a human figure, a sea otter, or an Ipiutak shaman doubling as both.*

164 *A 7.5-cm.-long walrus from Point Hope, Alaska, carved from the ivory tusk of the real animal, demonstrates the anatomical knowledge and x-ray vision of Ipiutak artists.*

165 *The function of this 26-cm.-long walrus-ivory object from Alaska's Seward Peninsula, with 'mouth' that hinges open, remains obscure, but it may have been used as a comb to clean bear skins before certain Ipiutak ceremonies. The central figure of a bear with its head between its paws is reminiscent of Scytho-Siberian motifs, and shows the relatively recent Asiatic heritage of all Eskimo-Aleut cultures.*

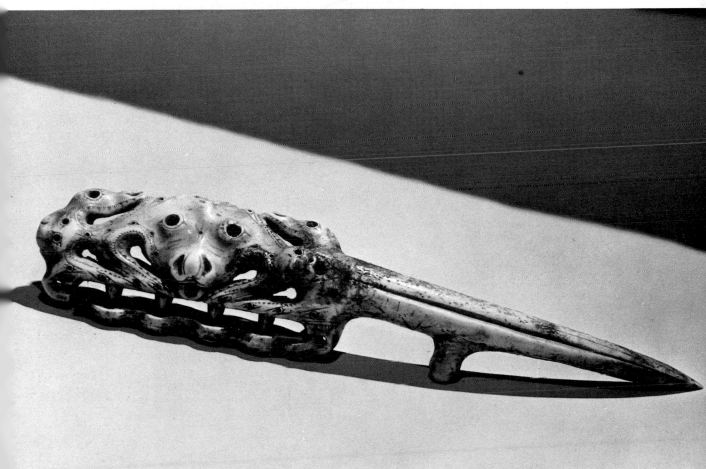

166 *Sets of mask-like ivory carvings are usually found associated with Ipiutak burials. The pieces of this 16-cm.-high mask from Point Hope, Alaska, may have had a backing of wood or leather.*

Opposite:
Eskimos of the Thule culture, which evolved out of Norton and Ipiutak in northern Alaska, moved eastward into the Canadian Arctic about 1000 years ago, swamping the Dorset Eskimos.

167 *With their igloos, dogsleds and other specialized equipment the Thule were well adapted to Arctic conditions, and often found time to make amulets such as this bone fish, 10 cm. long.*

168 *This bone-handled Thule knife, in the shape of a polar bear, 31.5 cm. long, bears an incised whale on its flank.*

With their inventory of weapons and other tools, virtually none of the food resources of the Arctic were closed to the Thule Eskimo. They had fully developed toggling harpoons, sometimes fitted with ice picks at the butts. There were special snow shovels carved from driftwood or bone, and sometimes edged with slivers of ivory. Fish were taken at stone weirs, or with finely made nets, spears, and hooks. 167 Birds were taken with nets and even small bolas. Men carried elaborate kits of bow drills, hand drills, hammers, flint flakers, scrapers, whalebone shavers, and other specialized tools. Women carried bone needles, elaborate winged needle cases of 168 bone or ivory, sealskin thimbles, bodkins, and thimble holders of ivory. Both sexes sported an array of amulets.

Stone lamps were better than they had been, and certainly better than they needed to be. Special bone trimmers were used to adjust the wicks. Pots were carved from soapstone, and occasionally thick clay pots were also made. Pottery was by now an old innovation, one inherited from the earlier Norton Eskimo. But it remained an undeveloped craft, appearing only as an occasional thick and poorly fired vessel.

The search by the Thule for raw materials sometimes led them to excavate the aged ivory of extinct mammoths which had been preserved in the frozen tundra. To the consternation of modern archaeologists, they even excavated the house sites of

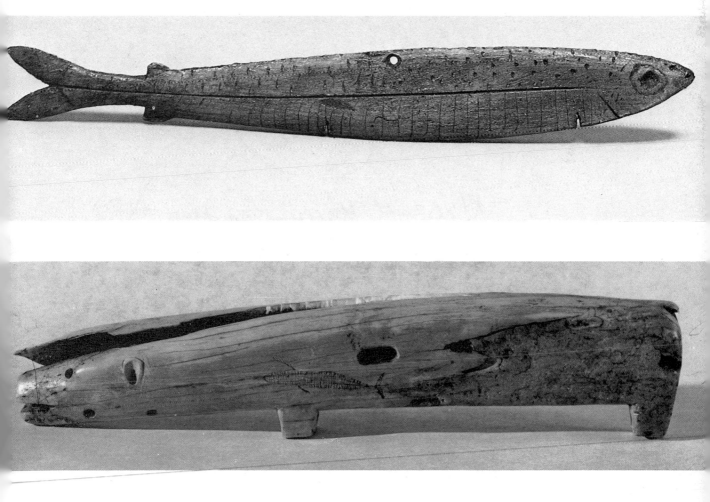

their Dorset predecessors, used the tools they found, and later discarded them out of context with their own implements.

The Thule Eskimos moved through their annual round, living in igloos or skin tents as the season required. Whale, walrus, seal, bear, musk ox, and caribou were their most important game. These were supplemented by many smaller species, and with the roots, berries, eggs, and shellfish they could gather in season. Sometimes their hunting techniques were unexpectedly simple, as when a long sliver of whale baleen was coiled and frozen within a ball of blubber. The innocent looking ball was thrown out on the snow where a wolf or bear would be tempted to gulp it down. Warmed by the animal's stomach, the blubber would melt and the lethal baleen coil would spring open. The animal eventually died in agony.

Other Thule hunting practices required almost infinite patience. Hunters were required to spend hours bending over breathing holes in the sea ice in order to spear an unlucky seal. Each seal maintained several such breathing holes and the hunter could never be sure which one would be visited. A tiny feather balance was sometimes placed at the edge of the hole so that it would move if a seal exhaled below. When it did move, the hunter plunged his harpoon downward through the hole, and if he was lucky the point lodged in the seal. The breathing hole then had to be enlarged so that the seal could be pulled out and taken home. Wound plugs kept the precious blood inside the animal until it could be drained and drunk.

Winter travel was often by dogsled, a framework sled introduced from the Asian Arctic. Near the fringes of the Subarctic forests, the sleds were often pulled by dogs harnessed in pairs. In the High Arctic, however, the dogs were usually tethered separately, and fanned out ahead of the sled. The sled was one of the last major innovations to reach the Thule from the outside before the advent of European trade goods.

Thule clothing was carefully tailored and each person had a sizeable wardrobe. Outer jackets were hooded. Boots of several types were made and used depending upon whether the season was wet or dry, warm or cold. Fish skins were tightly sewn to make waterproof slickers or coats. Special skins were cut and sewn with the fur on or off, inside or outside depending upon the requirements of use and season. Outer garments were embellished with carved buttons, buckles, and ornaments. Little wonder that the women responsible for it all required so much skill and specialized equipment. At death, each person was buried with his or her clothing and personal equipment, usually under a cairn of stones. Sleds and umiaks made travel with all the necessary equipment relatively easy, but there was little reason to retain the belongings of the dead, because most of the survivors already had all they needed for their own use.

Trade and barter was well developed among the Thule Eskimos. They traded with each other, and with the Indians who lived near them in the Subarctic forests. The Copper Eskimos mined nuggets of copper from the Coppermine River, which empties into the Arctic Sea in north central Canada. Sometimes they traded finished products, at other times raw nuggets. They traveled south to obtain wood in exchange, not for burning, but for making boats and sleds. In their own territory, the only available wood was that which drifted onto their shores. It was even scarcer farther north, and the Eskimos there were eager to trade for it.

169

169 *Tobacco spread from Virginia to Europe, finally reaching the Eskimos via Russian traders from Alaska. This early historical Huron effigy-pipe bowl from the Ottawa area was carved from soapstone, a precious commodity traded widely in the Arctic and Subarctic at this time.*

The Copper Eskimos were important middlemen for other goods as well. Their territory contained the largest source of soapstone in the Arctic, stone which was turned into oil lamps and pots. Other Thule Eskimos both east and west of the source area traded for the soapstone, and bands living as far away as Alaska and Labrador managed to obtain finished products.

Copper and soapstone are only the best examples. Trade in many goods was important prehistorically all across the area. The Eskimos traded with Indians for the iron pyrites, leather, snowshoes, and other goods they could not otherwise obtain. Eskimo bands traded with each other for virtually anything they might require. Finished products and raw materials moved in all directions. Recent history has seen the revival of work in some of these raw materials. Soapstone, for example, is now more valuable than ever. Eskimo craftsmen have found a ready market for soapstone carvings in Canada and the United States. Carvings in walrus ivory and whale baleen still remain popular.

Life in the Arctic was not easy, and it shaped the Eskimo cosmos in ways that we find sometimes engaging, sometimes shocking, but almost always logical. Death was taken for granted as the inevitable product of time. In lean months there was little room in polar bands for individuals who could not contribute to collective survival. If it was decided that a newborn child could not survive infancy anyway, it was put out to die rather than suffer and drain the resources of the band. Old people who could not contribute or keep up were left behind, or took it upon themselves to leave the band and die of exposure. Meat was often eaten raw because there was little heat for cooking. The stomach contents of walrus and caribou were eaten because they were often the only available source of vegetable food.

In the long months of winter darkness, the Eskimos often turned their extraordinary ingenuity toward songs, games, and other entertainment. Cat's cradle and a variety of amusements that are also familiar in European-derived cultures were well developed. Parents created an array of ingenious toys and games for their children, many of which are still being rediscovered and marketed by toy manufacturers. Adults competed in singing or story telling, and frequently engaged in rough but good-natured games of strength. One such game, still played today, required two men to stand side by side, so that each could reach his arm around the back of the other's head and hook his middle finger in the corner of his opponent's mouth. Each then pulled as hard as he could while spectators chose sides and cheered them on, and they remained locked together until one could no longer stand the strain and released his grip.

With their sophisticated technology, the Thule Eskimos penetrated deep into the High Arctic. They were the first residents of High Arctic Greenland, colonizing the northern end of the island and eventually moving southward along both the east and west coasts. The favorable climatic cycle that allowed them to expand so far, engulfing the Dorset culture as they went, also drew the Norse from Scandinavia.

The warm interval did not last long. The Norse settlers of Greenland found that the growing season had shortened, and they were no longer able to grow most of their crops. Gradually the Norse pulled back from Newfoundland and Greenland, leaving the North once again to the Thule. But the Eskimos were also hurt by the climatic change. Like the Dorset before them, they contracted into isolated refuges, abandoning many areas that had once been so attractive. The Arctic ice pack expanded and many sea mammals deserted water in which they had been plentiful. In certain areas the effects were tragic. Some bands near the mouth of Hudson Bay had abandoned much of their marine technology in favor of caribou hunting. But after a few generations the caribou were hunted out. The men who had known the old technology were all dead, and in their isolation the Eskimo bands could not recapture what they had lost. They died.

Elsewhere in the High Arctic isolated bands were out of contact for so long that they were quite taken by surprise when they first encountered European explorers. They had no reason to believe that they were not the only people on earth. Even harder for us to imagine is that they had no reason to believe that the earth was anything but a frozen expanse.

The richly painted and carved wooden masks of the lower Yukon and adjacent areas of Alaska are among the finest achievements of historical Eskimo art. Usually made by shamans, the masks were worn by male dancers in elaborate winter ceremonies designed to exorcise evil spirits and to appease the souls of game animals that had been killed, thus ensuring plentiful future supplies of food.

170 *Eskimo women did not dance with face masks, but used finger masks instead, like this 12-cm.-high example from western Alaska, with a mane of polar-bear fur.*

235

171 *This owl mask with
feathers was collected in the
late 19th century from St
Michael, west Alaska.*

172 *Facial features are blurred into crescents as they rotate wildly around the right eye of this 19th-century mask, 35.5 cm. high, from the lower Yukon. Two of the mask's arms are missing.*

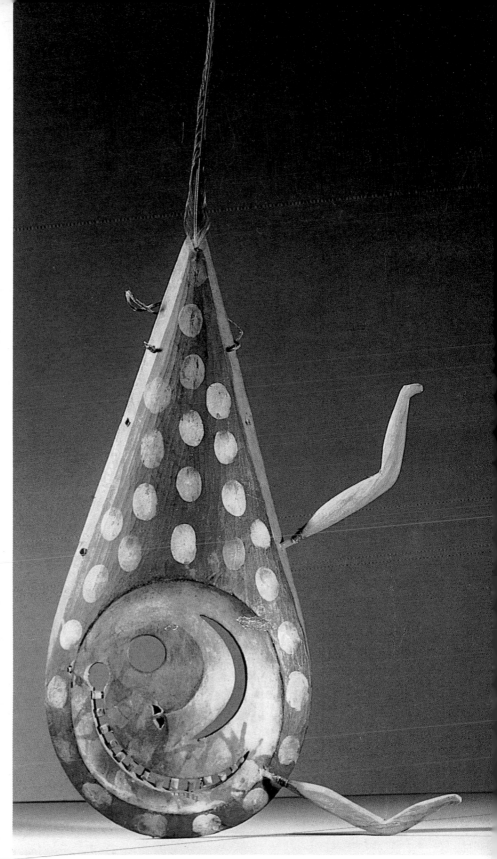

238

173 *The features of a cormorant are stretched to disguise the face of an Eskimo dancer on this 19th-century mask, 18 cm. high, from west Alaska.*

174 *Wooden masks like this historical green-and-white painted example from west Alaska are still carved by Eskimo craftsmen.*

240

The historical Thule Eskimos dominated the Arctic all the way from the Seward Peninsula of Alaska to Greenland. In southwest Alaska, however, other Eskimos 170–75 followed their own cultural traditions. These people, of whom the Kuskowagamiut are a good example, are less well-known to most readers, and they illustrate how stereotypes can obscure the colorful diversity of human culture. The Kuskowagamiut live along the Kuskokwim River, where they have been for centuries. They are and were fishermen and hunters, moving back and forth between the tundra and Subarctic forests of their area. The late prehistoric Kuskowagamiut retained the large permanent pit-house dwellings of the earliest Eskimos in this area. They burned fires in open hearths, but had oil lamps too. In this and other ways they combined the advanced technology of Eskimos farther north with an older and easier technology. They had all the advantages and fewer of the hardships of more northerly Eskimos.

The Kuskowagamiut were in close proximity to the Indian cultures of the Northwest Coast, and were therefore strongly influenced by them. For example, the mythological figure called Raven is found here as well as among Northwest Coast Indians. Even more interesting is the emphasis in kin relationships on descent through the female line, something not otherwise associated with Eskimos. Men and older boys of a community spent much of their time together in a special men's house, for their homes were dominated by women. After marriage, young couples lived in the house of the bride's mother. As a result, each house was filled with related women, their children and husbands. A man would sometimes take more than one wife, but under the prevailing circumstances, it is easy to see why they were usually sisters.

Trips were made for hunting and fishing, and at certain times of the year most of the villagers went to temporary camps. But for much of the year, the community of permanent houses was occupied at least by the women. The settlement system was important, because the female emphasis in Kuskowagamiut society would not have been possible without it.

Northwest Coast influences were felt in other ways too. The men's house was sometimes converted into a sweat lodge. Like many other Alaskan Eskimos, the men heated themselves by an open fire, and then doused themselves with cold water. But unlike other Eskimos, they also sometimes steamed themselves by pouring water over hot rocks, a practice they shared with most North American Indians. Eskimos outside of Alaska lacked the necessary wood, and practiced neither form of bathing. Similarly, only the southwest Alaskan Eskimos were near enough large trees to adopt the Northwest Coast practice of monumental wood carving. Poles decorated with feathers and carved wooden figures were often erected over the graves of the dead, but only a few of them were elaborately carved.

The Kuskowagamiut are striking, mostly because they diverge so far from the standard conception of what constitutes an Eskimo culture. No other large block of native Americans arrived as late or was as little fragmented by events as the Eskimos, yet even these people were and are still a spectrum of cultural variation. The prehistoric Indians of America spread into a far larger variety of environments than the Eskimos and their Aleut cousins, and they have been in the New World five times as long. We should not wonder that they developed such a bewildering array of life-

175 *This 19th-century mask of wood and feathers from St Michael, west Alaska, bears a black eye, perhaps a humorous detail to the shaman who carved it.*

ways, each with its own particular contribution to make to mankind. The mounted Indians of the Great Plains were only one ephemeral variation on the main theme of prehistoric America, but popular history and motion pictures of the twentieth century have elevated them to the quintessence of what was native to the New World. The elegant horsemen of the High Plains and the stolid Eskimos of the High Arctic deserve their glory, but to single them out as symbols of the larger whole is to ignore most of the greatness that was North America before it was engulfed by the Old World. This volume has been an attempt to encompass the depth and breadth of prehistoric North America in all its cultural variety. It has been written for people who are gone forever, but who contributed so much to the cultural history of the world. Like Ishi, the last of them, they kept their names.

Chronologies

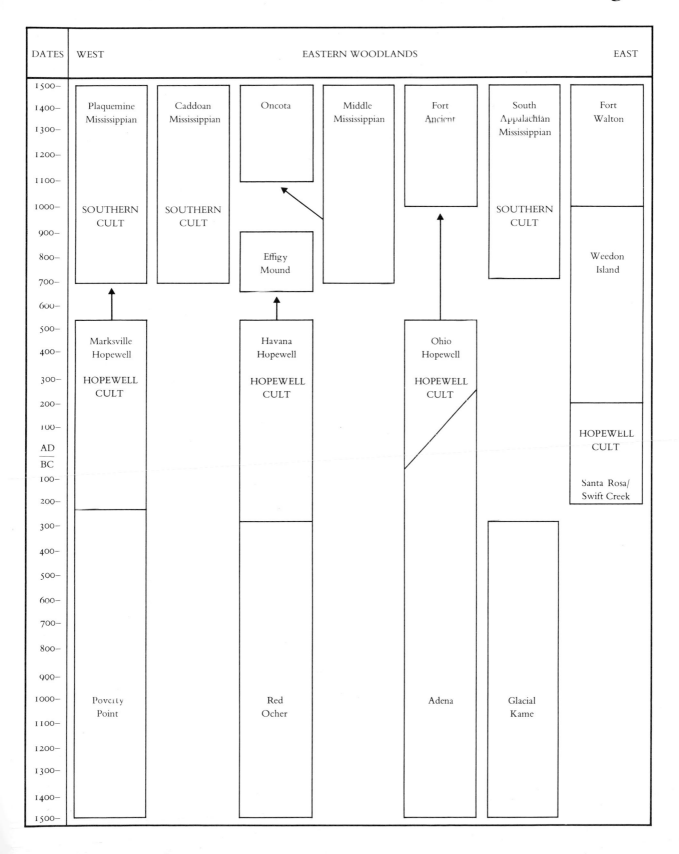

DATES	WEST	EASTERN WOODLANDS					EAST
1500–							
1400–	Plaquemine Mississippian	Caddoan Mississippian	Oncota	Middle Mississippian	Fort Ancient	South Appalachian Mississippian	Fort Walton
1300–							
1200–							
1100–							
1000–	SOUTHERN CULT	SOUTHERN CULT				SOUTHERN CULT	
900–							
800–			Effigy Mound				Weedon Island
700–							
600–							
500–							
400–	Marksville Hopewell			Havana Hopewell		Ohio Hopewell	
300–	HOPEWELL CULT		HOPEWELL CULT		HOPEWELL CULT		
200–							
100–							
AD							HOPEWELL CULT
BC							
100–							Santa Rosa/ Swift Creek
200–							
300–				Red Ocher			
400–							
500–							
600–							
700–							
800–							
900–							
1000–	Poverty Point				Adena	Glacial Kame	
1100–							
1200–							
1300–							
1400–							
1500–							

Mexico

c. 1500 BC	La Venta founded: Olmec civilization develops along Gulf Coast.
c. 100 BC	Teotihuacan founded in highland Mexico.
c. AD 100	Olmec civilization wanes.
c. AD 300–600	Early Classic period.
c. AD 500	Tula founded.
c. AD 600–900	Late Classic period.
c. AD 700	Teotihuacan sacked by hostile armies. Strong flow of Mexican traits to Eastern Woodlands.
c. AD 900–1200	Early Post-Classic period.
c. AD 1000	Toltec Empire founded with Tula as its capital.
AD 1168	Tula destroyed.
c. AD 1200–1500	Late Post-Classic period.
c. AD 1300	Mexico City founded.
c. AD 1500	Spanish Conquest.

The Eastern Woodlands

c. 3000 BC	Red Paint and Old Copper Archaic cultures develop in northern Woodlands.
c. 1500 BC	Poverty Point founded in Louisiana under influence from Olmecs.
c. 1400 BC	Adena cultures develop, centered on Southern Ohio and adjacent areas of Indiana, Kentucky, Pennsylvania, and West Virginia. First burial mounds appear.
c. 1000 BC	Archaic cultures wane.
c. 300 BC	Havana Hopewell religious cult develops in Illinois from Red Ocher and Adena cultures.
c. 100 BC	Hopewell cult develops in Ohio and then spreads south, forming Marksville Hopewell in Louisiana and Mississippi, and Santa Rosa/Swift Creek cultures in Northern Florida. Larger mound-earthwork complexes develop.

c. AD 200	Adena cultures wane.
c. AD 550	Hopewell cult wanes.
c. AD 550–700	'Dark age' in Eastern Woodlands.
c. AD 700	Mississippian culture develops under strong influence from the Classic Mexican center of Teotihuacan. First temple mounds and painted pottery appear. Chiefdoms develop. Burial mounds decline. Largest Mississippian settlement Cahokia in Illinois reaches 10,000–15,000 population focused around 100 mounds.
c. AD 1000	Mississippian fully formed, concentrated along Mississippi (Middle and Oneota Mississippian) and in southern Woodlands as an elaborate Southern Death Cult (Caddoan, Plaquemine and South Appalachian Mississippian).
AD 1540–42	De Soto visits Creek Indians in Southeast and observes strong hierarchical social system, public rituals on temple mounds and ball games played in town plazas. European diseases begin to decimate native populations.
17th century AD	Collapse of Mississippian culture under pressure of disease and European conquest. Temporary respite sought by some as mounted nomads on Great Plains.

The Great Plains

Early centuries AD	Plains Woodland culture emerges around Kansas City under influence from Eastern Hopewell cult and moves westward up river valleys, reaching Rocky Mountains by third century AD. Small burial mounds appear.
c. AD 750	Plains Woodland wanes.
c. AD 900	Plains Village culture develops from Plains Woodland along Missouri River with strong influence from Eastern Mississippian culture. Central Plains tradition develops in Kansas and Nebraska.
c. AD 1000	More permanent dwellings develop: large square pit houses with roofs of timber and earth.
c. AD 1470	Series of droughts spanning 40 years force abandonment of High Plains villages and contraction into smaller number of settlements called the 'Coalescent' tradition.
AD 1541	Coronado's Spanish expedition reaches Kansas.

17th century AD	Spanish horse introduced from the Desert West, which stimulates development of historical mounted nomadism.
AD 1804	Lewis and Clark expedition.
AD 1837	Epidemic kills 33 percent Hidatsa, 50 percent Arikara, and 98 percent Mandan populations.
AD 1876	Indians defeat Custer and U.S. Cavalry on the Little Bighorn in Montana.

End 19th century AD Indians defeated and subjugated.

The Desert West

The Great Basin

c. 9000 BC	Occupation of Danger Cave, Utah, by hunter-gatherers of the Desert Culture begins.
c. 7500 BC	Baskets in Danger Cave made by twining.
c. 4000 BC	Inventory of objects in Danger Cave – rattles, bone dice, gaming sticks, clay effigies – similar to those of historical period.
c. 2000 BC	Baskets in Danger Cave made by coiling.
c. AD 1000	Fremont culture, based on agriculture, flourishes briefly in northern Utah before warfare and drought force return to foraging lifeway.

The Southwest

Mogollon culture

c. 200 BC	Mogollon culture develops in Mogollon Mountains. Small villages of pit houses and part-time farmers emerge.
c. AD 300	Expansion of Mogollon culture into Hohokam and Anasazi areas.
c. AD 500–700	Crop failures create depression; partial emigration into Hohokam areas forms (with Anasazi migrants) Sinagua culture.
c. AD 700	End of depression; strong Anasazi influence. Further intermingling with Hohokam groups in south.
c. AD 900	Mimbres pottery style develops in southwestern New Mexico.

c. AD 1000	Trend away from pit to surface dwellings. Great Kivas appear.
c. AD 1100	Contraction of Mogollon culture in face of sporadic droughts and Athapascan influx. Emigration.
c. AD 1250	Abandonment reversed.
c. AD 1350	Abandonment resumes.
c. AD 1600	Historical Zuni.

Hohokam and Sinagua cultures

c. 300 BC	Hohokam culture develops in desert of southern Arizona. Sedentary life in shallow pit houses emerges based on irrigation agriculture.
c. AD 500	Sinagua culture develops in central Arizona from amalgam of Mogollon and Anasazi migrants.
c. AD 600	Influence from Mogollon. Mexican traits – ball courts, platform mounds – become prominent.
c. AD 1000	Chiefdoms emerge.
c. AD 1040–76	Sunset Crater eruption in Sinagua area. Sinagua emigration.
c. AD 1100	Mogollon immigration. Sinagua people return to central Arizona.
c. AD 1200	Anasazi immigration.
c. AD 1300	Climax of Sinagua culture based on successful farming on volcanic soils. Later, crop failures cause contraction and migration south to form Salado culture. Salado people coexist with Hohokam.
c. AD 1450	Series of crop failures and Athapascan influx cause decline of Salado and Hohokam and collapse of irrigation agriculture. Reversion to tribal organization.
c. AD 1600	Historical Pima and Papago.
AD 1694	Jesuit missionary Father Kino visits Hohokam area and observes irrigation network and towns in disrepair.

Anasazi culture

c. 500–100 BC	San Jose culture (Desert Culture variant) flourishes in upper Colorado and upper Rio Grande areas.

c. 100 BC	Anasazi culture (Basketmaker period) develops in four-corners area of Utah, Colorado, Arizona and New Mexico, based on hunting and gathering and some agriculture.
c. AD 400	Modified Basketmaker period begins. Pit houses grow deeper and smoke holes become entrances. Pottery appears for first time.
c. AD 550	Influence from Mogollon.
c. AD 650	First Great Kivas, some up to 20 meters in diameter.
c. AD 700	Pueblo period begins. First surface houses. Pottery styles influenced by Mogollon and Hohokam but technique of firing in reducing atmosphere unique to Anasazi.
c. AD 950	Aggregation of settlements, particularly in Chaco Canyon, leads to development of chiefdoms. Pueblo Bonito in Chaco Canyon and Cliff Palace on Mesa Verde flourish as centers of chiefdoms. Towers emerge.
c. AD 1050	Half villages on Mesa Verde are cliff dwellings. Cliff Palace has 200 rooms and 23 kivas, housing over 400 people.
c. AD 1276–99	Disastrous droughts and influx of Athapascans leads to general abandonment and contraction of Anasazi culture to Little Colorado River and upper Rio Grande areas.
AD 1540–42	Coronado's expedition through the Southwest opens Rio Grande to Spanish colonization.
c. AD 1600	Historical Hopi and Rio Grande Pueblos.
AD 1680	Indians revolt and expel Spanish.
AD 1692	Spanish reassert control.

The Athapascans

c. AD 825	Ancestral Apache bands break from northern Athapascan groups and migrate south.
c. AD 1025	Ancestral Navajo bands follow Apache.
c. AD 1200	Apache and Navajo raid settlements in Southwest, and warfare becomes endemic.
c. AD 1600	Historical Apache and Navajo groups.

The Far West

Baja California

c. 8000–1000 BC	Pinto Basin culture dominates southern California and Baja California with economy based on fish and shellfish.
c. 1000 BC	Peninsular Yumans migrate into region as Amargosa culture. Related to groups in southern California.
c. AD 1000	Amargosa evolves into Comondu culture, based on Desert Culture-type subsistence with fish and shellfish. Seed-grinding tools and basketry used in caves. Coastal shell middens emerge. Las Palmas culture develops in southern Baja California. Little basketry but sewn palm bark common. Spear-thrower used into historical times.
c. AD 1600	Historical Yumans evolve out of Amargosa culture in central Baja California. Historical Guaicurans evolve out of Las Palmas in south.

California

c. 5000 BC	Desert Culture-type tradition at Lake Mojave and San Dieguito sites. Food-grinding implements appear in south. La Jolla culture develops: marine animals not yet fully exploited.
c. 2000 BC	Possible influx of round-headed Penutian-speakers with bow and arrow into indigenous Hokaltecan-speaking areas. Development of hopper-mortar used in processing acorns. Coastal regions evolve strong maritime subsistence pattern.
c. AD 300	Canaliño culture develops in southern California, based on maritime resources and birds and game. Villages of circular houses and semisubterranean sweat houses cluster in valley bottoms near Santa Barbara coast.
c. AD 1600	Historical Chumash evolve out of Canaliño culture. Plank boats appears. Historical Pomo in central California develop elaborate coiled basketry.

The Northwest Coast and Plateau

c. 6000 BC	Salmon runs on Columbia River cease. Upper Columbia River tribes revert to Desert Culture lifeway.

c. 5000 BC	Athapascan influence from north on Fraser River.
c. 1000–0 BC	Earliest evidence of Coast Salish supported by marine economy with toggling harpoons. Ancestral Tsimshian arrive on lower Skeena River.
c. AD 0	Great increase in use of heavy woodworking tools in Fraser delta indicates development of cedar-log carving for houses and canoes.
c. AD 500	Northwest Coast emphasis on wealth and social stratification well established. First burial mounds appear.
c. AD 1265	Cascade Landslide reduces drop at Celilo Falls on Columbia River, allowing salmon to migrate upstream for first time in 7000 years. Sahaptin-speakers of area re-adapt to salmon-fishing.

The Arctic and Subarctic

The Subarctic

c. 8000 BC	Akmak microblade tool assemblage at Onion Portage on Kobuk River, where Paleo-Indians cull migrating caribou.
c. 6000 BC	Anangula Island in Aleutian Islands occupied by sea-mammal hunters.
c. 5000 BC	Athapascans migrate south from Alaska and northwestern Canada into western Subarctic, evolving a hunting-fishing-gathering lifeway well suited to environment. Algonquians migrate into eastern Subarctic from northern Eastern Woodlands.
c. AD 100	Dorset Eskimos colonize coast of Newfoundland.
c. AD 600	Dorset leave Newfoundland.
c. AD 1000	Norse arrive in Newfoundland.
c. AD 1200	Denetasiro tradition evolves from ancestral Athapascans in western Subarctic.
c. AD 1400	Norse leave Newfoundland.
c. AD 1600	Historical Algonquians and Athapascans.

The Arctic

c. 3000 BC	Aleuts and Eskimos migrate from Siberia to western Alaska. Aleuts settle in Aleutian Islands; Eskimos colonize Alaska, founding Arctic Small Tool tradition, shooting game and sea mammals with bow and arrow, and constructing meter-deep pit houses.
c. 2000 BC	Aleuts concentrate on sea mammals as source of food.
c. 1000 BC	Fragmentation of Small Tool tradition leads to growth of different local cultures. Choris culture emerges in north and west Alaska. Sarqaq culture emerges in north Canada and Greenland.
c. 800 BC	Dorset culture develops from Sarqaq culture and colonizes previously unexplored regions of Canadian Arctic.
c. 500 BC	Norton culture develops from Choris culture along coastal strip of west and north Alaska. Pottery introduced.
c. AD 0	On St Lawrence Island south of Bering Strait Okvik culture emerges from Small Tool tradition with inventory of distinctive artifacts such as 'winged' objects.
c. AD 200	Old Bering Sea culture develops out of Okvik culture on St Lawrence Island.
c. AD 300	Ipiutak culture, rich in ivory, bone and antler artifacts, evolves from Norton culture in northern Alaska.
c. AD 500–1000	Birnirk culture evolves from Ipiutak in northern Alaska. Punuk culture develops out of Old Bering Sea culture on St Lawrence Island.
c. AD 985	Norse arrive in Greenland.
c. AD 1000	Thule culture evolves from Birnirk in northern Alaska and rapidly colonizes most of Arctic. Full Eskimo inventory of tools and equipment now developed: igloos, dogsleds, toggling harpoons, snow shovels, stone lamps etc.
c. AD 1400	Norse settlements in Greenland deserted after decimation of population by Black Death and starvation.
c. AD 1600	Historical Yupic-speakers established in west Alaska; rest of Arctic occupied by Inupic-speakers.

Bibliography

General works

Baldwin, Gordon C. *America's Buried Past: The Story of North American Archaeology*. New York, 1962

Bushnell, G.H.S. *The First Americans*. London and New York, 1968.

Brandon, William, ed. *The American Heritage Book of Indians*. New York, 1961.

Ceram, C.W. *The First American: A Story of North American Archaeology*. New York, 1971.

Collier, John. *Indians of the Americas*. New York, 1947.

Dockstader, Frederick J. *Indian Art in America: The Arts and Crafts of the North American Indian*. Greenwich, 1967.

Driver, Harold E. *Indians of North America*. 2nd edn. Chicago and London, 1969.

Eggan, Fred. *The American Indian: Perspectives for the Study of Social Change*. Chicago, 1966.

Farb, Peter. *Man's Rise to Civilization as Shown by the Indians of North America from Primeval Times to the Coming of the Industrial State*. New York, 1968.

Fitting, James E., ed. *The Development of North American Archaeology*. New York, 1973.

Gorenstein, Shirley, ed. *North America*. New York, 1975.

Jennings, Jesse D. *Prehistory of North America*. 2nd edn. New York and London, 1974.

Josephy, Alvin M., Jr. *The Indian Heritage of America*. New York, 1968. London, 1972.

La Farge, Oliver. *A Pictorial History of the American Indian*. Revised edn. New York, 1974.

MacGowan, Kenneth, and Joseph A. Hester, Jr. *Early Man in the New World*. New York, 1962.

Martin, Paul S., George I. Quimby, and Donald Collier. *Indians before Columbus: Twenty Thousand Years of North American History Revealed by Archaeology*. Chicago, 1947.

Morgan, Lewis H. *Houses and House-Life of the American Aborigines*. Chicago and London, 1966.

National Geographic Society. *The World of the American Indian*. Washington, 1974.

Newcomb, William W., Jr. *North American Indians: An Anthropological Perspective*. Pacific Palisades, California, 1974.

Oswalt, Wendell H. *This Land Was Theirs: A Study of the North American Indian*. 2nd edn. New York and London, 1973.

Owen, Roger C., James J.F. Deetz, and Anthony D. Fisher. *The North American Indians: A Sourcebook*. New York and London, 1967.

Sanders, William T., and Joseph P. Marino. *New World Prehistory: Archaeology of the American Indian*. Englewood Cliffs, 1971.

Scherer, Joanna C. *Indians: The Great Photographs that Reveal North American Indian Life 1847–1929*. New York, 1974.

Sellards, E.H. *Early Man in America: A Study in Prehistory*. Austin, 1952.

Silverberg, Robert. *Mound Builders of Ancient America: The Archaeology of a Myth*. Greenwich, 1968.

Spencer, Robert F., Jesse D. Jennings, *et al. The Native Americans.* New York and London, 1965.

Underhill, Ruth M. *Red Man's America: A History of the Indians in the United States.* Revised edn. Chicago and London, 1971.

Walker Art Center. *American Indian Art: Form and Tradition.* New York, 1972.

Willey, Gordon R. *An Introduction to American Archaeology.* Vol. 1: *North and Middle America.* Englewood Cliffs, 1966.

Willey, Gordon R., and Jeremy A. Sabloff. *A History of American Archaeology.* London and San Francisco, 1974.

Wormington, H.M. *Ancient Man in North America.* Denver, 1957.

Regional works

Bandi, Hans-Georg. *Eskimo Prehistory.* College, 1969.

Collins, Henry B., *et al. The Far North: 2000 Years of American Eskimo and Indian Art.* Washington, 1973.

Drucker, Philip. *Cultures of the North Pacific Coast.* San Fancisco, 1965.

Erdoes, Richard. *The Pueblo Indians.* New York, 1967.

Fitting, James E. *The Archaeology of Michigan.* New York, 1970.

Gladwin, Harold S. *A History of the Ancient Southwest.* Portland, Maine, 1957.

Griffin, James B., ed. *Archaeology of the Eastern United States.* Chicago and London, 1952.

Heizer, Robert F., and M.A. Whipple. *The California Indians: A Source Book.* 2nd edn. Berkeley, 1971.

Holm, Bill. *Northwest Coast Indian Art: An Analysis of Form.* Seattle and London, 1965.

Jennings, Jesse D., and Edward Norbeck, eds. *Prehistoric Man in the New World.* Chicago and London, 1964.

Kidder, Alfred Vincent. *An Introduction to the Study of Southwestern Archaeology.* New edn. New Haven and London, 1962.

Kroeber, Theodora. *Ishi in Two Worlds: A Biography of the Last Wild Indian in North America.* Berkeley, 1961.

Martin, Paul S., and Fred Plog. *The Archaeology of Arizona: A Prehistory of the Southwest Region.* New York, 1973.

McGregor, John C. *Southwestern Archaeology.* 2nd edn. Urbana, 1965.

Ritchie, William A. *The Archaeology of New York State.* Revised edn. New York, 1969.

Watson, Don. *Indians of the Mesa Verde.* Colorado, 1961.

Webb, William S., and Charles E. Snow. *The Adena People.* Knoxville, 1974.

Wormington, H. M. *Prehistoric Indians of the Southwest.* Denver, 1964.

List of illustrations

The authors and publishers are grateful to the many museums, institutions and individuals mentioned below who have granted permission to photograph and helped in the identification of the objects illustrated in this book.
Unless otherwise acknowledged, all photographs are by Werner Forman.

Color Plates

Monochrome Plates

18 Sandal-sole gorget with animal on side. Glacial Kame culture, *c.* 1500 BC, *c.* 18 cm. long. Ohio State Museum.

19 Jade celt depicting were-jaguar. Olmec civilization, Mexican Gulf Coast, *c.* 1500 BC–AD 100, *c.* 31 cm. high. British Museum, London.

20 Serpent Mound. Adena-Hopewell cultures, near Locust Grove Ohio, *c.* 2000 years ago, *c.* 405 m. long and 1–2 m. high. Photo Tony Linck.

21 Man wearing copper ear-spools and pendants, and shellfish-pearl beads. Hopewell cult, *c.* 300 BC–AD 500. Field Museum of Natural History.

22 Hand cut from sheet mica. Hopewell cult, Ohio, *c.* 300 BC–AD 500, *c.* 25 cm. long. Field Museum of Natural History.

23 Stone disk engraved with hand. Hopewell cult, Illinois, *c.* 300 BC–AD 500, *c,* 32 cm. diameter. Smithsonian Institution.

24 Cannel coal thumb. Hopewell cult, *c.* 300 BC–AD 500, *c.* 18 cm. long. Field Museum of Natural History.

25 Platform effigy pipe depicting a frog. Hopewell cult, *c.* 300 BC–AD 500, *c.* 10.5 cm. long. Ohio State Museum.

26 Clay figurine of a woman. Hopewell cult, Turner Mound Group, Ohio, *c.* 300 BC–AD 500, *c.* 18 cm. high. Peabody Museum, Harvard University.

27 Fossil mammoth ivory figurine. Hopewell cult, *c.* 300 BC–AD 500 *c.* 8 cm. high. Field Museum of Natural History.

28 Human skull headdress. Hopewell cult, Mound City, Ohio, *c.* 300 BC–AD 500. Ohio State Museum.

29 Stone head possibly representing an ancestral figure. Cole culture, Ohio, *c.* AD 600, *c.* 15 cm. high. Ohio State Museum.

30 Pottery effigy-head vessel. Mississippian Southern Cult, *c.* AD 1000, *c.* 18 cm. high. Smithsonian Institution.

31 Pottery effigy-head vessel. Mississippian Southern Cult, *c.* AD 1000, *c.* 15 cm. high. Museum of the American Indian.

32 Pottery effigy vase depicting human being. Mississippian Southern Cult, *c.* AD 1000, *c.* 20 cm. high. Field Museum of Natural History.

33 Conch shell with an abstract face. Mississippian Southern Cult, Arkansas, *c.* AD 1000. Field Museum of Natural History.

34 Conch shell with a flying shaman. Mississippian Southern Cult, Oklahoma, *c.* AD 1000. Smithsonian Institution.

35 Shell gorget depicting a flying shaman with a death's head and mace. Mississippian Southern Cult, Tennessee, *c.* AD 1000, 10 cm. diameter. Museum of the American Indian.

36 Shell gorget depicting a flying shaman with wings and talons of bird of prey. Mississippian Southern Cult, Etowah, Georgia, *c.* AD 1000, *c.* 7 cm. diameter. Robert S. Peabody Foundation for Archaeology.

37 Shell gorget with a male face. Mississippian Southern Cult, *c.* AD 1000. Museum of the American Indian.

38 Shell head with weeping eye and other facial decoration. Mississippian Southern Cult, *c.* AD 1000, *c.* 6 cm. high. Museum of the American Indian.

39 Embossed copper face. Mississippian Southern Cult, *c.* AD 1000. Museum of the American Indian.

40 Bone long-nosed-god masks, patron gods of 'pochteca'. Mississippian Southern Cult, *c.* AD 1000, *c.* 5 cm. high. Museum of the American Indian.

41 Shell disk with crested woodpeckers. Mississippian Southern Cult, Tennessee, *c.* AD 1000, 8.5 cm. dia. Museum of the American Indian.

42 Shell disk with a spider. Mississippian Southern Cult, Illinois, *c.* AD 1000. Field Museum of Natural History.

43 Cedarwood deer mask inlaid with shell. Mississippian Southern Cult, Spiro Mound, Oklahoma, *c.* AD 1200, *c.* 29 cm. high. Museum of the American Indian.

44 Stone effigy pipe depicting a warrior decapitating a victim. Mississippian

Southern Cult, Spiro Mound, Oklahoma, *c.* AD 1200, *c.* 25 cm. high. Museum of the American Indian.

45 Stone effigy pipe depicting a man grinding maize. Mississippian Southern Cult, Spiro Mound, Oklahoma, *c.* AD 1200, *c.* 25 cm. high. Museum of the American Indian.

46 Pottery vessel with incised designs on scalloped collar. Iroquois, northeast Woodlands, *c.* AD 1500, *c.* 27 cm. high. National Museum of Man, Ottawa.

47 Basswood False Face mask. Iroquois, northeast Woodlands, historical, *c.* 5 cm. high. Field Museum of Natural History.

48 Map of Great Plains. Drawn by Allard Design Group Ltd.

49 Buckskin chart of the night sky. Pawnee, historical. Field Museum of Natural History.

50 Birchbark picture record of sacred song. Ojibwa, historical, *c.* 46 cm. long. Field Museum of Natural History.

51 Birchbark picture record of Midewiwin secret society seating plan. Ojibwa, Leech Lake, Minnesota, historical, *c.* 25 cm. wide. Field Museum of Natural History.

52 Bison-hide shield painted with a bison. Crow Indian, historical, *c.* 61 cm. diameter. Field Museum of Natural History.

53 Picture-writing on bison hide commemorating Sun Dance. Plains Indian, 19th century. Haffenreffer Museum of Anthropology, Brown University.

54 Detail of Plate 53.

55 Map of the Desert West. Drawn by Allard Design Group Ltd.

56 Danger Cave. Desert Culture, Great Salt Desert, Utah, after 9000 BC.

57 Petroglyph depicting shamans and sheep. Desert Culture, Glen Canyon, Colorado River, prehistoric. Utah Museum of Natural History.

58 Deer-leg hide moccasins. Desert Culture, Hogup Cave, Utah, *c.* AD 500. Utah Museum of Natural History.

59 Fiber and bone magical figures. De-

sert Culture, Hogup Cave, Utah, *c.* AD 1500, 6–7 cm. high. Utah Museum of Natural History.

60 Clay figurine. Fremont culture, northern Utah, *c.* AD 1000, *c.* 10 cm. high. Utah Museum of Natural History.

61 Painted ceramic bowl with insect decoration. Mogollon culture, Mimbres style, southwest New Mexico, *c.* AD 950, 30 cm. diameter. Peabody Mus. Harvard University.

62 Painted ceramic bowl with human figure decoration. Mogollon culture, Mimbres style, southwest New Mexico, *c.* AD 950, *c.* 30 cm. diameter. Maxwell Museum of Anthropology.

63,64 Details of Plate 62.

65 Painted ceramic bowl with guardians of the four directions. Mogollon culture, Mimbres style, southwest New Mexico, *c.* AD 950, *c.* 30 cm. diameter. Peabody Museum, Harvard University.

66 Painted ceramic bowl with waterbird decoration. Mogollon culture, Mimbres style, southwest New Mexico, *c.* AD 950, *c.* 30 cm. diameter. Peabody Museum, Harvard University.

67 Clay female figurine. Hohokam, Arizona, *c.* 2000 years old, *c.* 6 cm. high. Arizona State Museum.

68 Potsherd with ceremonial dance. Hohokam culture, Snaketown, *c.* AD 900. Arizona State Museum.

69 Potsherd with bird. Hohokam culture, Snaketown, *c.* AD 900. Arizona State Museum.

70 Pottery bowl with ceremonial dance. Hohokam culture, Snaketown, *c.* AD 900. Arizona State Museum.

71 Pottery bowl with flute players. Hohokam culture, Snaketown, *c.* AD 900, *c.* 27 cm. diameter. Arizona State Museum.

72 Stone pigment mortar in shape of toad. Hohokam culture, Snaketown, *c.* AD 900, *c.* 12 cm. long. Arizona State Museum.

73 Cotton fabric painted with geometric pattern. Hohokam culture, late prehistoric. Arizona State Museum.

74 Montezuma Castle National Monument, Verde Valley. Sinagua culture, prehistoric.

75 Brachiopod-valve toad ornaments. Sinagua culture, *c.* AD 500–1300. Museum of Northern Arizona.

76 Shell earrings in form of birds or animals. Sinagua culture, *c.* AD 500–1300. Museum of Northern Arizona.

77 Fiber female apron. Anasazi culture, Basketmaker period, pre-AD 700. Mesa Verde National Park Museum.

78 Coiled basket with bird decoration. Anasazi culture, Basketmaker period, pre-AD 700. Mesa Verde National Park Museum.

79 Doll of child swaddled to cradleboard. Mojave Indian, historical, *c.* 25 cm. long. Field Museum of Natural History.

80 Pottery bowl decorated with hermaphroditic figure. Anasazi culture, Pueblo period, Mesa Verde, Colorado, *c.* AD 900. Mesa Verde National Park Museum.

81 General view of Canyon de Chelly National Monument, Arizona.

82 The White House, Canyon de Chelly. Anasazi culture, Pueblo period, *c.* AD 1200–1300.

83 Cottonwood doll depicting kachina spirit. Pueblo Indian, historical. Collection G. Schindler.

84 Mortar with painted polychrome decoration. Anasazi culture, Pueblo period, Pueblo Bonito, Chaco Canyon, *c.* AD 1200, *c.* 20 cm. high. Museum of the American Indian.

85 Entrance to Cliff Palace, Mesa Verde, Colorado. Anasazi culture, Pueblo period, *c.* AD 1200.

86 Cliff Palace, Mesa Verde, Colorado. Anasazi culture, Pueblo period, *c.* AD 1200.

87 Pueblo Bonito, Chaco Canyon, New Mexico. Anasazi culture, Pueblo period, *c.* AD 1100, 3-acre site. National Geographic Society. Photo O. C. Havens.

88 Entrance ladders to ceremonial kivas, Spruce Tree House, Mesa Verde. Anasazi culture, Pueblo period, *c.* AD 1100.

89 Pottery pitcher decorated with geometric pattern. Anasazi culture, Pueblo period, *c.* AD 1000, *c.* 20 cm. high. Maxwell Museum of Anthropology.

90 Woven cotton shirt. Pueblo Indian, late prehistoric. Arizona State Museum.

91 Betatakin cliff dwelling, northeastern Arizona. Anasazi culture, Pueblo period, *c.* AD 1100–1300.

92 Skull of woman with point in forehead. Anasazi culture, Pueblo period, Mesa Verde, *c.* AD 1300. Mesa Verde National Park Museum.

93 Map of Far West. Drawn by Allard Design Group Ltd.

94 Abalone shell ladle or broach. California Indian, prehistoric, *c.* 13 cm. wide. Museum of the American Indian.

95 Basket decorated with feathers. Pomo Indian, central California, historical, *c.* 20 cm. long. Field Museum of Natural History.

96 Shell bead necklace with stone and abalone pendants. Kuksu cult, central California, historical. Field Museum of Natural History.

97 Hairpins. Kuksu cult, central California, historical. Field Museum of Natural History.

98 Ear Ornaments. Kuksu cult, central California, historical. Field Museum of Natural History.

99 Death mask of Ishi. The Robert H. Lowie Museum of Anthropology, University of California, Berkeley.

100 Points chipped by Ishi from beer bottles. The Robert H. Lowie Museum of Anthropology, University of California, Berkeley.

101 Whalebone club. Tsimshian, Northwest Coast, 17th century AD, *c.* 44 cm. long. National Museum of Man, Ottawa.

102 Fort Rock volcanic outcrop, central Oregon.

103 Painted cedarwood mask of woman with labret. Tlingit, Northwest Coast, 19th century AD. Washington State Museum.

104 Stone maul incised in shape of figure. Haida, Northwest Coast, 19th century AD, *c.* 22 cm. high.

National Museum of Man, Ottawa.

105 Steatite human seated figure. Fraser River area, prehistoric. British Columbia Provincial Museum.

106 Wooden bird-beak headdress. Kwakiutl, Northwest Coast, historical. Collection G. Schindler.

107 Section of wooden house post. Salish Indians, Quamichan, British Columbia, historical, *c.* 2.1 m. high (complete). British Columbia Provincial Museum.

108 Steatite pipe. Fraser River area, prehistoric, *c.* 12 cm. long. British Columbia Provincial Museum.

109 Steatite pipe. Fraser River area, prehistoric, *c.* 5 cm. long. British Columbia Provincial Museum.

110 Steatite screech-owl effigy bowl. Upper Skagit River area, British Columbia, prehistoric, *c.* 13.5 cm. long. British Columbia Provincial Museum.

111 Skeena River, British Columbia.

112 Basalt burial mask. Tsimshian, Northwest Coast, 19th century, *c.* 23 cm. high, National Museum of Man, Ottawa.

113 Cedar plank chest portraying totemic animal. Tlingit, northern Northwest Coast, 19th century, *c.* 50 cm. high. Portland Art Museum, Portland, Oregon.

114 Copper fighting knife with rawhide grip and ox-horn hilt. Tlingit, northern Northwest Coast, 19th century, *c.* 50 cm. long. University Museum, University of Alaska.

115 Detail of Plate 114.

116 Shaman's rattle of yellow cedarwood depicting face in bear's paw. Tlingit, southern Alaska, late 19th century, *c.* 14 cm. diameter. Washington State Museum.

117 Rattle in form of grebe. Possibly Tlingit, northern Northwest Coast, 19th century, *c.* 37 cm. long. Portland Art Museum, Portland, Oregon

118 Rattle of two pieces of unpainted wood. Unknown Northwest Coast origin, historical, *c.* 15 cm. diameter. Portland Art Museum, Portland, Oregon.

119 Argillite grease dish in form of frog. Tsimshian, northern Northwest Coast, historical, *c.* 13 cm. long. National Museum of Man, Ottawa.

120 Female mask with bird pendants. Tsimshian, northern Northwest Coast, historical. Portland Art Museum, Portland, Oregon.

121 Cedarwood figure. Bella Coola, British Columbia, historical, *c.* 60 cm. high. British Columbia Provincial Museum.

122 Cedarwood figure. Bella Coola, British Columbia, historical, *c.* 60 cm. high. British Columbia Provincial Museum.

123 Argillite ornament depicting killer whale. Northwest Coast, historical, *c.* 3 cm. high. National Museum of Man, Ottawa.

124 Goat-horn ceremonial spoon inlaid with abalone. Tsimshian, northern Northwest Coast, 19th century, *c.* 25 cm. long. National Museum of Man, Ottawa.

125 Trapezoidal Chilkat blanket detail showing killer whales. Tlingit, northern Northwest Coast, historical. Field Museum of Natural History.

126 Mortuary pole with an eagle. Haida, Queen Charlotte Islands, historical. British Columbia Provincial Museum.

127 Entrance to house carved in form of totem pole. Haida, Queen Charlotte Islands, historical. British Columbia Provincial Museum.

128 Shaman's crown of mountain goat horn. Tsimshian, northern Northwest Coast, 19th century, *c.* 15 cm. high. National Museum of Man, Ottawa.

129 Linked shaman's charms. Tsimshian, northern Northwest Coast, 19th century. National Museum of Man, Ottawa.

130 Shaman's necklace with bone and ivory amulets. Haida, Queen Charlotte Islands, historical. National Museum of Man, Ottawa.

131 Two-headed soul-catcher. Tsimshian, northern Northwest Coast, historical, *c.* 12 cm. long. National Museum of Man, Ottawa.

132,133 Shaman's charms cut from canine

teeth depicting fetal humans. Tsimshian, northern Northwest Coast, historical. National Museum of Man, Ottawa.

134 Mountain-goat-wool ceremonial robe. Tlingit, Alaska, 19th century. Portland Art Museum, Portland, Oregon.

135 Pattern board. Tlingit, Alaska, early historical. Portland Art Museum, Portland, Oregon.

136 Cedar plank drum with killer-whale design. Tlingit, Alaska, 19th century, *c.* 1 m. high. Portland Art Museum, Portland, Oregon.

137 Map of Arctic and Subarctic. Drawn by Allard Design Group Ltd.

138 Cedar-bark pouch. Athapascan, western Subarctic, 18th century. University Museum, University of Alaska.

139 Wooden hunting hat. Aleuts, Unalaska, Aleutian Islands, 18th century, 40 cm. long. Photo British Museum, London.

140 Wooden hunting hat. Eskimos, west Alaska, 19th century, *c.* 35 cm. long. National Museum of Man, Ottawa.

141 Wooden death mask. Aleuts, Unalaska Island, Aleutian Islands, 19th century, *c.* 35 cm. high. Smithsonian Institution.

142 Wooden death mask. Aleuts, Unga Island, Aleutian Islands, 19th century, *c.* 35 cm. high. Smithsonian Institution.

143 Chert microliths. Arctic Small Tool tradition, *c.* 3000 BC, *c.* 5 cm. long. Haffenreffer Museum of Anthropology.

144 Reconstructed pit house. Eskimos, Katmai National Park, Aleutian Range, late prehistoric, *c.* 5 m. diameter.

145 Female fertility figurine of walrus ivory, perhaps a bear mother. Okvik culture, St Lawrence Island, *c.* 2000 years ago, *c.* 17 cm. high. University Museum, University of Alaska.

146 Female fertility figurine, so-called 'Okvik Madonna'. Okvik culture, St Lawrence Island, *c.* 2000 years ago, *c.* 17 cm. high. University Museum, University of Alaska.

147 Ivory harpoon head with inset chert blades. Old Bering Sea culture, St Lawrence Island, *c.* AD 200, *c.* 12 cm. long. University Museum, University of Alaska.

148 Penis figurine. Punuk culture, St Lawrence Island, *c.* AD 700. University Museum, University of Alaska.

149 Socketed ivory shaft head for harpoon. Old Bering Sea culture, St Lawrence Island, *c.* AD 200, *c.* 21 cm. long. University Museum, University of Alaska.

150 Winged object: bird shape. Old Bering Sea culture, St Lawrence Island, *c.* AD 200, *c.* 21 cm. wide. Smithsonian Institution.

151 Winged object: butterfly shape. Early Punuk culture, St Lawrence Island, *c.* AD 700, *c.* 16 cm. wide. Museum of the American Indian.

152 Winged object: trident shape. Middle Punuk culture, St Lawrence Island, *c.* 10 cm. wide. Smithsonian Institution.

153 Winged object: coronet shape. Late Punuk culture, St Lawrence Island, *c.* AD 1000, *c.* 7 cm. wide. Smithsonian Institution.

154 Ivory animal head, perhaps a wolf. Old Bering Sea art, St Lawrence Island, *c.* AD 0–700, *c.* 7 cm. long. University Museum, University of Alaska.

155 Ivory animal head ornament. Old Bering Sea art, St Lawrence Island, *c.* AD 0–700, *c.* 10 cm. long. Smithsonian Institution.

156 Ivory box or pail handle. Old Bering Sea art, St Lawrence Island, *c.* AD 0–700. Smithsonian Institution.

157 Ivory adze handle. Old Bering Sea art, St Lawrence Island, *c.* AD 0–700, *c.* 31 cm. long. Museum of the American Indian.

158 Ivory-handled slate 'woman's knife'. Norton Eskimos, Alaskan coast, *c.* 500 BC, *c.* 10 cm long. Smithsonian Institution.

159 Lip plugs or 'labrets'. Eskimos, prehistoric, max. 5 cm. long. National Museum of Man, Ottawa.

160 Incised bone comb. Dorset Eskimos, Canadian Arctic, *c.* 500 BC. Haffenreffer Museum of Anthropology.

161 Figurine. Yupic Eskimos, south-western Alaska, after AD 1100, c. 9 cm. high. Haffenreffer Museum of Anthropology.

162 Ivory mask. Dorset Eskimos, Sugluk, Quebec, c. 500 BC, c. 4 cm. high. National Museum of Man, Ottawa.

163 Bone carving of human figure or otter. Ipiutak culture, northern Alaska, c. AD 500, c. 14 cm. long. The American Museum of Natural History.

164 Ivory walrus. Ipiutak culture, northern Alaska, c. AD 500, c. 7.5 cm. long. The American Museum of Natural History.

165 Ivory object, perhaps a comb. Ipiutak culture, Seward Peninsula, Alaska, c. AD 500, c. 26 cm. long. University Museum, University of Alaska.

166 Mask-like ivory carvings. Ipiutak culture, Point Hope, Alaska, c. AD 500, c. 16 cm. high. The American Museum of Natural History.

167 Bone fish amulet. Thule Eskimos, Canadian Arctic, c. AD 1000, c. 10 cm. long. National Museum of Man, Ottawa.

168 Bone-handled knife in shape of polar bear. Thule Eskimos, Arctic, after AD 1000, c. 31.5 cm. long.

169 Soapstone pipe bowl. Huron, Ottawa area, historical, c. 6 cm. high. National Museum of Man, Ottawa.

170 Finger mask used by women. Yupic Eskimos, western Alaska, historical, c. 12 cm. high. The Robert H. Lowie Museum of Anthropology, University of California, Berkeley.

171 Owl mask with feathers. Yupic Eskimos, St Michael, west Alaska, historical. The Robert H. Lowie Museum of Anthropology, University of California, Berkeley.

172 Mask with crescents as facial features. Yupic Eskimos, lower Yukon River, west Alaska, 19th century, 35.5 cm. high. The Robert H. Lowie Museum of Anthropology, University of California, Berkeley.

173 Mask depicting cormorant. Yupic Eskimos, west Alaska, 19th century, c. 18 cm. high. The Robert H. Lowie Museum of Anthropology, University of California, Berkeley.

174 Green-and-white painted mask. Yupic Eskimos, west Alaska, historical. The American Museum of Natural History.

175 Mask with black eye and feathers. Yupic Eskimos, St Michael, west Alaska, 19th century. The Robert H. Lowie Museum of Anthropology, University of California, Berkeley.

Index

Numerals in italics refer to numbered illustrations

weaving 49, 155
Weeden Island culture 59, 115, *14*
weight, spear-thrower 37, 43; *see also* atlatl, bannerstone, birdstone, boatstone, 'winged' objects
whale *see* sea mammals
wheel 19, 29
White House site *81*, *82*
Wichita 75, 91, 92, 93
wild rice 93
winged-eye motif 61, 68, *30*, *32–35*, *38*, *XI*
'winged' objects (bannerstones) *see* bannerstones
'winged' objects (Eskimo) 216–217, *150–153*
Winnebago 78, 91
Wiyot 176

wool, mountain-goat 196, *134*, *XXII*
'woman's knife', Eskimo 37
Wounded Knee, battle of 93

Y
Yahi 169–170
Yana 169–170
Yellowknife 206
Yukon artifact 23, 204
Yumans, California and Peninsular 159
Yupic languages *see* languages
Yupic Eskimos *see* Eskimos
Yurok 176

Z
Zuni 119, 148

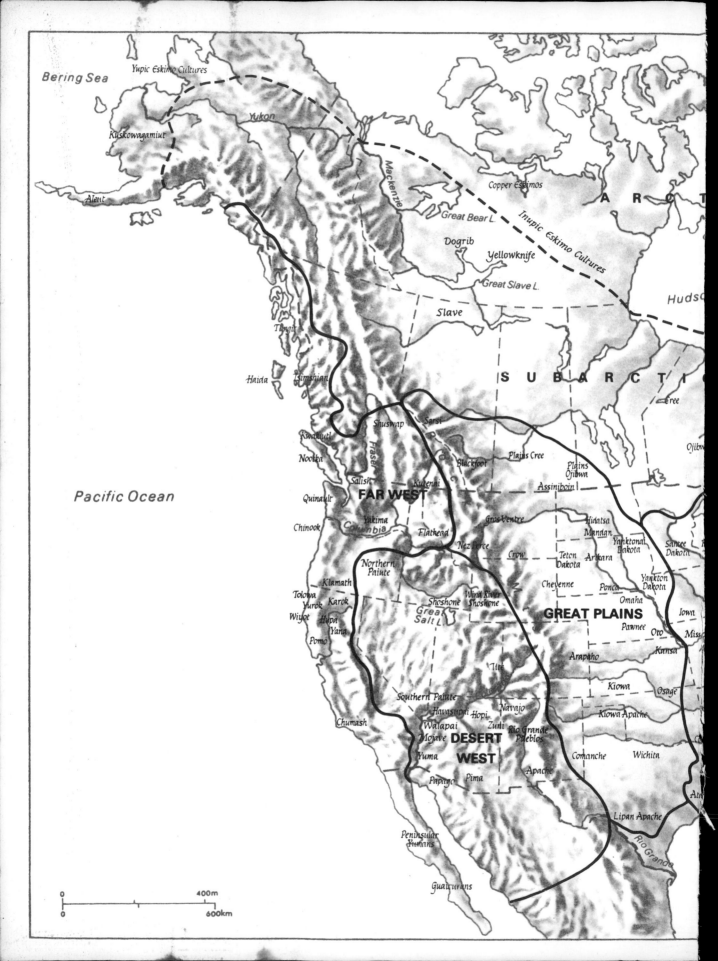

Bering Sea

Yupic Eskimo Cultures

Yukon

Kuskowagamiut

Aleut

Copper Eskimos

Great Bear L.

Inupic Eskimo Cultures

A R C T

Mackenzie

Dogrib

Yellowknife

Great Slave L.

Hud

Slave

S U B A R C T I

Tlingit

Cree

Haida

Tsimshian

Ojibw

Shuswap

Sarsi

Kwakiutl

Blackfoot

Plains Cree

Plains
Ojibwa

Noolka

Fraser

Assiniboin

Salish

Kutenai

FAR WEST

Quinault

Yakima

Gros Ventre

Hidatsa

Mandan

Chinook

Columbia

Flathead

Yanktonal
Dakota

Santee
Dakota

Nez Perce

Crow

Teton
Dakota

Arikara

Northern
Paiute

Cheyenne

Ponca

Yankton
Dakota

Pacific Ocean

Klamath

Wind River
Shoshone

Omaha

Iowa

Tolowa
Yurok
Wiyot

Karok

Shoshone

Great
Salt L.

GREAT PLAINS

Hupa

Yana

Pawnee

Oto

Miss

Pomo

Kansa

Arapaho

Ute

Kiowa

Osage

Southern Paiute

Havasupai Hopi

Navajo

Kiowa Apache

Chumash

Walapai

Zuni

Rio Grande
Pueblos

Comanche

Wichita

Mojave

DESERT

Yuma

WEST

Apache

Papago

Pima

Ate

Lipan Apache

Peninsular
Yumans

Rio Grande

Guaicurians

0 ____ 400m
0 ____ 600km